THE GEOMETER'S SKETCHPAD®

**Dynamic Geometry™
for the 21st Century**

User Guide and Reference Manual

Macintosh Version

D1468492

KEY CURRICULUM PRESS
Innovators in Mathematics Education

The Geometer's Sketchpad®

Macintosh Version 3

April 1995

Project Design: Nicholas Jackiw
Program Implementation: Nicholas Jackiw and Scott Steketee
Editors: Dan Bennett, William Finzer, Greer Lleud, Joan Meyers, and Steven Rasmussen
Mathematicians: Eugene Klotz, Doris Schattschneider, and Cynthia Schmalzried
Curriculum Development: Dan Bennett and William Finzer
Technical Writing: Dan Bennett, William Finzer, Nicholas Jackiw, Jacqueline Hale, Josh Markel, and Scott Steketee
Production: William Finzer, Ann Rothenbuhler, and Luis Shein
Cover Design: Luis Shein and Tessera
Field Testing: Rob Berkelman
Special Thanks: Steven Fought, Jed Hartman, Philip Ivanier, James King, Peter Rasmussen, John Schiener, and Jay Scott

The Geometer's Sketchpad is the product of a collaboration between the Visual Geometry Project at Swarthmore College and Key Curriculum Press. The Visual Geometry Project was directed by Drs. Eugene Klotz and Doris Schattschneider. Portions of this material are based upon work supported by the National Science Foundation under award number III-9203421. Any opinions, findings, and conclusions or recommendations expressed in this publication are those of the author(s) and do not necessarily reflect the views of the National Science Foundation.

Key Curriculum Press
P.O. Box 2304
Berkeley, California 94702
510-548-2304

Replacement Policy

Once you have filled out our Product Registration Card and returned it, you are covered by our warranty. Key Curriculum Press guarantees that The Geometer's Sketchpad disks in this package are free of defects. Defective disks will be replaced free of charge if returned within 90 days of the purchase date. After 90 days, there is a $10.00 replacement fee for each disk returned.

Backup Policy

Key Curriculum Press authorizes the original purchaser of this software to make one copy of the program for archival purposes, or copy the software onto the purchaser's hard disk and retain the original disks for archival purposes. We remind you that your backup copy is to be used for archival purposes only. Unauthorized copying of The Geometer's Sketchpad is a violation of Federal Law. The Software End-User License Agreement printed on the disk envelope contains the full text of your rights to use The Geometer's Sketchpad.

Welcome to Dynamic Geometry

The Geometer's Sketchpad is a powerful tool for exploring geometry.

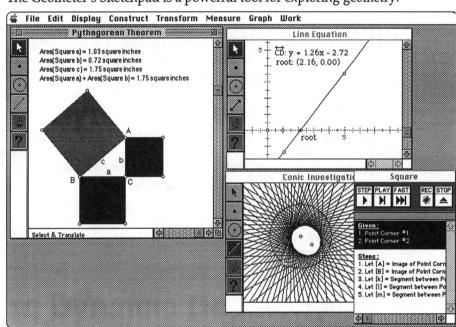

With Sketchpad you can construct an amazing variety of figures:

- Simple textbook figures

- Working models of the Pythagorean Theorem

- Perspective drawings

- Escher-like tessellations

- Fractals

- Animated sine waves

- Graphs

- Curves

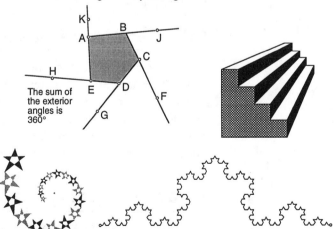

The sum of the exterior angles is 360°

Once you have drawn a figure, you can use Sketchpad's dynamic geometry to transform your figures with the mouse—preserving the geometric relationships of your construction. Every construction leads naturally to generalizations as you see which aspects of the geometry change and which stay the same. Discovering geometry was never so exciting!

A Powerful Tool for Visualization

The mechanical drawbacks of standard tools—paper and pencil, compass and straightedge—often limit drawings and obscure vital geometric principles. With The Geometer's Sketchpad, you construct points, lines, and circles using geometric constraints. Constrain a point to be the the midpoint of a line segment; set one line to be parallel to another; fix a circle's radius equal to a given length; construct a graph of a geometric relationship. Drawing is fast, precise, and accurate, revealing essential relationships with ease and clarity.

As you transform parts of your figure, all related parts update continuously. Whereas a paper and pencil drawing demonstrates only one case of a geometric relationship, with Sketchpad you examine a vast set of similar cases.

If you record your figure in a script, Sketchpad models your construction as an abstract system of geometric relationships, independent of any particular drawing or diagram. When you play back the script, you can investigate the construction in both related and special cases, observing dynamically which conjectures hold true, and which conjectures prove false.

Opens Windows on the World of Geometry

The Geometer's Sketchpad models geometry in two linked views. Sketches depict concrete geometry and emphasize spatial reasoning, while scripts describe constructions verbally and abstractly.

Sketches: Graphic Exploration

In the sketch window, you draw with electronic versions of Euclid's tools. Sketchpad's menus offer more sophisticated constructions and planar transformations. As you work, you can measure quantities ranging from simple distances to complex expressions of your own devising. Best of all, since Sketchpad embodies the mathematics of your sketch, it preserves all geometric relationships as you move components with the mouse or the built-in animation tool.

Scripts: Logical Abstraction

Scripts are generalized descriptions of constructions. You can record scripts step-by-step yourself, or have Sketchpad generate a script to describe a construction you've already sketched. Scripts become part of your basic geometric toolbox: use them again and again to generate figures, or portions of figures, while sketching. You can even use individual scripts to build larger ones, deriving more and more complicated constructions just as Euclid derived all geometry from a handful of definitions and postulates centuries ago.

A Powerful Tool for Communicating Mathematics

Sketchpad's variety of display and formatting options encourage you to explore new ways of presenting findings—dynamically and elegantly. As you work, you can color, label, and annotate your drawings. Scripts can also be annotated, printed, and saved to provide tools for future investigations and a forum for discussing your work. You can present geometry interactively with Sketchpad as your dynamic blackboard!

Table of Contents

Getting Started

System Requirements

The Geometer's Sketchpad will work on any Macintosh® from the Macintosh Plus up. It requires a minimum of one megabyte (1M) of random access memory, or RAM, and System 6 or higher of the Macintosh operating system. Certain features are only available on computers running System 7 (or higher) of the Macintosh operating system.

Quick Install

1. Insert Disk 1 in the floppy disk drive of your computer.

2. Double-click on the icon labeled "Install Sketchpad."

3. In the resulting installer dialog box, press the button labeled "Easy Install."

4. Follow the remaining directions that appear on screen.

The installer places the correct edition of Sketchpad for the given machine and several folders of sketches and scripts in a folder on your computer's hard disk. It does not do anything to your system folder.

Once you have installed the program on your hard disk, store the original disks in a safe place—this will protect you in case of mistake or misfortune.

The section below explains some details relating to installation of a lab pack or site license in a networked environment.

Custom Installation

You need to do a custom installation if you are installing Sketchpad on a network server and there are different types of computers that will access the software. Custom installation allows you to install more than one edition of Sketchpad so that users can choose the edition appropriate to the computer they are using.

You may also wish to do a custom installation in order to install only certain of the auxiliary files on the disks; e.g., the program but not the sample sketches, scripts, or tour.

Pressing "Custom Install" instead of "Easy Install" lets you choose among various options, explained here.

Editions of Sketchpad

There are three different editions of Sketchpad, each suited to different Macintosh computers. If you accidentally attempt to use an improper edition, Sketchpad will alert you to this fact when you start it, and identify the edition which is best suited to your computer.

Except for speed and the absence of color in the standard edition, all three editions are identical.

Standard Edition	This edition works on all Macintosh computers. However, it is specifically intended for use with the Macintosh Plus, SE, PowerBook 100 or 140, and Classic computers. It does not support color.
Enhanced Edition	This edition works on the 68020/030/040 Macintosh line. This includes most of the LC, Performa, Powerbook, and Duo lines of computers, as well as several older Macintoshes. It is slightly faster than the Standard Edition and allows the use of color. It is also the correct edition to use with Power Macintoshes.
FPU Edition	This edition will work only on computers with floating-point units (math coprocessors)—the SE/30 and the Macintosh II line, many Quadras, and high-end Powerbooks, Centrises, or Duos. It is significantly faster than other editions.

Sketches, Scripts, and Presentation

These sample documents are designed to illustrate what Sketchpad can do and to aid you in your mathematics learning and teaching. You'll want to explore at least some of these as you gain proficiency with the software. Therefore, if you have room on your disk, you should choose to install them.

Using Sketchpad on a Macintosh with two floppy disks

1. On a Macintosh with a hard disk, use Custom Install to install the desired edition of Sketchpad.

2. Copy the program onto a floppy disk.

3. Use this disk in one drive and your regular System disk in the other.

To start Sketchpad, double-click the icon of the program. Once the program starts, click again anywhere in the sketch plane to dismiss the title page.

Documentation

This manual contains general information for the new user, guided tours of instructions for getting acquainted with Sketchpad, comprehensive information about sketches and scripts, and command and tool references. In addition, there is a table of contents and a general index. The manual contains nine chapters:

Getting Started	Describes the installation procedure and gives a brief overview of the User Guide and Reference Manual.
Quick Start	Provides a fast way for experienced computer users to acquire an overview of Sketchpad's capabilities.
The Basics	Details general Macintosh and Sketchpad procedures, such as using the mouse, choosing from menus, selecting tools, and using the controls in a script window.
Guided Tours	Provides step-by-step exercises that guide you through the most common Sketchpad activities.

Sketches	Discusses creating and manipulating geometric constructions in sketches.
Scripts	Discusses creating and using scripts.
Command Reference	Describes every command in the menus.
Toolbox Reference	Describes every tool in the Toolbox.
Advanced Applications	Describes advanced features of the software which experienced users may find helpful.
What's New in Version 3	Describes significant enhancements as compared to previous versions of Sketchpad.
General Issues	Provides information on memory management and other issues which may come up as you grow in using Sketchpad.

You may want to read about what Sketchpad does and how you can use it to explore geometric principles. The Sketches and Scripts chapters provide an overview of Sketchpad's capabilities. If you want to get your hands on the computer right away, begin with the Guided Tours; they give complete instructions for using the mouse and menus, while providing an overview of sketches and scripts. The reference chapters give complete information for each command and tool so that you can look up specifics.

Notes and Teacher Tips

You'll find notes and teacher tips in the left margins of this manual. Those tips that are especially for teachers are marked with a ⌦ symbol.

Quick Start

Some people like to get started using new software quickly, paying minimal attention to the documentation and lots of attention to what is happening on the screen. If you are such a person, this chapter is for you. *But, if you want a complete, step-by-step guide to getting started with Sketchpad,* skip this chapter and proceed with the next chapter—The Basics.

What You Should Already Have Done

You should already have installed Sketchpad on your computer as described in the installation section that begins on page 1. In addition, you should have started Sketchpad. (Starting Sketchpad is described on page 26.) You should see a Sketchpad window on your screen similar to the one below.

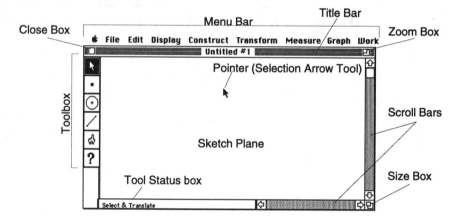

Overview

What can you do with Sketchpad?

1. You can accomplish Euclidean constructions with the drawing tools in the toolbox and with the commands in the Construct menu.

2. The commands in the Transform menu allow you to go beyond Euclidean construction to accomplish translation, rotation, and dilation by fixed, computed, and dynamic quantities.

3. The Measure and Graph menus take you into the realm of analytic geometry where you can measure properties of your sketch and work in rectangular or polar coordinates.

4. Combine the Edit and Display menus with the text tool, and you can add labels and captions, change the visual properties of displayed objects, and create animations.

5. With scripts you can encapsulate complex constructions in single steps, extending Sketchpad's capabilities.

What makes Sketchpad special? In a word, *dragging*. Because constructed relationships remain valid while you drag, geometry becomes dynamic. Sketchpad is a dynamic geometry environment.

Drawing

Three of the tools in the Toolbox on the left side of the Sketchpad window allow you to draw points, circles, and lines.

To choose a drawing tool, click and release on it. Do not attempt to drag the tool into the drawing area.

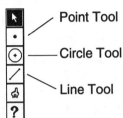

— Point Tool

— Circle Tool

— Line Tool

Notice that when you click on a tool, the Tool Status Box in the lower left corner of the window shows you which tool you have selected.

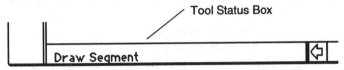

Tool Status Box

Draw Segment

1. Try out each of the drawing tools. See if you can draw each of the figures shown below. (Don't delete your sketches. Keep them for when you learn about dragging in the next section.)

Notice that Sketchpad drawing tools snap to the nearest point or segment if there is one. This makes it easy to connect the sides of a polygon or inscribe a triangle inside a circle.

Triangle

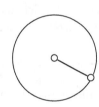

Circle with radius

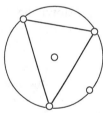

Triangle inscribed in a circle

2. The Line drawing tool is actually three tools in one. Hold the mouse button down on the tool to reveal a pop-up menu of drawing tools. While holding down the mouse button, move to the tool you want to use and release the mouse button.

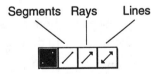

Segments Rays Lines

Try out these tools. See if you can make the drawings shown below.

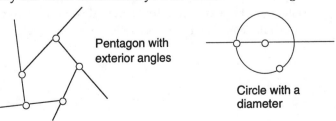

Pentagon with exterior angles

Circle with a diameter

3. Anything you do with Sketchpad you can undo. You can undo actions back to the last time you saved or, if you have not saved, to the beginning of the sketch. (This is different from most other programs, which let you undo only the most recent action.) If you hold down Option before pulling down the menu, the command becomes Undo All.

Try it!

Dragging and Selecting

You experience the *dynamic* aspects of Sketchpad when you drag objects you have drawn or constructed. Use the Selection Arrow tool for dragging.

3. Try dragging sketches that you have already made. The following questions are meant to give you some ideas about drag behavior.

   a. The points at the ends of a line segment are *control points*. What happens to the line segment when you drag these points?

   b. Most anything you see in a Sketchpad document can be dragged. When you drag a line segment, what properties of that segment remain constant?

   c. How can you change the radius of a circle without changing the location of its center?

   d. How can you change the location of the center of a circle without changing its radius?

   e. With the Point tool, place a point on the circumference of a circle. What happens when you drag that point?

   f. Draw two line segments that cross each other. Place a point at their intersection. What happens to the point when you drag a segment so that the two segments no longer intersect? What happens when you drag the point?

4. With the Selection Arrow tool, you can select more than one object at a time by holding down the Shift key as you click in the document window. This is useful when you want to drag more than one object at a time, and, as you'll see in the next section, for doing constructions.

   Draw a quadrilateral similar to the one below. With the Selection Arrow, click on one side of the quadrilateral. Hold down the Shift key and click on an adjacent side. You should see selection handles on both of the sides you clicked on.

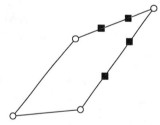

   • Now drag one of the sides. Notice how both sides drag together.
   • Click in an empty place in the window to deselect.

5. Another way to select more than one object is to draw a *selection marquee* around them. Imagine a rectangle that will surround the objects you wish to select. Click and drag, starting at one corner of that rectangle and releasing at the opposite corner. All objects partially contained in the selection marquee are selected.

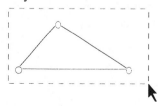

Constructing

Because the drawing tools contain a Euclidean compass and a straightedge, you can use them to do constructions. You can also use the Construct menu to accomplish certain constructions more easily and quickly than you can with the drawing tools.

You can hide auxiliary circles and points by selecting them and choosing Hide Objects from the Display menu. (The keyboard shortcut for Hide is ⌘H.)

6. Try, using the drawing tools, to construct a perpendicular bisector for a line segment. You can do this by constructing two circles, each one using an endpoint of the segment as its center and the other endpoint as its radius. Then you can connect the two intersection points of the circles with a line. You might get something similar to this.

Does your construction hold together when you drag the endpoints of the line segment? Try several other compass-and-straightedge constructions.

7. The Construct menu contains shortcuts for common constructions. The items in the Construct menu will be disabled (grayed out) until you have selected the objects Sketchpad needs to do a construction. For example, if you want to construct a perpendicular, you must first select a line and a point so that Sketchpad can construct a perpendicular to the line through the point.

Here you can see what you must select to do the constructions indicated in the Construct menu.

To undo any construction command, type ⌘Z.

Construct		Select
Point On Object		One or more objects
Point At Intersection	⌘I	Two paths
Point At Midpoint	⌘M	One or more segments
Segment	⌘L	Two or more points
Perpendicular Line		A straight object and one or more points, or
Parallel Line		a point and one or more straight objects
Angle Bisector		Three points, the 2nd being the angle's vertex
Circle By Center+Point		Two points
Circle By Center+Radius		A point and a segment
Arc On Circle		Three points, or a circle and two points
Arc Through 3 Points		Three points
Interior	⌘P	A set of points, a circle, or an arc
Locus		An object and a point on a path
Construction Help...		

To construct a line parallel to a given line through a given point,

• Draw a line and a point not on the line.

- Use the arrow tool to select both the line and the point. (Remember, you have to hold down the Shift key to select the second object.)

- Choose Parallel Line from the Construct menu. That should give you the desired construction.

If the desired item in the Construct menu remains gray, it may be because you have too many objects selected. To deselect everything, click in an empty place in your sketch. Then start selecting again.

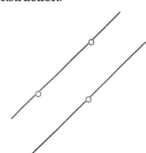

Experiment with dragging all the parts of your construction.

8. Try out each of the other constructions on the Construct menu.

    Each time you construct something, drag things around and notice how your constructed relationships hold up.

    Here are some interesting constructions to try.
    - The quadrilateral joining the midpoints of a quadrilateral.
    - A square.
    - The incenter for a triangle (i.e., the center of the inscribed circle determined by the intersection of the angle bisectors of the triangle). Find the incenter, then construct the incircle.

Transforming

Translations, reflections, rotations, and dilations are easily accomplished with Sketchpad. There are two basic methods. First, the Selection Arrow tool lets you transform objects as you drag them. Second, you can use commands in the Transform menu to create transformed images of the original objects. The menu commands let you transform by fixed quantities; e.g., translating by 2 inches in the x-direction, or rotating by 45° around a center. The menu commands also let you transform by dynamic quantities that will change as you drag. These dynamic quantities can be specified geometrically by marking a vector, angle, or ratio; or, they can be specified by marking measurements.

A quick way to obtain an empty sketch is to Undo All by holding down Option while you choose Undo All from the Edit menu.

9. You already know how to translate objects in a sketch—that's what dragging with the Selection Arrow tool is all about. What about rotating and dilating?

    - First draw a triangle. Select one of the vertices.

The point will flash briefly to indicate that it will be used as a center. The shortcut for marking a center is ⌘F or double-click with the Selection tool.

- To accomplish a rotation or a dilation, you must specify a center of rotation or a center of dilation. With the vertex still selected, choose Mark Center from the Transform menu.

- Press and hold the mouse button down on top of the Selection tool. The palette displays the Selection Arrow tools.

- Let's do rotation first. Drag the mouse over to the rotation tool and release.

- Now drag the *side* of the triangle opposite the vertex you marked as a center. You should see the triangle rotate around that vertex.
- With the side still selected, choose Trace Segment from the Display menu. As you drag with the Rotate tool, you should get a trace similar to the one shown below.

The trace will disappear when you move to the next step in your sketch. To turn off tracing, select the segment and choose Trace Locus in the Display menu again. The shortcut for tracing is ⌘T.

- Dilation works just like rotation. First select the Dilate tool.

- Now drag the side of the triangle opposite the marked center. If tracing for that segment is still turned on, you should get a tracing like the one shown below.

10. Reflection requires an axis of reflection—that is, a mirror. First you mark a straight object as the mirror, then you reflect something.

- Draw a line and, while it is selected, choose Mark Mirror from the Transform menu.
- Draw something else in your sketch and select it.

The line will flash briefly to indicate that it will be used as a mirror. The shortcut for marking a mirror is ⌘G or double-click with the Selection Arrow tool.

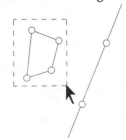

- Choose Reflect from the Transform menu. The reflected image of the selected objects should appear.

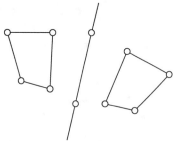

11. You can use the Translate command in the Transform menu to translate an object by a fixed distance in a fixed direction. For example, suppose you want to construct a segment that will always be one inch long. Here's how.

- Place a point in your sketch.
- With the point selected, choose Translate from the Transform menu. This brings up a dialog box in which you can specify the desired translation.

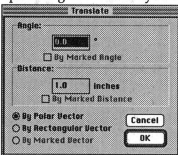

Clicking OK should give you a second point, constrained to be one inch to the right of the original point. Try dragging the original. Can you drag the translated point?

- Use the Segment tool to connect the original point to its transformed image. This segment will always be one inch long.

12. Rotation by a fixed angle and dilation by a fixed ratio require a marked center.

- Draw a polygon and place a point near it.

- Select point *A* and choose Mark Center from the Transform menu.
- The Rotate and Dilate commands in the Transform menu work are very much alike. To try them, first select the polygon, and then choose the command from the Transform menu. You will get one of these two dialog boxes.

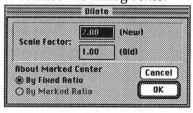

Experiment with dragging. What happens when you drag the center? The original polygon? The rotated and dilated image?

- The result of applying first one transformation and then the other is shown below. Which transformation was applied first?

- What happens when you dilate by a ratio greater than one? What happens when you dilate by a negative ratio?

13. Transformations by fixed quantities are limiting when you want to experiment with different amounts of transformation. Sketchpad uses marked vectors, angles, and ratios to achieve dynamic transformations. Here we'll show only a dynamic translation.

   - To try out dynamic translation, set up a sketch like the one below.

   - Select point *A*. Hold down the Shift key and select point *B*.
   - Choose Mark Vector in the Transform menu.

When you choose Mark Vector, you should see a brief animated flash from point A to B to show you what vector is being marked.

   - Select the polygon and choose Translate from the Transform menu. Click on the By Marked Vector radio button, then click OK. You should get something similar to what is shown here. (The image is gray, the original is black.)

   - Now drag points *A* and *B* to see how the transformation changes dynamically.
     For more detail on dynamic transformations, see Tour 13: Dynamic and Custom Transformations on page 79.

Measuring and Calculating

Sketchpad can measure many different quantities, and the measurements will update dynamically as you drag things around.

14. To measure something in Sketchpad, select the objects that define the quantity you want to measure, and then choose the appropriate command from the Measure menu.

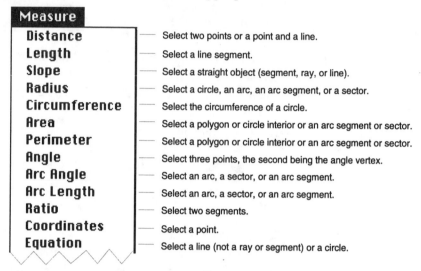

Measure	
Distance	— Select two points or a point and a line.
Length	— Select a line segment.
Slope	— Select a straight object (segment, ray, or line).
Radius	— Select a circle, an arc, an arc segment, or a sector.
Circumference	— Select the circumference of a circle.
Area	— Select a polygon or circle interior or an arc segment or sector.
Perimeter	— Select a polygon or circle interior or an arc segment or sector.
Angle	— Select three points, the second being the angle vertex.
Arc Angle	— Select an arc, a sector, or an arc segment.
Arc Length	— Select an arc, a sector, or an arc segment.
Ratio	— Select two segments.
Coordinates	— Select a point.
Equation	— Select a line (not a ray or segment) or a circle.

- Draw a triangle and measure its three angles. You measure an angle by selecting the three points that define an angle in order. Select the first point, then hold down the Shift key and select the other two points. Then choose Angle from the Measure menu.

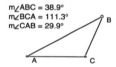

$m\angle ABC = 38.9°$
$m\angle BCA = 111.3°$
$m\angle CAB = 29.9°$

Notice that the angle measurements change dynamically as you drag the vertices of the triangle.

Another way to use existing measurements in the calculator is to click on them while the calculator is open.

15. To calculate a new quantity from existing measurements, select the measurements you wish to use in your calculations (using the Shift key to get more than one) and choose Calculate from the Measure menu. As shown, the calculator contains a pop-up menu from which you can choose the measured or calculated quantities you selected.

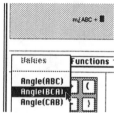

- Calculate the sum of the three angles of the triangle. Notice that this sum does not change as you drag the triangle's vertices.

$m\angle ABC = 38.9°$
$m\angle BCA = 111.3°$
$m\angle CAB = 29.9°$

$m\angle ABC + m\angle BCA + m\angle CAB = 180.00°$

Animating and Tracing

Dragging lies at the heart of dynamic geometry. Animating allows you to automate dragging so can you create beautiful or funny or illuminating sketches that move. Buttons make it easy to replay an animation. Often, a need to see the trace of an object is reason to animate.

Here is a way to use animation to study hyperbolas with Sketchpad.

16. First set up the animation.

- Draw a circle, then draw a line segment with one end on the circumference of the circle, as shown.

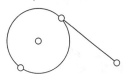

- Animation requires a point and a path. In this case, you want a point to animate around the circle. Select the end of the line segment on the circle's circumference and Shift-select the circle.

- From the Edit menu, choose Animation in the Action Button submenu.

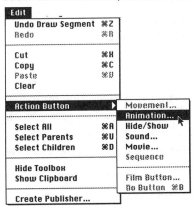

- This command brings up a dialog box that allows you to change the speed and direction of the animation. Click the Animate button.

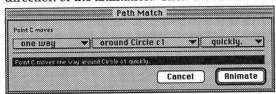

- Now you should see a button in your sketch.

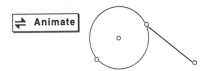

- Double-click the button with the Selection Arrow tool to see the point drag the line segment around the circle.

To stop the animation, click with the mouse

17. A trace of the line segment's perpendicular bisector will create a hyperbola's envelope.

- Construct the perpendicular bisector of the line segment. (To do so, select the segment. Choose the Midpoint command from the Construct menu. Select the midpoint and segment and choose Perpendicular Line from the Construct menu.)

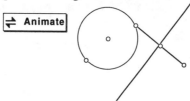

- With the perpendicular bisector selected, choose Trace Line from the Display menu.
- Double-click the Animate button again. You should see something like this.

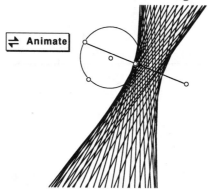

Try different locations for the endpoint of the line segment not attached to the circle. Try different sizes for the circle.

Scripting

When you want to do a particular construction more than once, you can record your construction as a script. Suppose, for example, you are working on a sketch that shows the Pythagorean theorem. You have three squares to construct. Wouldn't you like to be able to construct one and have Sketchpad construct the other two for you?

18. Prepare a sketch and script to record the construction of a square.

- Open a new sketch window.
- Use the New Script command in the File menu to open a new script window. Resize the sketch window so that you can see both the sketch and script windows at the same time.

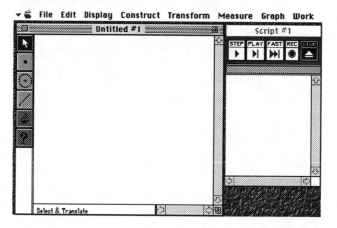

- Press the Record button in the script window.

  The sketch becomes active and the script will record your constructions.

19. Now you'll record the steps needed to construct a square. We'll use rotation as the method for construction, but you can use any method you choose.

- Draw a line segment. Notice that the script window records points *A* and *B* as givens for the construction and shows a single step, namely the construction of the segment.

- Select one endpoint of the line segment and choose Mark Center from the Transform menu.
- Select the other endpoint of the segment and the segment itself.

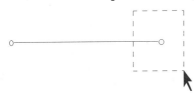

Notice that the script does not record marking. Scripts only record actual construction steps.

- Choose Rotate from the Transform menu and rotate by 90°.
- Mark a center and rotate again to get the four vertices of the square.
- To finish the square, connect the first and fourth vertices with a line segment.
- Press the Stop button in the script window to indicate you are done recording. The steps recorded in your script should be similar to these.

Steps:
  1. Let [j] = Segment between Point [B] and Point [A].
  2. Let [C] = Image of Point [B] rotated 90.0 degrees about center Point [A].
  3. Let [k] = Image of Segment [j] rotated 90.0 degrees about center Point [A].
  4. Let [D] = Image of Point [A] rotated 90.0 degrees about center Point [C].
  5. Let [m] = Image of Segment [k] rotated 90.0 degrees about center Point [C].
  6. Let [n] = Segment between Point [D] and Point [B].

---

20. Your script is now ready to assist you in making squares.

- In a new sketch select two points.
- Press the Play button in the script window. You should see the script go through the steps of your construction.
- Experiment with using the Step button and the Fast button to play the script.
- With the script window activated, choose Save from the File menu. Name your script "Square."
- Construct a right triangle and use your script to place squares on each side.

  If you end up with a square that's on the inside of a side of the triangle instead of on the outside, you've selected the end points in the wrong order. Undo the construction of that square, select the end points of that side of the triangle in the reverse order, and then play the script again.

Where to Go from Here

If you've been successful with this QuickStart, there are a number of places you could go next.

- Try the sample activities in the *Teaching Geometry* booklet that comes in the binder with this user manual.
- Look at the sample sketches that come with Sketchpad. They contain many useful and instructive ideas.
- Select tours featured later in this manual that deal with parts of the program that especially interest you. For example, you may be interested in learning more about scripting or analytic geometry.
- Wing it! Make sketches that interest you.

The Basics

This chapter describes using Sketchpad: how to select tools, how to choose from menus, and how to use dialog boxes. It also describes the difference between sketch windows and script windows.

If you are relatively new to the Macintosh, you should read this entire chapter. If you know how to use a Macintosh but have not used any drawing programs, you might skip to the Toolbox section in this chapter. If you are very familiar with the Macintosh and drawing programs, you may want to skip this chapter completely and start with the Guided Tours.

What You Should Know About the Macintosh

If you have never used a computer before, or if you are new to the Macintosh, you should read the *Getting Started With Your Macintosh* manual that came with your computer.

Throughout this manual, the following terms are used for mouse activities:

Point   Move the mouse until the tip of the pointer is over what you want to select.

Click   Point, then press and release the mouse button quickly.

Double-click   Point, then click the mouse button twice in rapid succession.

Drag   Point, then press and hold down the mouse button. Move the pointer to a new location and release the mouse button.

What You Should Know About Sketchpad

When you use Sketchpad, you will be working with sketches—which contain geometric objects, constructions, and transformations—and scripts, which contain statements about geometric constructions.

Sketches   Sketches are geometric drawings. You can start with a blank sketch and explore geometry from scratch. When you create sketches, you combine objects—points, circles, segments, rays, and lines—to construct figures and investigate geometric principles. You can also just have fun drawing interesting geometric figures and constructing clever animations.

Scripts   Scripts are recordings (in English) of geometric constructions (that is, of objects and their relationships to each other). You can play back a script, and it will construct the objects it describes in a sketch.

Many of Sketchpad's features are like those in other Macintosh programs. The major exception is that Sketchpad has two types of documents—sketches and scripts. These documents appear in windows like those illustrated below. Both sketch windows and script windows have many of the same elements: title bar, scroll bars, close box, zoom box, and size box.

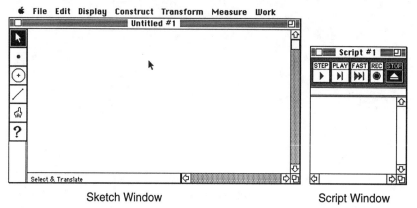

Sketch Window   Script Window

The Sketch Window section of this chapter describes all the features common to sketches and scripts and the features unique to sketches. The Script Window section describes features unique to scripts.

Sketch Window

The illustration below shows the menu bar and components of a sketch window.

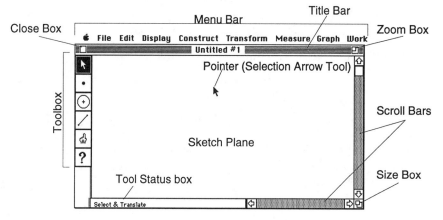

Close Box	Closes the document. If you haven't saved your document in a file when you click this box, Sketchpad gives you the opportunity to save it before closing.
Menu Bar	Lists the menus of commands. The menus that work on sketches are different from those that work on scripts. Some menus are disabled (shown in gray) when the active window is not a sketch window.
Toolbox	Contains the sketch tools for creating and changing geometric objects, displaying and editing labels and captions, and getting information about objects.
Title Bar	Contains the name of the document and the close and zoom boxes. You can drag the window around the screen by dragging the title bar.
Zoom Box	Toggles the size of the window between normal size and full size.

Pointer	Indicates your location in the window. It moves when you move the mouse. When the pointer is in the sketch plane, it takes on a shape representing the current tool.
Sketch Plane	The area where you construct and manipulate geometric objects.
Size Box	Makes the window larger or smaller. Drag these elements to new locations to resize the window.
Scroll Bars	Move the contents of the sketch plane within the window either horizontally or vertically.

Menus

The menu bar shows the names of Sketchpad's individual pull-down menus. Each menu contains related commands, such as commands to measure objects or commands that work on files.

⬢ File Edit Display Construct Transform Measure Graph Work	**Sketch Menu Bar**

When a script window is active, only the menus pertinent to scripts are available; all others are dimmed.

Apple	Standard Desk Accessories.
File	Commands for opening, closing, saving, and printing files (sketches and scripts).
Edit	Commands for selecting objects and editing sketches and scripts.
Display	Commands for changing the appearance of your sketch and for setting preferences about how Sketchpad works.
Construct	Commands for constructing geometric figures in your sketch.
Transform	Commands for translating, rotating, dilating, and reflecting existing geometric figures in your sketch.
Measure	Commands for displaying objects' measurements and making calculations and tables in your sketch.
Graph	Commands for controlling axes, the grid, and the form of coordinates and equations. Allows plotting of points.
Work	Commands for making a script window from an existing sketch and for arranging or manipulating your windows. Choose the name of a script window while holding down the Option key to play the script.

Choosing a command from a menu

1. Move the pointer to the name of the menu that contains the command you want to use.

2. Press and hold down the mouse button.

The menu drops down to display the commands. Each command highlights as you move the pointer over it. If a command is dimmed, it is not available.

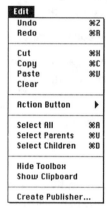

3.   Drag the pointer down the menu to the command you want.

4.   When the pointer is on the command you want, release the mouse button.

Why are some commands dimmed?

When you look at the menus, you see that some commands appear in gray, dim text. These commands are not available because they require some special condition. For example: the Paste command is not available on the Edit menu unless you have already cut or copied something; the commands on the Construct menu are not available until you have selected certain prerequisite objects. Don't worry if you don't understand these reasons; they are explained as you go though this manual. For now, all you need to know is that if the command appears in bold, black text it is available, and if it appears in dim, gray text it is not available.

Choosing menu commands with keystrokes

You can choose some commands from the keyboard by holding down the ⌘ key and pressing the letter indicated to the right of the command you want to choose.

You can use menus either by pulling them down and choosing a command, or by using ⌘ key shortcuts from the keyboard. The available shortcuts appear beside the commands on each menu.

⌘ key shortcuts allow some menu commands to be chosen by holding down the⌘ key and pressing another key. For instance, if you wanted to choose Copy, you could hold down the ⌘ key and press C. This operation is referred to from here on as ⌘C. (The ⌘ key, also known as the Command key, is sometimes referred to as the Open Apple key or the Apple key. It will be referred to here *only* as the ⌘ key.)

Use the F1 function key for help with menu commands.

Submenus

Commands that display an indicator (▶) contain a submenu of choices. When the command is highlighted, the submenu appears.

Choosing a command from a submenu

1.   Display the menu.

2.   Drag the pointer to the command you want.

The submenu appears.

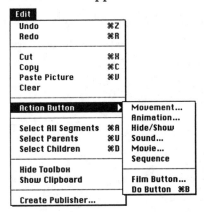

3. Continue holding down the mouse button, and drag the pointer to the right and down the submenu to the command you want.

4. Release the mouse button.

Dialog Boxes

A menu command ending in an ellipsis (...) will bring up a dialog box asking for additional information.

Dialog boxes allow you to supply additional information needed for some commands. For example, when you choose the Open command, the Open dialog box appears.

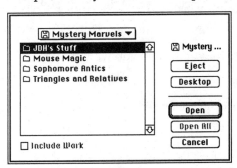

Once you make your selections in the dialog box, click Open to proceed. Some dialog boxes have OK and Cancel buttons; OK executes the request and Cancel dismisses the dialog box without making any changes or executing the request.

Toolbox

The Toolbox contains the tools to draw, label, and change your geometric sketches, as well as a tool to provide information about the current selections.

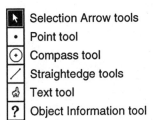

Selection Arrow tools
Point tool
Compass tool
Straightedge tools
Text tool
Object Information tool

Selection Arrow   The Selection Arrow tools not only select objects in the sketch plane, they transform selected objects. Individual Selection Arrow tools translate, rotate, and dilate selected objects.

Point   The Point tool creates points.

Compass	The Compass tool creates circles.
Straightedge	The Straightedge tools create segments, rays, and lines.
Text	The Text tool creates labels and captions for annotating your sketch.
Object Information	The Object Information tool displays information about an object or group of objects in your sketch.

The tools are described in more detail in the Toolbox Reference chapter.

Choosing a tool from the Toolbox

Click the mouse on the tool you want to select. The active tool remains active and highlighted until you click another tool.

Choosing a tool from a palette

The Selection Arrow tools and the Straightedge tools are palettes of tools.

1. Move the pointer to the Selection Arrow tool or Straightedge tool in the Toolbox.

2. Press and hold down the mouse button to display the palette.

3. Drag the pointer to highlight the tool you want to use.

4. Release the mouse button.

   The tool you chose becomes active and highlighted.

Script Window

The script window has many of the same elements as the sketch window. When this window is active, the menus act on it rather than the sketch window. The script window contains five areas: the control deck, the status pane, the comment pane, the comment bar, and the script pane. The comment pane only appears when you drag the comment bar.

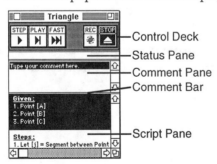

Control deck

This area of the script window contains tape recorder-like controls for recording and playing back steps that create geometric figures in the active sketch.

STEP	Plays back the script one step at a time.
PLAY	Plays back all steps in the script.
FAST	Plays back the script as quickly as possible.

| **REC** | Records the steps of your construction in the active sketch. |
| **STOP** | Stops the recording or playback of a script. |

Buttons are dimmed if their function is not available. For example, if you have not recorded anything, the playback buttons are not available.

Status pane	This area of the script window shows the current state of the script (for instance, whether it is currently being recorded or played).
Comment pane	This portion of the window shows any comment that has been typed in about the script. Comments often include the name of the person who created the script and information about how to use it. The comment pane can be displayed or hidden by dragging the comment bar.
Comment bar	This double bar just above the script pane can be dragged down or up to show or hide the comment pane.
Script pane	This area of the script window shows the script itself. The Given items required for the construction are shown at the top of the script pane, followed by the actual steps of the construction.

Scripts are described in detail in the Scripts chapter.

Guided Tours

Introduction

The tours in this chapter give you a chance to use most of Sketchpad's features. These tours do not teach geometric principles; they teach you how to use Sketchpad to explore geometry. Each tour contains five parts.

- **Free Play** lists the tasks covered in the tour but doesn't tell you how to do them. If you like to figure things out on your own, this section is for you. Try to accomplish each task by yourself. You can always peek at the step-by-step instructions if you need help on any of the tasks. Once you complete the tasks, skip ahead to Further Play.

- **Step-By-Step** lists the instructions for accomplishing each of the tour's tasks. If you prefer to be guided, this is the section for you. Numbered items break each task down into its parts, and each numbered item is followed by detailed directions on what to do.

- **Further Play** lists additional activities for you to explore. You don't have to do them all, but they will give you excellent practice to make sure you've mastered the tour.

- **Questions** allow you to check your understanding of the topics of the tour.

- **Answers** let you check yourself. If this check reveals any missing knowledge, you should repeat the tour. It's very important to master each tour before going on, because the next tour builds on the skills you've just learned.

As you proceed through the tour, the instructions provide alternative methods for performing tasks. For example, one tour may have you save your sketch by using the File menu and another tour may tell you to use ⌘S on the keyboard. There isn't a right or wrong way to execute the Save command; the tours simply illustrate the alternatives so that you are aware of them.

The notes in the margins of the tours provide extra information. You can omit reading these notes and still perform the tasks described. If you want to learn more about Sketchpad, however, you should read them as they appear or come back to them once you finish the exercise.

Do as many tours as you are comfortable with at one sitting. By all means, if a task inspires you to try something different, open a new sketch or script and play with your ideas. The purpose of Sketchpad is to explore geometry, so don't feel hesitant about deviating from a tour as your analytical mind and creativity provide the impetus!

What If You Make a Mistake?

Everyone makes mistakes, especially while learning something new. While you're doing these tours, you may want to get rid of some objects or backtrack to an earlier step. Sketchpad has a very handy feature for just this situation: the Undo command.

The Undo command on the Edit menu undoes your work step by step—all the way back to the empty sketch plane (or the last time you saved) if you want. To retrace just a few steps, choose Undo from the Edit menu, or press ⌘Z. Each time you choose it, the next-most recent step of your construction is undone. To get rid of everything, hold down the Option key while choosing Undo All from the Edit menu, or press Option-Z.

Tour 1: Using Points and Segments

This tour describes points and lines—how to draw them, how to put them together to make geometric shapes, how to select them, and how to move them.

What You Should Know Before Starting

You should already know how to turn on your computer and start Sketchpad as described in the Getting Started chapter of this manual. You should also be able to use the standard Macintosh interface—pointing, clicking, double-clicking, and choosing from menus as described in The Basics chapter.

Free Play

Free Play lists the tasks covered in the tour. If you like to figure things out on your own rather than follow step-by-step instructions, this is the section for you. Just play with the program until you figure out how to do each of the tasks listed. If you have trouble with any of the tasks, you can go through the numbered steps.

If you've experimented with Sketchpad and learned about every task listed in Free Play, skip the numbered steps and go to the Further Play section of the tour. Finally, check to see if you understand everything by answering the questions. Once you think you understand all the concepts of this tour, proceed to the next tour.

✔ Start Sketchpad.

✔ Draw two points, connect the points with a segment, and create a triangle with additional segments.

✔ Select segments and points, using the Selection Arrow tool and the Select All command with the active tool as a filter.

✔ Deselect individual points, segments, and, finally, all objects.

✔ Drag a marquee to select multiple objects.

✔ Move segments and points.

Step-By-Step

1. Open a new sketch. If Sketchpad is already started, quit and start again so that you begin in the same place the tour begins. (You do not have to turn off the computer, just quit and restart Sketchpad.)

    • If necessary, turn on your Macintosh.

    • Double-click on the Sketchpad icon.

The application starts and a new, empty sketch appears.

- Click anywhere in the Sketchpad window to remove the title page from the screen.

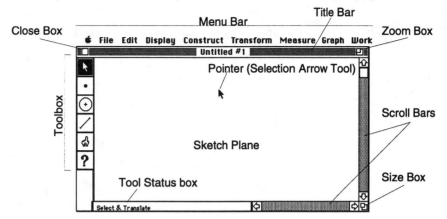

2. Draw two points.
    - Choose the Point tool.

Geometric points have no length or breadth, but point objects in Sketchpad are represented by small circles so that you can see them.

- Move the pointer to the sketch plane.

  The pointer changes to a crosshair pointer. The Point tool is in effect.

The shape of the pointer when it's in the sketch plane tells you which tool is active.

- Click anywhere in the sketch plane.

  The point appears where you clicked. The point is selected—it becomes highlighted.

  ◉

  The Point tool is still in effect.

- Move the pointer in any direction in the sketch plane and click about 2 inches from the first point.

  A second point appears. The second point is selected, and the first one is not selected.

When you create an object, it is automatically selected so that you can easily change it.

   o   ◉

Unselected Point   **Selected Point**

3. Connect the points with a segment.
    - Choose the Segment tool.

    - Move the mouse until the crosshair pointer is centered on one of the two points.

                   ◉

    - Press the mouse button and hold it down.

- While holding down the mouse button, drag the mouse until the crosshair pointer is centered over the other point.

- Release the mouse button.

  The two points are connected with a line segment.

  The segment is selected. When a segment is selected, it displays two black square indicators.

4. Draw two more segments to create a triangle.

   - Move the pointer to one of the endpoints of the first segment.

   - Drag in any direction to create another segment.

     The segment is drawn with a new endpoint at the end.

   - Drag a third segment between the free endpoints of the previous segments.

     Notice that as the pointer gets close to the original point, the tool status box in the bottom left of the window changes to show you that you are on top of the point.

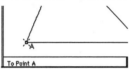

     The triangle is complete.

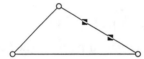

     If you don't quite hit an already existing end point when drawing one of the new segments, the sides of your triangle will not quite connect. Use the Undo Draw Segment command from the Edit menu to erase the segment that missed and try again.

5. Once you have created an object, it must be selected before you can do anything to it such as move it or change its size. The last segment you drew is selected, but no other objects in your sketch are selected. Explore selecting the points and segments you created.

   - Choose the Selection Arrow tool.

   - Move the pointer to one of the segments that is not selected.

     The pointer displays a different, horizontal arrow when the Selection Arrow tool is pointing at an object that can be dragged.

   - Click one of the segments that is not selected.

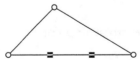

     The new segment is selected but the previously selected segment is no longer selected.

   - Click one of the points.

You can select one object at a time by clicking. You can select and deselect multiple objects by holding down the Shift key while you click.

- Hold down the Shift key and click another point.

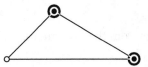

- Continue holding down Shift and clicking until every point and segment is selected.

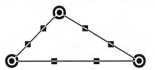

6. Deselect individual segments.

   - With Shift still held down, click each of the selected segments to deselect it.

   Only points are still selected.

There are three methods for selecting multiple objects.

1. Use the Shift key while clicking with the Selection Arrow tool.

2. Drag a selection marquee with the Selection Arrow tool.

3. Use Select All (in conjunction with the current tool for a filter, if you want to limit selections to a single object type).

7. Use a selection marquee to select objects.

   - Visualize a rectangle that would surround all the points and segments.

   - Move the pointer to the upper left corner of the imaginary rectangle.

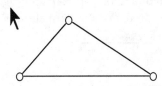

   - Press and hold down the mouse button.

   - Drag the mouse down and to the right until the rectangle surrounds all the objects.

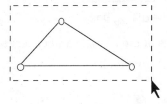

   - Release the mouse button.

   All objects are selected.

   - Click any empty place in the sketch plane.

   All objects are deselected.

8. Use the Select All command with a filter for selecting and deselecting objects.

The current tool acts as a filter for the Select All command, which selects all objects of the same type as the current tool. If the Selection Arrow tool is chosen, Select All selects every object, regardless of its type.

   - Choose Select All from the Edit menu.

   All objects are selected.

   - Click in any empty place in the sketch plane.

   All objects are deselected.

   - Choose the Segment tool.

   - Notice that the Select All command now says Select All Segments. Choose Select All Segments from the Edit menu.

   All segments are selected.

   - Click any empty place in the sketch plane.

- Choose the Point tool.

- Choose Select All Points from the Edit menu.

  All points are selected.

9. Display a list of the selected objects.

   - Move the pointer to the Object Information tool.

   - Press and hold down the mouse button.

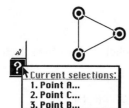

You will learn more about how points and segments are labeled in Tour 3.

- Drag down the list and select Point A.

  An Object Information dialog box appears, telling you about the selected object and its parents and children. (You'll learn about these terms later.)

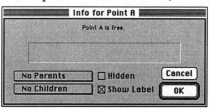

Parents and children are explained in a later tour.

- Click OK to dismiss the dialog box.

10. Move various components of the triangle and observe the effect.

    - Choose the Selection Arrow tool.

    - Click an empty place in the sketch plane to deselect everything.

    - Click on one of the vertices, hold the mouse button down, and drag the point around.

      The point you've selected moves, changing the triangle as you drag. Drag the vertex to make different types of triangles: acute, obtuse, isosceles, equilateral, and right.

When you move an object, many related objects change.

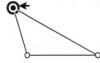

    - Release the mouse button.

    - Drag one of the segments.

      The position of the segment changes, but its length and slope remain constant.

*The heart of **dynamic geometry** is the ability to drag objects and watch how the figure changes.*

The two endpoints of the segment move with it, and since each of them is attached to another segment, those segments stretch and move with their endpoints.

Further Play

A. Try selecting other points and segments and moving them.

B. Try selecting two segments by holding down the Shift key while selecting them, and then drag them around. Do the same with two points.

C. Try selecting all three segments or all three points and moving them.

D. Draw another triangle that has a side or a vertex in common with the one you've already constructed and see what happens when you move various points or segments.

E. Add circles to your drawing. Choose the Compass tool, then drag to indicate a center point and a point on the radius of the circle. The center is located where you press the mouse button, and the end of the radius is located where you release the mouse button. You must drag to create the circle—you can't simply click two locations to create the circle with the Compass tool.

You can create rays and lines in the same manner that you create segments—select the tool and drag in the sketch plane.

F. Experiment with the Ray and Line tools as well as the Point and Segment tools. To select the Ray tool, move the pointer to the Segment tool and hold down the mouse button. The Ray and Line tools appear to the right of the Segment tool. Drag to the Ray tool and release the mouse button.

Questions

1. How do you start Sketchpad from the Finder desktop?

2. What tools would you use to draw a triangle?

3. How would you select all of the points on the screen at once?

4. If all the points on the screen are selected, how can you deselect only one of them and leave the others selected?

5. How can you change the shape of a triangle?

Answers

1. Double-click the Sketchpad icon.

2. Use the Segment tool (possibly, though not necessarily, in conjunction with the Point tool).

3. Choose the Point tool, then choose Select All Points from the Edit menu.

4. Hold down Shift and click the point you want to deselect.

5. Use the Selection Arrow tool to drag a vertex or edge.

Tour 2: Construction Commands

In this tour you will use the Construct menu to create a triangle and use the midpoints of the sides to construct another triangle.

Free Play

To get a blank sketch, you can choose New Sketch from the File menu or you can clear the current sketch by holding down the Option key while choosing the Undo command from the Edit menu.

Try experimenting with Sketchpad to learn how to do each of the tasks listed here in Free Play. If you need more help on any of the tasks, use the Step-By-Step instructions. When you've mastered all the tasks, go on to the Further Play section of the tour. Finally, check to see if you understand everything by answering the questions. Once you think you understand all the concepts of this tour, proceed to the next tour.

✔ Clear the sketch.

✔ Use the Shift key to create points.

✔ Use the Option key to temporarily invoke the Selection Arrow tool while using another tool.

✔ Use the Construct menu to construct segments.

✔ Use the Construct menu to construct midpoints.

Step-By-Step

1. Clear the current sketch.

   • Press and hold the Option key.

   • Choose Undo All from the Edit menu.

     Every object on the sketch disappears.

2. Construct a triangle using the Construct menu.

   • Create one point with the Point tool.

   • Hold down the Shift key and create another point.

     The two points are selected. Release Shift.

To switch to the Selection Arrow tool temporarily while using any drawing tool, hold down the Option key.

   • Choose Segment from the Construct menu or use its keyboard shortcut, ⌘L.

     A segment appears between the selected points.

   • The Point tool is still in effect. Hold down Option and observe that while the key is held down, the pointer in the sketch plane changes into the Selection Arrow.

   • While holding down Option, select one of the endpoints of the segment.

   • Release Option.

     The Point tool is now the current tool.

The difference between the Segment tool and the Segment command is that the tool creates new endpoints if they don't exist, whereas the command requires that the endpoints exist and be selected.

   • Hold down Shift and click another location to create another point.

     Two points are selected.

   • Choose Segment from the Construct menu again.

- Use any method you like to construct the third segment.

  The triangle is complete.

3. Construct the midpoints of the segments.
   - Select all three segments (but not the points).
   - Choose Point At Midpoint from the Construct menu or use its keyboard shortcut, ⌘M.

     A midpoint appears on each segment.

If Point At Midpoint isn't available in the Construct menu, click and hold on the Object Information tool to verify that only segments are selected.

   - Use any method you want to construct a triangle, using the midpoints as vertices.

Further Play

If a command is dimmed, it is not available. If you want to figure out what objects are required for each construction command, think about the mathematics behind what you want to construct.

Every command on the Construct menu requires you to select one or more objects before using the command. These prerequisite selections for commands appear in the Quick Reference sheet as well as in Construction Help in the Construct menu. Construction commands are available according to the types of objects you have selected. Selecting too many, too few, or the wrong kind of object will prevent you from using these commands.

A. Experiment with the Construct menu commands for circles, parallel and perpendicular lines, and points on objects.

B. Go through the Construct menu one command at a time, selecting the appropriate objects to make each command available.

C. Create an angle from two line segments, then create the bisector of that angle. (As in geometry texts, three points identify an angle. The order in which you select the three points is important: you must select the vertex second.)

If your Macintosh doesn't have a color monitor, the Display menu contains a command for Shade but not Color.

D. Select a circle and use the Construct menu to create the circle interior. Use the Display menu to see the shade and color of the interior. To look at the current Shade setting, drag to Shade and the Shade submenu appears. What happens if you choose a different shade?

Questions

1. How can you clear all the objects from the current sketch?

2. If you've got one selected point, what would you do to create another one without deselecting the first point?

3. How can you select a segment while keeping the Point tool the active tool?

4. How can you create a segment without using the Segment tool?

5. How can you create a point at the midpoint of a segment?

Answers

1. Hold down Option while selecting Undo All from the Edit menu.

2. Hold down Shift while using the Point tool to place a new point in your sketch.

3. Hold down Option to use the Selection Arrow tool temporarily.

4. Select two points and use the Segment command in the Construct menu or its keyboard shortcut, ⌘L.

5. Choose the Midpoint command in the Construct menu, or ⌘M.

Tour 3: Labels, Captions, and Measurements

In this tour you will display and move labels for segments and points, create a title for a drawing, and display measurements. Once you observe the different types of text used for labels, captions, and measurements, you will edit the text and its display characteristics.

Text Samples

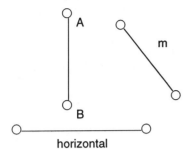

m $\overline{AB}$ = 0.96 inches
m = 0.95 inches
Slope k = -1.23
horizontal = 1.39 inches

horizontal

Free Play

Experiment with Sketchpad to learn about every task listed in Free Play, using the numbered steps if you need more guidance. Then go to the Further Play section of the tour. Finally, check to see if you understand everything by answering the questions. Once you think you understand all the concepts of this tour, proceed to the next tour.

✔ Display the label for a segment.

✔ Move and change the label.

✔ Create a caption for a drawing.

✔ Display the length of a segment.

✔ Change the text style for the caption.

✔ Change the length of a segment.

✔ Save a sketch on a disk.

Step-By-Step

1. Choose New Sketch from the File menu.

   A new, empty sketch opens on top of any other sketches that may be open.

Holding down the Shift key while drawing assists you in making segments that are horizontal, vertical, or at 15° angle intervals.

2. Construct three segments: one vertical, one horizontal, and one at any angle you want. (If you draw the segments in this order, your labels will more closely match the example.)

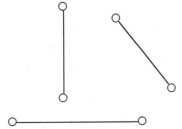

Every object has a label whether it is visible or not.

3. Display the labels for the segments and points.

- Choose the Text tool.

- Move the pointer's finger to one of the existing points until the hand turns black.

Labels for segments are lower-case and point labels are upper-case.

- Click the point.

  A label appears when you click the point.

- Continue clicking points until you have labeled all the points.

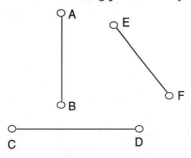

When the Text tool is active, clicking an object toggles between displaying and hiding its label.

- Click each point again to turn off the labels.
- Click each segment.

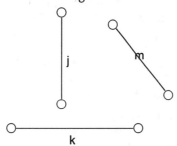

4. Move a label. Sometimes the position of a label on an angled segment isn't in a good location, as is true for the *m* in the illustration above.

- Move the pointer's finger to the label until an *A* appears in the hand. (The letter *A* indicates that the finger points to an editable label instead of a geometric object.)

- Drag the *m* to a new location while the Text tool is still in effect.

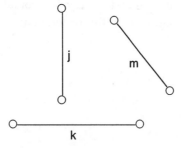

5. Change a label.

- With the Text tool still in effect, double-click the *k* label.

The Label dialog box appears with the label entry box selected.

- Type `Horizontal`.

  The word *horizontal* replaces the selected entry.

- Click the OK button.

  The dialog box disappears and the label changes.

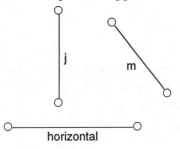

6. Add a caption to your sketch.

   - With the Text tool still in effect, press and drag a blank area in your sketch. Your drag defines a dotted-line box in the sketch.

   - Release the mouse button when the box seems to be about the right size for what you want to type.

     The I-beam will flash in the upper left corner of the box. The height of the box is not very important, because it will automatically resize to accommodate whatever amount of text you enter.

- Type something about your sketch.

> It seems that there are a variety of ways to create a given object! Objects can be created by using the Toolbox, commands in the different menus, or with a combination of the two.

Note that the text wraps to the next line automatically when it reaches the right-hand edge of the box. If you type beyond the bottom of the box, the box expands to accommodate the text.

- Choose the Selection Arrow tool.

Clicking on any other tool or clicking in the sketch completes your caption. The box resizes to fit the text and appears black with white text, indicating that it's selected. It will remain selected until you select or create something else.

7. Move and resize this caption.

- Use the Selection Arrow tool to drag the caption around your sketch.
- Drag one of the white corner boxes of the caption to resize it.

The text reflows to adjust to the new caption size.

> It seems that there are a variety of ways to create a given object! Objects can be created by using the Toolbox, commands in the different menus, or with a combination of the two.

8. Reformat the text in this caption.

- If it's not selected already, select the caption.
- Choose a different text font, style, and/or size in the Display menu.

9. Reformat some labels on your construction.

It's useful to be able to change font sizes and styles when using Sketchpad with an over-head projector. Most fonts can be seen from anywhere in a classroom if they're formatted in 14 pt bold.

- Select the three segments.
- Choose a different text font, style, and/or size from the Display menu.
- While the segments are still selected, press the Shift, ⌘, and > (greater-than) keys. Continue to hold down Shift and ⌘, and press > again.

Each time you press Shift, ⌘, and >, the labels' font size increases by one size.

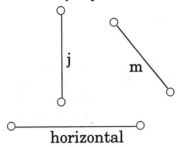

Point labels can also be reformatted by double-clicking the label (not the object) with the Text tool or by using commands in the Text Font and Text Style submenus when the points are selected.

- Continue to hold down Shift and ⌘, and press the < (less-than) key twice.

  Each time you press Shift, ⌘, and <, the labels' font size decreases by one size.

10. Change the text in the caption.

    - Choose the Text tool.

    - Bring the Text tool over the first letter of the text. It will change into an I-beam.
    - Highlight the text by dragging the I-beam over it.
    - Type Text Samples. This replaces the previous text.

11. Display and observe measurements for the segments.

    - Select a segment.
    - Choose Length from the Measure menu.

      The length of the segment appears in the upper left corner of the sketch plane. You can select and move the measurement text with the Selection Arrow tool if you want.

    - Display the length of every segment.

Text Samples

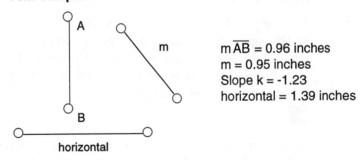

$m\overline{AB} = 0.96$ inches
$m = 0.95$ inches
Slope $k = -1.23$
horizontal $= 1.39$ inches

12. Change the length of a segment and observe the measurement.

    - Choose the Selection Arrow tool if it isn't the active tool.
    - Drag the right endpoint of the horizontal segment to the right.

As the segment stretches, the measurement changes and the label moves.

Text Samples

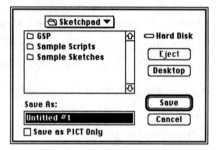

k

m $\overline{AB}$ = 0.96 inches
k = 0.95 inches
Slope k = -1.23
horizontal = 2.07 inches

horizontal

13. Save the document.

   • Choose Save from the File menu.

     The Save As dialog box appears because this document has not been named or saved before.

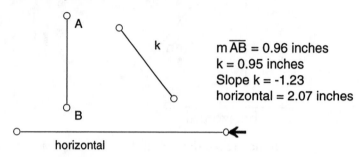

   • Type Tour Practice and click Save.

     The document is saved in the current disk and/or folder, and the sketch remains open for further work.

Further Play

A. Draw circles and measure them.

B. Try changing labels, adding captions and comments, changing the text in measures, and changing the style of the text. Notice that when you change the style of a particular type of text (labels, for example), all future text of that type displays in the new style. This style setting remains in effect—even for new sketches—until you change it again or until you quit Sketchpad.

C. Change the style by selecting text, then choosing the Text Style or Text Font commands in the Display menu. Experiment with different fonts and point sizes.

D. See if you can find different ways to change the font size of a label.

Questions

1. What tool or command do you use to display, move, and change object labels?

2. What's the difference between a caption and a label? (In particular, where can each be displayed and where can each be moved?)

3. With which tool can you create a caption?

4. Describe how to reformat an object label without using the Text tool.

5. How can you find the length of a segment?

6. How do you get a displayed length of a segment to change?

Answers

1. Use the Text tool.

   - Click an object to display or hide its label.
   - Click and drag a label to move it.
   - Double-click a label to edit it.

2. A label is created automatically with the object. You have to create a caption explicitly. When a label is shown, it appears near the object and cannot be moved far away from it. A caption can be created in any blank space in the sketch and can be moved anywhere in the sketch plane.

3. Drag the Text tool in a sketch to create a caption.

4. Select the object and use a text formatting submenu (Text Style or Text Font) in the Display menu.

5. Select the segment, then choose Length from the Measure menu.

6. Drag either endpoint of the segment, and the displayed length updates as you change the segment's length.

Tour 4: Measurements, Calculations, and Polygon Interiors

In this tour you'll learn more uses for commands from the Measure menu, and you'll learn how to calculate measurements that Sketchpad does not directly provide. You will also construct a polygon interior.

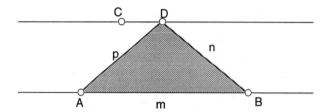

n = 1.19 inches

Distance A to n = 1.13 inches

$$\frac{n \cdot (\text{Distance A to n})}{2} = 0.67 \text{ inches}^2$$

Area ADB = 0.67 inches^2

Free Play

Experiment with Sketchpad to learn about every task listed in Free Play, using the numbered steps if you need more guidance. Then go to the Further Play section of the tour. Finally, check to see if you understand everything by answering the questions. Once you think you understand all the concepts of this tour, proceed to the next tour.

✔ Set your Preferences to display the labels of all new points and straight objects.

✔ Use the Line tool from the Straightedge palette.

✔ Measure the distance from a point to a line.

✔ Use the Calculate command to compute measurements.

✔ Create a polygon interior.

✔ Measure the area of a polygon interior.

Step-By-Step

1. Start with a new sketch.
    *   Close all other sketches, saving as you wish.
    *   Choose New Sketch from the File menu.

2. Set the Preferences to show labels for straight objects and points.

- Choose Preferences from the Display menu.

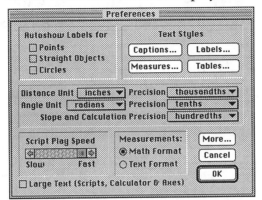

- Click Points and Straight Objects in the Autoshow Labels section, then click OK.

  Observe how this affects the objects you create in subsequent steps.

  After you finish this tour, you can turn off this option so that new objects appear unlabeled by going back to the Preferences dialog box and clicking in the check boxes again.

3. Draw two parallel horizontal lines.

- Move the pointer to the Segment tool and press and hold the mouse button.

The Straightedge palette appears.

- Drag to highlight the Line tool, then release the mouse button

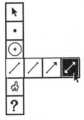

The Line tool is active, and its icon replaces the Segment tool on the tool palette.

- Construct a horizontal line, holding down the Shift key while dragging the Line tool.

- Construct a point several inches above the segment.

- Select the point and the line.

- Choose Parallel Line from the Construct menu.

Alternatively, you can use Translate in the Transform menu to construct a parallel line.

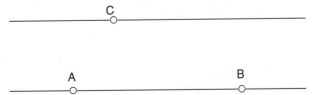

The line through the point is parallel to the first line.

4. Construct a triangle with one side collinear to the lower line and the opposite vertex on the upper line.

- Construct a new point on the top line with the Point tool.

- Drag to select the Segment tool from the Straightedge palette.

- Construct the triangle shown here.

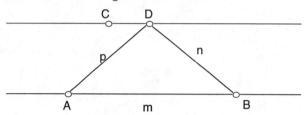

- Use the Text tool to adjust the labels so that you can see them. (They need not be the same letters pictured here.)

5. Find the area of the triangle with the Calculate command.

The area of a triangle is usually calculated by multiplying the length of the base of the triangle by its height, and then dividing by 2. This produces the same result no matter which side of the triangle is considered the base.

- Assume the right edge is the base of the triangle. Measure its length.

  The segment's length appears in the upper left corner of the sketch window. Your sketches probably won't have the same measurements as the measurements illustrated in these tours.

  n = 1.19 inches

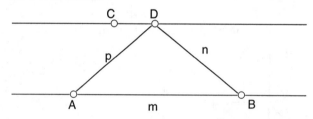

- Using the Selection Arrow tool as the active tool, hold down Shift and select the lower left vertex.

  Both the vertex and the base are selected.

- Choose Distance from the Measure menu.

  The distance between the vertex and the base appears. This measurement is the length of the altitude.

  n = 1.19 inches
  Distance A to n = 1.13 inches

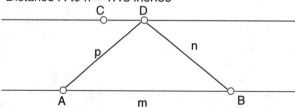

- Select both the segment length measurement and the distance measurement.
- Choose Calculate from the Measure menu, or double-click the selected measurements.

The Calculator appears.

The Value pop-up menu contains the measures you selected in the sketch as well as π and e.

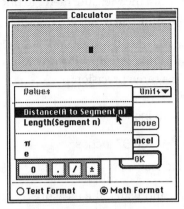

- Click the Value pop-up menu to select Distance (A to segment n).

The Distance value appears in the calculation display rectangle at the top of the dialog box.

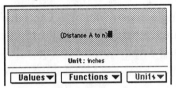

- Click the asterisk in the numeric keypad diagram to indicate multiplication.

- Press on the arrow in the Value pop-up menu and drag to choose the Length value.

The Length value appears in the display rectangle as just the name of the segment.

(Distance A to n)·n

Instead of using the mouse to click on the numeric keypad buttons in the dialog box, you can type any of the keypad numbers or characters (*, /, +, -, etc.) from the keyboard. You will achieve the same result with both methods.

- Click the slash in the keypad diagram to indicate division.

- Click 2.

- Click OK.

n = 1.19 inches
Distance A to n = 1.13 inches
$$\frac{n \cdot (\text{Distance A to n})}{2} = 0.67 \text{ inches}^2$$

The calculation and result appear beneath the other two measurements.

When one object is on top of another, you can click one with the Selection Arrow tool to select it. You can select the second object by clicking again with the Selection Arrow tool.

6. Construct the interior of the triangle.

- Select all three vertices of the triangle.

- Choose Polygon Interior from the Construct menu.

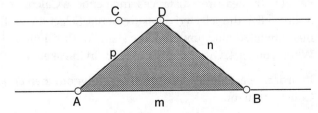

The triangle fills with a color or a shade of gray. The interior flashes when it is selected.

7. Use the Area command from the Measure menu to find the area of the triangle directly.

   - With the polygon interior still selected, choose Area from the Measure menu.

     The measurement indicating the area of the triangle appears under the others. This number is the same as that given by the previous calculation, although it may not be displayed with the same precision.

     $n = 1.19$ inches

     Distance A to $n = 1.13$ inches

     $$\frac{n \cdot (\text{Distance A to } n)}{2} = 0.67 \text{ inches}^2$$

     Area ADB $= 0.67$ inches^2

8. Move parts of the sketch and watch the measures change.

   - Move either of the bottom vertices.

     Both of the area measurements change as you move the vertices.

   - Now try moving the top vertex left and right along its line.

     The area of the triangle doesn't change. Though the base and the height you first calculated both change when you move the top vertex, the second base and height don't change. Thus, the area doesn't change.

This lack of change in the area measurement demonstrates a mathematical idea known as Cavalieri's Principle.

Further Play

A. Use the Measure menu to measure the perimeter of a polygon interior, then add the lengths of the sides together (using Length or Distance and Calculate) to show that the perimeter measure is accurate.

B. Measure all three internal angles of your triangle and add them together. Then move parts of the triangle around to see that no matter what the shape or size of the triangle, its angles total 180°.

Questions

1. How do you measure the distance between a point and a line?

2. How would you find the ratio of two distances?

3. What steps do you use to create a polygon interior?

4. How do you find the area of a polygon interior?

Answers

1. Use the Distance command in the Measure menu.

2. Select both measured distances, then choose Calculate from the Measure menu or double-click the selected measurements. Select one of the distances from the pop-up menu in the dialog box, click the slash for division, and then select the other distance. When you click OK, the ratio appears in the sketch.

3. In order, select all the vertices of the polygon, then choose Polygon Interior from the Construct menu.

4. Select the polygon interior, then choose Area from the Measure menu.

Tour 5: Measuring Circles, Angles, and Arcs

In this exercise, you use more of the commands on the Measure menu and you learn to construct arcs.

Circumference$\odot$AB = 3.21 inches

Radius $\odot$AB = 0.51 inches

$$\frac{\text{Circumference}\odot\text{AB}}{\text{Radius}\odot\text{AB}} = 6.28$$

arc angle a1 = 114.8°

m∠CAB = 114.8°

m∠CDB = 57.4°

$$\frac{\text{arc angle a1}}{\text{m}\angle\text{CDB}} = 2.00$$

arc length a1 = 1.02 inches

$$\frac{\text{arc length a1}}{\text{Circumference}\odot\text{AB}} = 0.32$$

$$\frac{\text{arc angle a1}}{360.0°} = 0.32$$

Area p1 = 0.26 inches^2

Area $\odot$AB = 0.82 inches^2

$$\frac{\text{Area p1}}{\text{Area}\odot\text{AB}} = 0.32$$

Free Play

Experiment with Sketchpad to learn about every task listed in Free Play, using the numbered steps if you need more guidance. Then go to the Further Play section of the tour. Finally, check to see if you understand everything by answering the questions. Once you think you understand all the concepts of this tour, proceed to the next tour.

✔ Measure the circumference and radius of a circle and calculate their ratio.

✔ Construct an arc on a circle and measure its arc angle and arc length.

✔ Measure and compare central and inscribed angles.

✔ Construct a sector and compare its area to the area of the circle.

Step-By-Step

The default measurement unit for arcs and angles is degrees, and the default measurement unit for lengths and distances is inches, but you can change either or both defaults using Preferences from the Display menu.

1. Start with a new blank sketch. Make sure the Preferences are set to autoshow labels for points and the angle units are degrees.

2. Place a total of three points on a circle.

    • Construct a circle using the Compass tool.

    • With the Point tool, place two new points, evenly spaced with the original point on the circumference of the circle.

    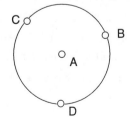

3. Measure the circumference and radius of the circle and calculate their ratio.

    • Select the circle by clicking on it with the Selection Arrow tool.

    • Choose Circumference from the Measure menu.

    The measurement of circumference displays.

- The circle should still be selected. If not, select it again.
- Choose Radius from the Measure menu.

  The measurement of radius appears underneath the measurement of circumference.
- Select the two measurements and use Calculate on the Measure menu to compute the ratio of the circumference and the radius.

  Circumference⊙AB = 3.21 inches
  Radius⊙AB = 0.51 inches
  $$\frac{\text{Circumference}⊙AB}{\text{Radius}⊙AB} = 6.28$$
- Drag point *B* to change the radius of the circle. Notice that the circumference and radius measurements change as you drag. What happens to their ratio? What familiar number is this?

4. Construct an arc on a circle and measure its arc angle and arc length.
   - Select points *A*, *B*, and *C*. These points will define an arc.
   - Choose Arc on Circle from the Construct menu.

     The arc appears on top of a portion of the circle and is selected.
   - In order to make the arc more visible, use the Line Weight command in the Display menu to change the arc's line weight to thick.

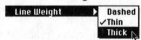

   - With the arc still selected, choose Arc Angle from the Measure menu.

     The measurement of the arc angle appears. Drag the endpoints of the arc and notice how the measurement changes.
   - Select the arc again, then choose Arc Length from the Measure menu. Drag the arc's endpoints and notice how the measure of arc length changes.
         arc angle a1= 114.8°
         arc length a1 = 1.02 inches

5. Show that an arc angle is equal to the measure of its corresponding central angle and equal to twice the number of degrees of its corresponding inscribed angle.
   - Select points *C*, *A*, and *B* in order.
   - Choose Angle from the Measure menu.

     The measure of angle *CAB* appears. Notice that it is equal to the corresponding arc angle no matter what you drag.
   - Similarly, select the inscribed angle, *CDB*, and measure it.

     Notice that the inscribed angle appears to be about half the arc angle.
   - Select the measurement of the arc angle and the measurement of the inscribed angle and choose Calculate from the Measure menu.
   - In the calculator, compute the arc angle divided by the measure of the inscribed angle.
   - Click the OK button.

The ratio appears and is equal to 2 no matter how you drag things.

arc angle a1 = 114.8°

m∠CAB = 114.8°

m∠CDB = 57.4°

$$\frac{\text{arc angle a1}}{\text{m∠CDB}} = 2.00$$

6. Compare two ratios: the ratio of the arc angle to the total number of degrees in the circle and the ratio of the arc length to the circumference of the circle.

   • Using Calculate, divide the previously-measured arc angle measure by 360 degrees. Use the Units pop-up menu to set degrees as the unit of measure for 360.

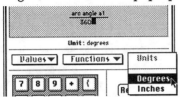

   • Press the OK button. The result should be a number with no units because degrees divided by degrees is unitless.

   • Use Calculate to divide the arc length by the circle's circumference.

$$\frac{\text{arc angle a1}}{360.0°} = 0.32$$

$$\frac{\text{arc length a1}}{\text{Circumference} \odot \text{AB}} = 0.32$$

Note that these two values are equal; they both indicate the fraction of the circle taken up by the arc.

7. Construct a sector and compare its area to the area of the circle.

   • Select the arc.

   • Choose Arc Sector Interior in the Construct menu.

   The sector appears inside the circle.

   • With the sector still selected, choose Area from the Measure menu.

   The measurement of the area of the sector appears. Notice how it responds to dragging the points that define the arc.

   • Select the circle by clicking on its circumference.

   • Choose Area from the Measure menu.

   • Select both area measurements and use the Calculate command to compute the ratio of the circle's area to the sector's area.

Area p1 = 0.26 inches^2

Area⊙AB = 0.82 inches^2

$$\frac{\text{Area p1}}{\text{Area} \odot \text{AB}} = 0.32$$

Note that this is the same as the ratio of arc angle to 360°.

Further Play

A. Move all the parts of the circle around, noticing which measures change and which don't. Figure out why.

When one object lies on top of another (as the circle lies on top of the arc) pay close attention to the selection handles to tell which object you have selected. If you get the wrong object, click again to get the next object in that location.

B. Calculate a value for π using Calculate and some of the measures you already have, without using the π value given by the Calculator dialog box.

C. Figure out a way to compute the area of the sector of the circle for your chosen arc, without directly measuring it.

D. Place three points in your sketch, select them, and use the Arc Through 3 Points command to construct an arc. Investigate some of the properties of this arc.

E. Inscribe a triangle in half of a circle, using the circle's diameter as one edge. What is the measure of the angle of the triangle opposite the diameter?

F. Select an arc and use the Arc Segment Interior command to construct an arc segment. Investigate the relationship between the area of the arc segment and the angle of the arc.

G. Make a pretty design using circles, arcs, sectors and arc segments.

Questions

1. How do you measure the number of degrees of an angle?

2. How do you find the distance along the circumference between two points on the circumference of a circle?

3. How do you measure the total circumference of a circle?

4. How do you find the area of a sector of a circle?

5. Given the circumference of a circle, how would you use Calculate to find the radius?

Answers

1. Select the three points that define the angle (with the vertex of the angle as the second point), then choose Angle from the Measure menu.

2. Select the center of the circle followed by the two points and choose Arc on Circle in the Construct menu. Then choose Arc Length from the Measure menu.

3. Use the Circumference command in the Measure menu.

4. Construct an arc corresponding to the desired sector. Select the arc and use Area in the Measure menu.

5. Select the circumference measurement, then use Calculate to divide by 2π.

Tour 6: Tables and Action Buttons

In this tour, you'll learn how to create tables and add entries for measured values that change over time as you manipulate your figure. If your computer has a microphone, you'll learn how to record a sound and play it in your sketch.

Free Play

Experiment with Sketchpad to learn about every task listed in Free Play, using the numbered steps if you need more guidance. Then go to the Further Play section of the tour. Finally, check to see if you understand everything by answering the questions. Once you think you understand all the concepts of this tour, proceed to the next tour.

✔ Construct a parallelogram.

✔ Measure angles.

✔ Create a table.

✔ Add entries using the Measure menu, the keyboard, and the mouse.

✔ Record a sound and create an action button to play it.

Step-By-Step

1. If you have not already done so, close all open sketches and scripts, and open a new sketch.

2. Construct a parallelogram with labeled vertices.

   • Construct a segment.

   • Construct a point not on the segment.

   o

   • Select the point and the segment and choose Parallel Line from the Construct menu.

   • Construct a segment from the lower-left segment endpoint to the point on the parallel line.

   • Select this new segment and the lower-right endpoint and choose Parallel Line from the Construct menu.

- Construct the lines' point of intersection by clicking the intersection with the Selection Arrow tool.

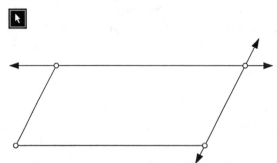

- Select the two lines and choose Hide Lines from the Display menu.

You can show point labels automatically by choosing Autoshow Labels for Points in Preferences.

- Use the Segment tool to complete the parallelogram.

- Use the Text tool to show the labels of the four vertices (points) of the parallelogram.

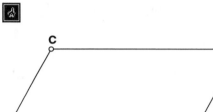

3. Measure the four angles.
   - Select three vertices of the parallelogram.
   - Choose Angle from the Measure menu.

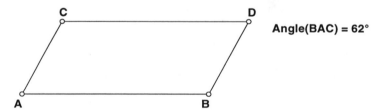

Angle(BAC) = 62°

Sketchpad can measure directed angles if you so choose under Preferences. Directed angles can be negative. Angles measured counterclockwise, as in this example, are positive.

Sketchpad measures the angle according to the order in which you selected the points. In this example, the points were selected in order, *B-A-C*. Point *A* is the vertex of the angle.

   - Repeat for the other three angles of the parallelogram.

     You should now have four measures in your sketch.

4. Drag the vertices of your parallelogram and observe how the measures change.

5. Create a table for these four measures.
   - Select the four angle measures by holding down Shift and clicking them with the Selection Arrow tool, or by blanketing them with a selection marquee.

- Choose Tabulate in the Measure menu.

Angle (ACD)	123.0
Angle (CDB)	57.0
Angle (DBA)	123.0
Angle (BAC)	57.0

Sketchpad lists the four measure labels in a table with four rows, showing one entry for each measure label. Each entry is the value of that measure at the time you created the table.

6. Add entries to this table.

- Move a vertex or side of your parallelogram so that the angle measures change.

  While the measures change, the table entries do not. Table entries represent measurements taken at specific times and are thus fixed.

- Click on the table with the Selection Arrow tool and choose Add Entry from the Measure menu.

Angle (ACD)	123.0	115.2
Angle (CDB)	57.0	64.8
Angle (DBA)	123.0	115.2
Angle (BAC)	57.0	64.8

Another column is added to the table showing the four measures of your angles in this new state.

- Manipulate the figure again. Select the table, then press the letter E while holding down the ⌘ key.

  A third column of entries is added to the table. ⌘E is the keyboard shortcut for Add Entry.

- Manipulate the figure again, then double-click the table with a Selection Arrow tool.

Angle (ACD)	123.0	115.2	109.5	100.5
Angle (CDB)	57.0	64.8	70.5	79.5
Angle (DBA)	123.0	115.2	109.5	100.5
Angle (BAC)	57.0	64.8	70.5	79.5

A fourth column of entries is added to the table. Double-clicking is the mouse shortcut for Add Entry.

7. Select the table and choose Flip Direction from Measure menu.

Angle (ACD)	**Angle (CDB)**	**Angle (DBA)**	**Angle (BAC)**
123.0	57.0	123.0	57.0
115.2	64.8	115.2	64.8
109.5	70.5	109.5	70.5
100.5	79.5	100.5	79.5

The measure labels and their entries flip from being listed in rows to being listed in columns.

8. Edit one of the measure labels on the table and reformat all text in the table.

- Double-click the table's measure label, "Angle (ACD)," with the Text tool.

This dialog box appears. It's similar to the dialog boxes for editing object labels and measures.

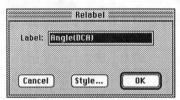

- Edit the text in the highlighted text-entry box. (For example, type   Angle C if you wish to edit the label "Angle (DCA).")
- Click the Style button.
- Choose a new font, style, and/or font size from the options in the Style dialog box.
- Click OK once to dismiss the Style dialog box and again to dismiss the Label dialog box.

You can also reformat a table's text by selecting it and choosing commands from the Text Font and Text Style submenus in the Display menu.

Angle (ACD)	Angle (CDB)	Angle (DBA)	Angle (BAC)
123.0	57.0	123.0	57.0
115.2	64.8	115.2	64.8
109.5	70.5	109.5	70.5
100.5	79.5	100.5	79.5

The table now shows the edited text for the label which you double-clicked, and reformatted text for all the labels and the table entries. Labels can be edited individually, but text formatting changes apply to all the text in the table.

9. Hide the table's labels by clicking the table (not its labels) once with the Text tool.

10. Show the table's labels again by clicking it again with the Text tool.

11. If your Macintosh is equipped with a microphone, add a sound to your sketch.
    - Choose Sound from the Action Buttons submenu of the Edit menu. (This command won't be available if your Macintosh doesn't have a microphone. If that's the case, the tour's over. Go on to Further Play and the questions.)

      You see this dialog box.

    - Click Record and speak into the microphone.
    - When you're finished speaking, click Stop.
    - Click Save.

      An action button labeled "Play Sound" appears in your sketch.

      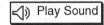

    - Play the sound by double-clicking the action button.

Action buttons have numerous uses for turning sketches into multi-media presentations. See the Reference section for more details.

12. Double-click the action button with the Text tool to change its label to   My Voice.

Further Play

A. Measure other quantities in your sketch and create a table to analyze them.

B. Construct a right triangle and create a table of trigonometric functions.

C. Experiment with other action buttons to see what they do.

Questions

1. Where is the Tabulate command found?

2. What needs to be selected before you can create a table?

3. Name three ways to add an entry to a table.

4. Where is the Sound command found?

Answers

1. In the Measure menu.

2. One or more measures need to be selected before you can create a table.

3. Add entries to a table by selecting the table and choosing Add Entry in the Measure menu. ⌘E is a keyboard shortcut for Add Entry. Or you can simply double-click the table with the Selection Arrow tool.

4. Sound is in the Action Buttons submenu of the Edit menu.

Tour 7: Introducing Scripts

A script is a way to record a series of actions and repeat them later. Once you have recorded the steps, you can replay the script to create the same geometric figures using new, selected objects for the Givens in the script.

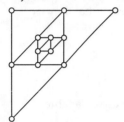

Free Play

Experiment with Sketchpad to learn about every task listed in Free Play, using the numbered steps if you need more guidance. Then go to the Further Play section of the tour. Finally, check to see if you understand everything by answering the questions. Once you think you understand all the concepts of this tour, proceed to the next tour.

✔ Close a document.

✔ Size a window so that you can see both windows at the same time.

✔ Create a script for constructing a triangle with midpoints.

✔ Replay the script using the midpoints as the Given points.

Step-By-Step

1. Start with a new sketch.
   - Close the sketch from the previous tour by clicking the close box in the upper-left corner of the title bar.

     Sketchpad gives you the opportunity to save the changes you have made since the last time you saved.
   - If you want to save, click Save. If you don't want to save, click Don't Save.
   - Choose New Sketch from the File menu.

2. Set Preferences to hide labels for straight objects and points.
   - Choose Preferences from the Display menu.

     Turn off Autoshow Labels by clicking the boxes with checks in them and then clicking OK.

3. Begin a script.
   - Choose New Script from the File menu.

     The controls for a script are like the controls on a cassette tape player.

     A blank script window appears.

4. Change the size of the sketch window so that you can see both windows at the same time.

   - Click the title bar of the sketch window to make it the active window.

   - Move the pointer to the size box at the lower-right corner of the sketch window.

   - Drag the size box to the left until you can see both windows.

   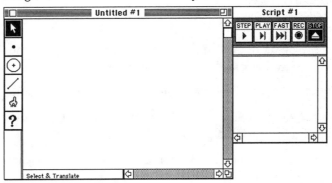

5. Record the construction of a triangle.

   - Click the REC button in the script window.

   The sketch becomes active and the script records your actions.

   - Construct a triangle.

6. Create midpoints.

   - With the Segment tool active, choose Select All Segments from the Edit menu.

   - Choose Point At Midpoint from the Construct menu.

   The midpoints appear and are selected; the segments are no longer selected.

7. Stop the script recording.

   - Click the STOP button in the script.

8. Play back the script.

   - With the midpoints selected in the sketch, click the PLAY button in the script.

   A new triangle appears with vertices at the midpoints of the sides of the first triangle. The midpoints of sides of the new triangle are selected.

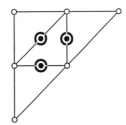

9. Play the script again.

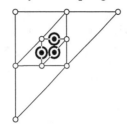

The midpoint triangles in this activity converge upon the triangle's centroid.

10. Use FAST to play the script.

   The script plays quickly. If the script is on top of the sketch, the script window moves to the back so that you can watch what happens in the sketch.

11. Create three selected points that are unrelated to the triangle, and play the script.

12. Create three selected points, and try the STEP feature of the script.
    - Select three points.
    - Click the STEP button in the script window each time you want to execute a step.
    - Step through to the end of the script, or click the STOP button when you want to stop.

13. Save the script, if you wish.

If the sketch is active, the Save command saves the sketch. If the script is active, Save saves the script.

    - Click the close box in the script window.

      You have the opportunity to save the script.

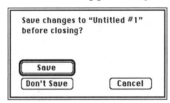

    - Click the Save button to save the script if you wish.

Further Play

A. Open a new sketch and script. Start recording the script. Create a four-sided figure. After you stop the script, create four selected points that are not the corners of a rectangle and play the script for those points.

B. Replay the script on the same four selected points, selected in a different order. (Deselect all four points, and then select them again, selecting diagonally opposite points as your first two points.)

C. Experiment with creating other shapes and selecting points at the end of the recording session before clicking STOP.

Questions

1. Where do you click to close an open sketch or script?

2. How do you change the size of an open sketch or script?

3. Assuming that a script window is not open, what commands and buttons do you use to record a construction in a script?

4. Once a script is recorded, what buttons do you click to play it back?

Answers

1. The close box in the upper-left corner of the window.

2. Drag the size box in the lower-right corner of the window.

3. Choose New Script from the File menu, click the REC button, and proceed with the construction. When you have completed the construction, click STOP.

4. Any of the STEP, PLAY, or FAST buttons will play the script.

Tour 8: Transformations

In this tour you'll use the Transform commands and the Selection Arrow tools to work with transformational geometry. You can translate, rotate, and dilate with either the commands or the tools but you can reflect a selection only with the command.

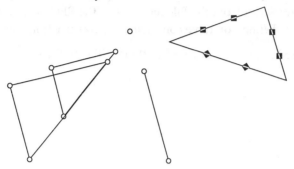

Free Play

Experiment with Sketchpad to learn about every task listed in Free Play, using the numbered steps if you need more guidance. Then go to the Further Play section of the tour. Finally, check to see if you understand everything by answering the questions. Once you think you understand all the concepts of this tour, proceed to the next tour.

✔ Mark the center for future transformations.

✔ Dilate a triangle using the Dilate tool.

✔ Dilate a triangle using the Dilate command.

✔ Create a mirror image.

Step-By-Step

1. Construct a triangle using any method you like.

2. Construct a point anywhere outside the triangle and mark it as the center for rotation and dilation.

   Rotation and dilation are transformations that require a center in order to be mathematically well-defined.

   - Construct a point outside the triangle.

     The point is selected.

   - Choose Mark Center from the Transform menu.

     The point flashes briefly to indicate that it is the center. It remains the center of rotation or dilation until you choose a different center.

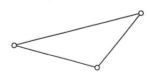

3. Use the Dilation tool from the Selection palette to select and dilate the triangle.

   - Move the pointer to the current Selection Arrow tool in the Toolbox.

   - Press and hold down the mouse button.

     The palette displays the Selection Arrow tools.

- Drag to select the Dilate tool.

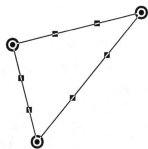

- Drag one of the edges of the triangle.

  The edge dilates relative to the center of dilation.

4. Use the Dilate command to dilate the triangle.

   - Use the Selection Arrow tool to drag a marquee around the triangle.

You can use each of the Selection Arrow tools to select objects in the same way.

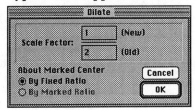

   - Choose Dilate from the Transform menu.

     The Dilate dialog box appears.

   - Type 1 in the upper edit-box and 2 in the lower edit-box for a ratio of $1/2$.

   - Click OK to dilate the triangle by a factor of $1/2$.

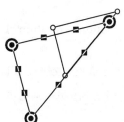

     The new $1/2$ scale triangle appears.

Dilation is a similarity transformation; when you dilate a figure, you change its size but not its shape.

5. Repeat the dilation with a new ratio that makes the triangle larger.

   - Choose Dilate from the Transform menu. The dialog box appears.

   - Type 3 in the upper edit box and click OK.

     A new triangle appears at $1^1/2$ scale.

Reflection is a transformation that requires a mirror line in order to be mathematically well-defined.

6. Add a segment to your sketch and reflect the larger triangle.

   • Draw a segment to the right of the triangles.

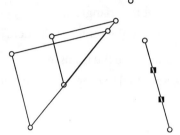

   The segment is selected.

   • Choose Mark Mirror from the Transform menu.

   • Select the segments but not the vertices of the larger triangle.

   • Choose Reflect from the Transform menu.

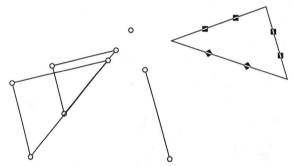

   • Notice that the segments of the triangle are reflected, but not the points. Only selected objects are reflected.

Further Play

A. Use the Selection Arrow tool to drag some of the points and segments of the original two triangles. Notice how all of the triangles are affected. Try dragging a segment you marked as a mirror or a point you marked as the center.

B. Experiment with the Rotate command and the Rotate tool.

C. Try drawing an asymmetric letter, such as F, using segments. Reflect it. Observe what happens when you move the segments making up the letter individually. Then reflect the reflection with another mirror.

Questions

1. How do you mark a point as the center of rotation? How do you mark a segment as a mirror?

2. What must you do before using the Dilate tool to dilate an object?

3. Other than using the Dilate tool, how else can you change the size of an object?

Answers

1. Select the point, then choose Mark Center from the Transform menu. Select the segment, then choose Mark Mirror from the Transform menu.

2. Mark a point as the center of dilation.

3. Use the Dilate command in the Transform menu.

Tour 9: Dynamic Geometry and Dragging

In this tour you will explore more about dragging objects and learn how some drag operations are constrained.

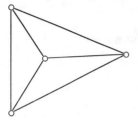

Free Play

Experiment with Sketchpad to learn about every task listed in Free Play, using the numbered steps if you need more guidance. Then go to the Further Play section of the tour. Finally, check to see if you understand everything by answering the questions. Once you think you understand all the concepts of this tour, proceed to the next tour.

✔ Construct an intersection point.

✔ Drag intersecting segments.

✔ Observe parents and children.

✔ Construct the angle bisectors of a triangle.

✔ Construct a point at the intersection of the angle bisectors of the triangle.

✔ Hide the angle bisectors.

✔ Construct segments from the vertices of the triangle to the intersection point.

✔ Use Undo to return to the original triangle.

✔ Rotate the triangle.

Step-By-Step

1. Construct a point at the intersection of two segments.
   - Construct two segments that intersect.

   - Select the segments.
   - Choose Point At Intersection from the Construct menu.

You can also create a point at an intersection by clicking with the Point tool or the Selection Arrow tool on the intersection of the lines.

2. Move the segments and the intersection point.
   - Drag one of the segments.

     The intersection point moves.
   - Drag the selected segment so that it no longer intersects with the other segment.

     The intersection point disappears.
   - Drag the segment until it once again intersects with the other segment.

     The intersection point reappears.
   - Select the intersection point and drag it.

     Notice that the segments move with the point of intersection.

The segments are the parents of the intersection point because they define it. The point is a child of the segments.

3. Observe the relationships between the segments and the intersection point.

   • Select the intersection point.

   • Choose Select Parents from the Edit menu.

     The segments are selected.

   • Choose Select Children from the Edit menu.

     The intersection point is selected.

4. Construct the angle bisectors in a triangle and label the intersection of the angle bisectors as `incenter`.

   • Construct a triangle.

   • Select the three vertex points.

   • Choose Angle Bisector from the Construct menu.

   • Construct the remaining angle bisectors.

When you define an angle, Sketchpad assumes the second point is the vertex.

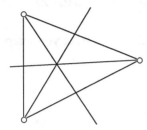

You can't construct a point at the intersection of three objects. If three or more straight objects pass through a single point, you can use the Construct menu to construct a point at the intersection of any two of them.

   • Drag the segments and vertices of the triangle one by one.

     The angle bisectors always intersect at a single point.

   • Construct a point at the intersection. (Select two of the angle bisectors and construct a point at the intersection using the Construct menu.)

   • Click the intersection point with the Text tool.

   • Double-click the label.

   • Type `incenter` and click OK.

   • Drag the point and observe what moves.

5. Hide the angle bisectors.

   • Select the three angle bisectors.

   • Choose Hide Rays from the Display menu.

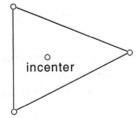

   • Drag the sides of the triangle and watch the incenter move.

- Construct segments from the vertices to the incenter.

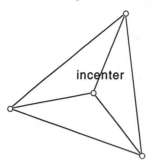

incenter

- Try dragging the new segments.

6. Go back to your original triangle.
   - Choose Undo from the Edit menu to go back one step in your construction.
   - Hold down the ⌘ key and press the letter Z. This is the keyboard shortcut for Undo.
   - Repeatedly use either method to retrace your steps to the original triangle.

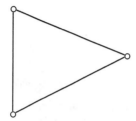

7. Rotate the triangle.
   - Mark one of the vertices as the center of rotation.
   - Drag the various elements with the Rotate tool in the Selection palette.

     Sketchpad constrains the rotation to circular paths around the center. You can't drag the center point.

Further Play

A. Explore dilating the triangle.

B. Try constructing points where a segment intersects a circle. Observe the constraints for dragging the segment, circle, and intersections.

C. Construct circles, then rotate and reflect them using different centers and mirror lines.

D. Try constructing an incircle (a circle inscribed in a triangle with its center at the incenter). Does the circle remain inscribed as you change the triangle? What do you need to do to ensure that the inscribed circle remains tangent to the three sides of the triangle?

Questions

1. Give two ways for creating a point at the intersection of two segments.

2. How can you move the point of intersection between two segments?

3. How can you select the parents of a selected object?

4. How do you bisect an angle?

5. How can you create a point at the intersection of three segments?

6. What command makes objects invisible? How can you display them again?

7. If you start with a triangle and then perform a complicated construction, how can you get back to the original triangle?

Answers

1. Select both segments, then choose Point At Intersection from the Construct menu. You can also click the intersection with a Selection Arrow tool.

2. You must move the segments that intersect to move the point at the intersection.

3. Choose Select Parents from the Edit menu.

4. Select one endpoint, then the vertex point, and finally the other endpoint of the angle. Then choose Angle Bisector from the Construct menu.

5. Select two of the intersecting segments, then choose Point At Intersection from the Construct menu.

6. The Hide command in the Display menu makes objects invisible. Choose Show All Hidden to display hidden objects.

7. Use Undo (or ⌘Z) from the Edit menu repeatedly until you arrive back at the original triangle.

Tour 10: Coordinates and Equations

In this tour you'll learn how to use Sketchpad's coordinate system to measure coordinates and plot points. You'll also get the equation of a line and check that the coordinates of a point satisfy the equation.

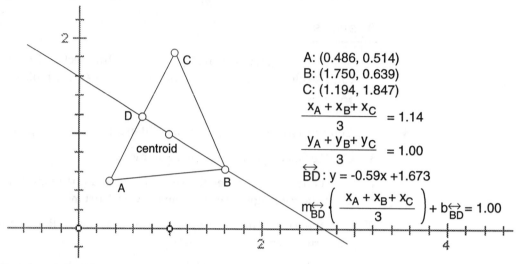

$$A: (0.486, 0.514)$$
$$B: (1.750, 0.639)$$
$$C: (1.194, 1.847)$$

$$\frac{x_A + x_B + x_C}{3} = 1.14$$

$$\frac{y_A + y_B + y_C}{3} = 1.00$$

$$\overleftrightarrow{BD}: y = -0.59x + 1.673$$

$$m_{\overleftrightarrow{BD}}\left(\frac{x_A + x_B + x_C}{3}\right) + b_{\overleftrightarrow{BD}} = 1.00$$

Free Play

Experiment with Sketchpad to learn about every task listed in Free Play, using the numbered steps if you need more guidance. Then go to the Further Play section of the tour. Finally, check to see if you understand everything by answering the questions. Once you think you understand all the concepts of this tour, proceed to the next tour.

✔ Find the coordinates of the vertices of a triangle.

✔ Use the calculator to compute the mean of the x-coordinates and the mean of the y-coordinates of the vertices.

✔ Plot the two means as an (x, y) pair and compare its position with the centroid of the triangle.

✔ Find the equation of the median line of the triangle and show that a plotted point satisfies this equation.

Step-By-Step

1. Starting with a new sketch, draw a triangle and find the coordinates of its vertices.
   - Use the segment tool to draw a triangle.
   - Select the three vertices and choose Coordinates from the Measure menu.

The coordinates and also a pair of axes appear.

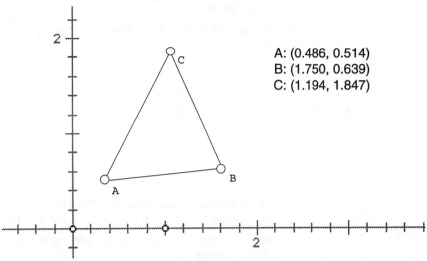

- Try dragging the vertices of the triangle and notice how the coordinates change. Try dragging the origin.

  Dragging the point at (1, 0) will also change the coordinates. As you drag the point, notice that the unit size on each axis changes.

2. Compute the mean of the x-coordinates of the three points.

   - Select the three coordinates.
   - Choose Calculate from the Measure menu.
   - Start by pressing the open parenthesis key. This will enable you to get the sum of the x-values all in the numerator of a fraction.
   - Hold down the mouse pointer on the Values pop-up menu. Move the pointer to Point A, then move to the right to choose x in the submenu. The calculator display shows x_A.

   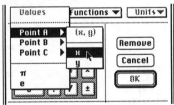

   - Press the + key (plus) on the keypad.
   - Choose x_B from the Values pop-up menu.
   - Press the + key (plus) on the keypad again.
   - Choose x_C from the Values pop-up menu.
   - Press the OK button

     The desired calculation appears in the sketch window.

     $$\frac{x_A + x_B + x_C}{3} = 1.14$$

3. Repeat the above calculation for the mean of the y-coordinates.

   $$\frac{y_A + y_B + y_C}{3} = 1.00$$

4. Use the mean of the x-coordinates and mean of the y-coordinates to plot a new point.

- First select the mean of the *x*-coordinates, then Shift-select the mean of the *y*-coordinates.
- Choose Plot as (x,y) from the Graph menu.

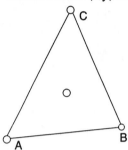

A new point appears in the middle of the triangle. Drag the vertices of the triangle and notice how the new point responds. Try dragging the origin and unit of the coordinate system. Even though the coordinates all change, the computed point remains stationary.

5. The plotted point appears to be the centroid of the triangle. Check out this conjecture by drawing one or more median lines.
   - Select segment *AC*.
   - Choose Midpoint from the Construct menu.
   - Use the Line tool (not the Segment tool) to draw a line through point *B* and the midpoint of segment *AC*.

     Notice that the median line appears to go through the plotted point no matter how you drag the triangle.
   - Label the plotted point `centroid`.

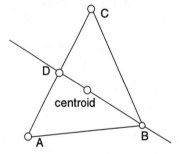

6. Obtain the equation for the median line and determine whether the coordinates of the centroid satisfy this equation.
   - Select the median line and choose Equation from the Measure menu.

     Notice that as you drag the vertices of the triangle, the equation of the median line changes dynamically.
   - Select the mean of the *x*-coordinates and the equation of the line.
   - Choose Calculate in the Measure menu.
   - In the Value pop-up menu, choose the slope of the line.
   - Press * key (asterisk) on the keypad.
   - In the Value menu, choose the mean of the *x*-coordinates.
   - Press + key (plus) on the keypad.
   - In the value pop-up menu, choose the intercept of the line.
   - Press OK.

$$\frac{x_A + x_B + x_C}{3} = 1.14$$

$$\frac{y_A + y_B + y_C}{3} = 1.00$$

$$\overleftrightarrow{BD}: y = -0.59x + 1.673$$

$$m_{\overleftrightarrow{BD}}\left(\frac{x_A + x_B + x_C}{3}\right) + b_{\overleftrightarrow{BD}} = 1.00$$

The result of substituting a particular x into the equation of the line appears. Compare it with the mean of the y-coordinates. Drag the vertices of the triangle to check that the equality of the two computations continues to hold.

It is a short step from here to an analytic proof that the medians of a triangle all go through a single point.

Further Play

A. Use analytic techniques to construct the intersection of two lines given their equations.

B. Carry through an analytic proof that the three medians of a triangle intersect at a common point.

C. Draw a circle centered at the origin of the coordinate system and a line passing through the origin. Get the equations of both the circle and the line and use them to calculate the coordinates of a point of intersection. Plot the point to see if it matches the observed intersection.

Questions

1. How do you get the coordinates of a point and the equation of a line?

2. How do you use the x-coordinate of a point in a calculation?

3. Given the computed coordinates of a point, how do you plot that point in a coordinate system?

4. Does the computed position of the centroid of a triangle depend on the origin or unit of the coordinate system?

Answers

1. To measure the coordinates of a point, select the point and choose Coordinates in the Measure menu. (If you want the coordinates in polar form, first use the Grid Form sub-menu in the Graph menu.) To get the equation of a line, select the line and choose Equation in the Measure menu.

2. To use the x-coordinate of a point in a calculation, select the measurement of the point's coordinates and choose Calculate in the Measure menu. Then the Values pop-up menu gives access to each individual component of the point's coordinates.

3. To plot a point from computed coordinates, select first the x (or r) coordinate, then the y (or θ) coordinate and choose Plot as (x,y) from the Graph menu.

4. Though the values of the x- and y-coordinates of the computed centroid change as the origin or unit of the axes change, the actual plotted position remains the same. This makes sense because the centroid is defined as the intersection of medians, independent of the coordinate system.

Tour 11: Script Tools

In this tour you will learn how to make a script from existing geometric objects and use that script as a tool. Script tools are scripts that you have placed in a specified folder.

Free Play

Experiment with Sketchpad to learn about every task listed in Free Play, using the numbered steps if you need more guidance. Then go to the Further Play section of the tour. Finally, check to see if you understand everything by answering the questions. Once you think you understand all the concepts of this tour, proceed to the next tour.

✔ Set Sketchpad's Script Tool folder.

✔ Construct a circumcircle of a triangle.

✔ Make a script from the circumcircle figure.

✔ Save the script as Circumcircle and install it in the Script Tools folder.

✔ Use your new script tool to construct a circumcircle on a new triangle.

Step-By-Step

See the documentation that comes with your Macintosh for details on creating folders.

1. Create a script tools folder and set Sketchpad's Script Tool folder to that folder.
   - Go to the Finder. Create a new folder inside the folder that contains Sketchpad. Name the new folder `My Tools`.
   - Choose Preferences from the Display menu.
   - Press the More button in the dialog box.

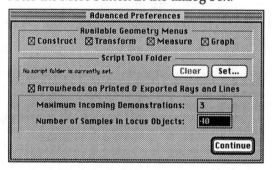

   The Advanced Preferences dialog box appears. It probably says that "No script folder is currently set."
   - Press the Set button. In the resulting dialog box, locate and select the `My Tools` folder you created above.
   - Press the Continue button in the Advanced Preferences dialog box and the OK button in the Preferences dialog box.

   A new tool appears in the toolbox. You can put any number of tools in the script tool folder.

2. Construct the circumcircle of a triangle.
   - Open a new sketch.
   - Draw a triangle.
   - Construct the perpendicular bisectors of two of the sides of the triangle.
   - Place a point at the intersection of the two perpendicular bisectors.

- Using the Circle tool, construct a circle whose center is at the intersection of the two perpendicular bisectors and whose radius control point is at one of the triangle's vertices.

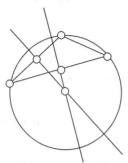

- Hide the midpoints, perpendiculars, and intersection point.

3. Use the above construction to create a script for drawing a circle through three points.
    - Choose Select All from the Edit menu. (Make sure the selected tool is the Selection Arrow tool. Otherwise you won't get all objects in the sketch.)

Make Script gives you a way to create a script from an existing construction.

    - Choose Make Script from the Work menu.

        A new script window opens and the script appears. It should have three points as givens and approximately nine steps. You can try playing your script on three new points in your sketch if you wish, but the object here is to create a new tool that appears in the tool bar.

    - With the script window active, choose Show Comment in the Edit menu.

The name of a script tool is taken from the first line of the script's comment.

    - In the first line of the comment area of the script, type `Circumcircle of a triangle`.

4. Save the script in the Script Tools folder.
    - Click the title bar in the script window.
    - Choose Save from the File menu.
    - Set the folder to My Tools.
    - Type `Circumcircle` and press Return.

5. Use your new script tool to construct a circumcircle on a new triangle.
    - Press the mouse button down on top of the script tool icon in the toolbar. Choose "Circumcircle of a triangle" from the pop-up menu.

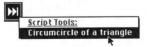

    - Move the mouse pointer into the sketch window and click three times in three different places.

        Notice that the tool status box tells you what you need to select at each stage of the construction. As soon as you have placed the first point, Sketchpad makes as much of the construction as it can based on the first point and on the position of the mouse pointer for the second point. After the second click, Sketchpad can show you the completed construction, using the position of the mouse pointer for the third point.

Further Play

A. Use your circumcircle tool on some existing points or on points that you place on existing lines or circles.

B. Make script tools for other useful or interesting constructions, such as constructing regular pentagons, inscribing a circle in a triangle, or trisecting an angle.

C. Try moving into your script tools folder some of the sample scripts that come with Sketchpad.

Questions

1. If you've completed a construction, what is the simplest way to make a script of it?

2. How do you set the location of script tools?

3. How do you add a new script tool?

Answers

1. Select the objects in the figure. Then choose Make Script from the Work menu.

2. Use the Preferences command from the Display menu and get the Advanced Preferences dialog box. There you can clear or set the location of Script Tools.

3. Move the script you wish to use as a tool into the script tools folder.

Tour 12: Recursive Scripts

In this tour you'll learn how to use the LOOP button to create recursive scripts. You can use recursion to create fractals, among other things.

Free Play

Experiment with Sketchpad to learn about every task listed in Free Play, using the numbered steps if you need more guidance. Then go to the Further Play section of the tour. Finally, check to see if you understand everything by answering the questions. Once you think you understand all the concepts of this tour, proceed to the next tour.

✔ Record a script and use LOOP to repeat the script on objects constructed by it.

✔ Dilate objects about a marked center.

✔ Use recursive scripts to create fractals.

Step-By-Step

1. If you have not already done so, close all open sketches and scripts, and open a new sketch.

2. Open a new script and click REC to begin recording. Position the sketch and script side by side.

3. In the sketch, construct a horizontal segment using the Segment tool. Drag from left to right so that the Givens in your script will appear from left to right.

4. Divide the segment in thirds using dilation.
   - Select the right endpoint.

   - Choose Mark Center from the Transform menu.
   - Select the left endpoint to be dilated.
   - Choose Dilate from the Transform menu. This dialog box appears:

   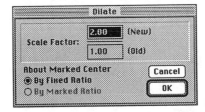

   - If necessary, click By Fixed Ratio.
   - Type 1 in the New box. Press tab to highlight the Old box. Type 3. Click OK (or press Return).

   A point is constructed one-third of the left endpoint's distance from the marked center.

   - Returning to the Dilate dialog box, type 2 in the New box to dilate the left endpoint by a scale factor of $2/3$.

Points are labeled "¹/₃" and "²/₃" in this tour for explanation purposes. These are not the labels the points in your sketch will have, unless you choose to edit them.

Another point is constructed two-thirds of the left endpoint's distance from the marked center. The segment is now divided in thirds.

5. Construct an equilateral triangle on the middle third of this segment.

- Mark the $^2/_3$ point as center in the Transform menu.
- Select the $^1/_3$ point and choose Rotate from the Transform menu. Click By Fixed Angle and enter 60. Click OK to rotate the $^1/_3$ point 60° about the $^2/_3$ point.
- Construct segments to connect the $^1/_3$ and $^2/_3$ points to this new point, thus constructing an equilateral triangle.

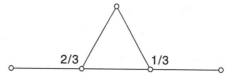

6. Hide the original segment.

- Click the Selection Arrow tool.
- Click the center of the original segment.
- Choose Hide Segment from the Display menu.

7. Construct segments from the original endpoints to the $^1/_3$ and $^2/_3$ points to create the figure shown:

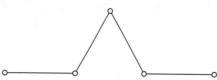

This is the first stage of the Koch curve. The simple rules that create a Koch curve fractal are: Divide a segment in thirds. Build an equilateral triangle on the middle third, and remove the middle third, leaving four equal segments. Apply this rule again and again to the segments so created.

8. Recurse the steps of your script on the four segments the script creates.

- Moving from left to right, select the first two points. (For the recursive script to work properly you must select these points in the same left-to-right order as the Givens in your script.)

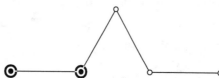

- Click LOOP in the script window.

  Your script records the step to recurse on those two points.
- Select the next two points in the figure, from left to right (first the $^2/_3$ point and then the equilateral triangle vertex).
- Click LOOP in your script.
- Selecting from left to right, recurse on the other two pairs of consecutive points in your figure: vertex and $^1/_3$ point; $^1/_3$ point and right endpoint.

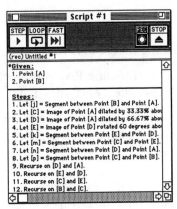

Your script should now contain four recursive steps. You've created a script that divides a segment into thirds, builds four equal segments to form an equilateral "bump," then repeats the procedure on the four segments.

9. Select the three vertices of the equilateral bump and choose Hide Points from the Display menu.

10. Click STOP in your script. Save your script with a descriptive name like Koch Curve.

11. Open a new sketch.

12. Play your script to three levels of recursion.

    - Construct a point, hold down Shift, and construct a second point.

      Your two points should be selected, ready to have your script played on them.

    - Click FAST in the script.

      The following dialog box appears on your screen.

      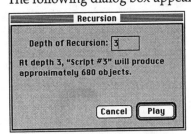

    - Type 3 in the highlighted box to indicate you wish to play your script to three levels of recursion. This means your script will loop three times.

      The dialog box gives an approximate number of objects this level of recursion would create. It also indicates whether you have enough memory to create that number of objects. If you don't have enough memory, it will say "not enough memory," and you'll have to try two levels instead.

    - Click Play.

      Your script produces this figure—a stage-four Koch curve.

      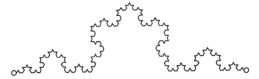

Further Play

A. Experiment with playing the Koch Curve script on different recursion levels.

B. Close your sketch and open a new one. Play your Koch Curve script on the three sides of an equilateral triangle to create a Koch snowflake.

C. Record a script to construct a triangle and the midpoints of each side. Loop this script on the midpoints. Experiment by playing this script to different recursion levels.

Questions

1. What needs to be selected before you can click LOOP in a script?

2. What does clicking LOOP do?

3. When you play a script with a recursion step, what does Sketchpad ask you to specify?

Answers

1. You need to select objects in your sketch to correspond to the script's Givens.

2. Clicking LOOP records a step in the script to recurse on the objects you select. This allows you to apply a script's steps to objects created by the script.

3. Sketchpad asks you to specify the desired recursion depth when you play a script with recursion steps.

Tour 13: Dynamic and Custom Transformations

In this tour you will create a spiral design using a two-step transformation you define your-self. You can manipulate this design easily because you'll perform your transformations using a dynamic angle of rotation and ratio of dilation.

Free Play

Experiment with Sketchpad to learn about every task listed in Free Play, using the numbered steps if you need more guidance. Then go to the Further Play section of the tour. Finally, check to see if you understand everything by answering the questions. Once you think you understand all the concepts of this tour, proceed to the next tour.

✔ Mark a dynamic angle of rotation in a sketch.

✔ Rotate an object by a marked angle.

✔ Mark two segments as a dynamic ratio for dilation.

✔ Dilate an object by a marked ratio.

✔ Define a multi-step custom transformation.

Step-By-Step

1. If you have not already done so, close all open sketches and open a new sketch.

2. Construct an angle and mark it as an angle of rotation.

   - Construct a small angle by using the Segment tool to construct two segments with a common endpoint.

   - Select the three angle points in order: bottom endpoint, angle vertex, top endpoint.

   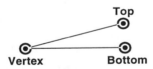

   - Choose Mark Angle from the Transform menu.

     A brief animation shows the angle has been marked to act as a counterclockwise angle of rotation.

If you had selected the points in the opposite order, you would have marked the angle for a clockwise rotation.

3. Construct two segments and mark them as a ratio for dilation.

   - Use the Segment tool to construct two segments, one shorter than the other.
   - Select the short segment, then the long one.

   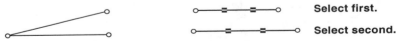

By selecting the shorter segment first, you told Sketchpad you want a scale factor less than one. A scale factor comprised of a smaller quantity over a larger quantity will shrink objects dilated by it.

   - Choose Mark Ratio from the Transform menu.

     A brief animation shows that the two segments have been marked to serve as a ratio for dilation.

4. Construct a point and while it's selected choose Mark Center in the Transform menu.

At this point, you've constructed an angle for rotation, a ratio for a dilation, and a center about which to rotate and dilate any object.

5. Construct a polygon interior.

- While holding down the Shift key, use the Point tool to create several selected points.

- Choose Polygon Interior from the Construct menu.

If you carefully locate points in the correct order, you can create an interesting figure for your polygon interior.

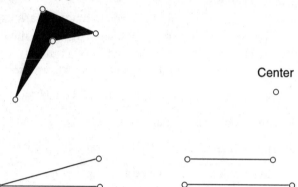

9. Rotate this interior by the marked angle and give it a different shade.

- Select the polygon interior.

- Choose Rotate from the Transform menu.

  This dialog box appears:

- Click By Marked Angle.

- Click OK (or press Return).

  Sketchpad constructs a rotated image of your original polygon.

- Select the image and choose a different shade and/or color by selecting Color or Shade from the Display menu.

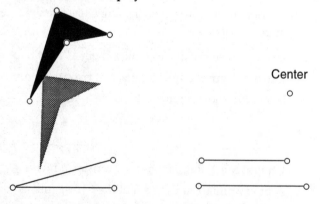

10. Drag the points on your angle to see how this affects the rotated image.

11. Dilate this rotated image by the marked ratio and give it a third shade.

- Select the rotated polygon interior.

- Choose Dilate from the Transform menu.

This dialog box appears.

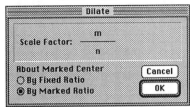

- By Marked Ratio should already be chosen.
- Click OK (or press Return).

  Sketchpad constructs a dilated image of the rotated image of your original polygon.

- Select the image and choose a shade and/or color in the Display menu that's different from both your original and the first rotated image.

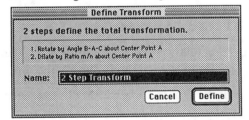

Center

12. Drag the endpoints of the segments that define the marked ratio and observe how that affects the dilated image.

13. Define a custom transformation for the rotation-dilation sequence.
    - Select the original polygon and the second image (the darkest and lightest in the figure above). Make sure you hold down Shift to select more than one object.
    - Choose Define Transform in the Transform menu.

      You'll see this dialog box listing the two transformation steps that constructed the second image from the original.

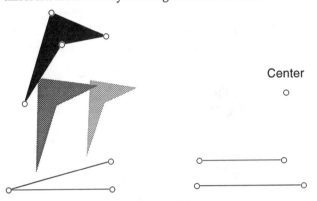

    - Type a descriptive name like `Twist'n Shrink`.
    - Click Define (or press Return).

      You've now defined a custom transformation of a rotation followed by a dilation. This two-step transformation, Twist'n Shrink, now appears in the Transform menu, ready to be applied to any object.

14. Apply Twist'n Shrink to the rotated-dilated image several times.
    - Select the rotated-dilated polygon interior.
    - Choose Twist'n Shrink from the Transform menu.

Sketchpad constructs a rotated image and a rotated-dilated image. The new rotated-dilated image is selected, ready to have the transformation applied to it again.

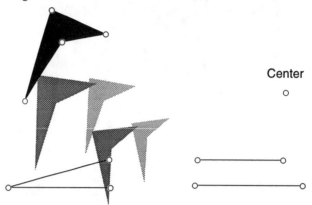

Note that the polygon resulting from the two-step transformation and the intermediate polygon have the same shade and/or color you gave their corresponding pre-images when you defined the custom transformation. Likewise, if you had hidden the intermediate polygon before defining the transformation, the custom transformation would have hidden it too.

- Hold down the ⌘ key and press 1 several times to create a spiral towards the center. (⌘1 is the keyboard shortcut for the first custom transformation you define.)

15. Adjust the angle and ratio to manipulate the spiral. Also, move the original polygon and center point.

Further Play

Try other combinations of transformations:

A. Define a reflection followed by a translation as a custom transformation. Apply it to some polygon interior several times. What's the result?

B. Define two reflections across intersecting lines as a custom transformation. What's the result?

C. Define two reflections across parallel lines as a custom transformation. What's the result?

D. Try a translation followed by a dilation.

E. Experiment with translation by marked vector.

Questions

1. How do you mark an angle of rotation?

2. How do you mark a ratio of dilation?

3. What else do you need to mark in order to rotate or dilate an object?

4. What do you need to select in order to define a custom transformation?

5. What's the keyboard shortcut to apply a custom transformation?

Answers

1. Select three points, vertex in the middle, and choose Mark Angle in the Transform menu.

2. Select two segments and choose Mark Ratio in the Transform menu. Selecting a short and then a long segment will define a scale factor that will shrink objects. Selecting a long and then a short segment will define a scale factor that will enlarge objects.

3. Rotations and dilations require a marked center.

4. Select an object and its image constructed by a sequence of one or more transformations.

5. Press ⌘1 to perform the first-defined custom transformation.

Tour 14: Animation

In this tour you will explore animated objects.

Free Play

Experiment with Sketchpad to learn about every task listed in Free Play, using the numbered steps if you need more guidance. Then go to the Further Play section of the tour. Finally, check to see if you understand everything by answering the questions. Once you think you understand all the concepts of this tour, proceed to the next tour.

✔ Animate points on circles and straight objects.

✔ Create an action button that starts an animation.

Step-By-Step

1. In a new sketch draw a circle and a line segment with one endpoint on the circle.

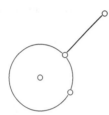

2. Animate the segment's endpoint around the circle.
   - Select the circle and the segment's endpoint on the circle.
   - Choose Animate from the Display menu.

     The Path Match dialog box appears.

If you were animating several points along several different paths, the Path Match dialog would allow you to select which path each point moves along, as well as selecting the type and speed of movement for each point.

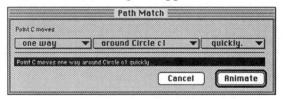

   - Click the Animate button.

     The animated point follows the circular path. Since the point defines the segment, the segment is animated too.
   - Press and hold the mouse button to stop the animation.

3. Create an animation button which you can double-click to start the animation.
   - Once again, select the circle and the segment's endpoint on the circle.
   - From the Edit menu, choose the Action button submenu.
   - Choose Animation from the Action button submenu. The Path Match dialog box appears.

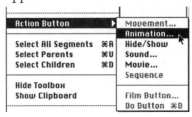

- Once again, click the Animate button in the Path Match dialog box. An animation button appears.

⇌ Animate

- Double-click the Animate button to start your animation. Click anywhere to stop the animation.

Further Play

A. Create some original animations.

Questions

1. What must be selected before you animate a point on a path?

2. What kind of objects can be paths?

3. How do you create an animation button?

Answers

1. The point and the path to animate it on.

2. Circles, straight objects, arcs, and interiors.

3. Select the points to be animated and the objects on which they should move. Then Choose Animation from the Action Button submenu of the Edit menu.

Tour 15: Tracing

In this tour you will explore the Sketchpad's tracing feature.

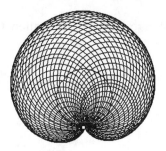

Free Play

A trace is the image of an object across some transformation. When you trace an object in Sketchpad, the object leaves a trail of images as it moves, illustrating where it has been.

Experiment with Sketchpad to learn about every task listed in Free Play, using the numbered steps if you need more guidance. Then go to the Further Play section of the tour. Finally, check to see if you understand everything by answering the questions.

✔ Trace a point.

✔ Create a trace by animation.

✔ Animate without the Path Match dialog box.

Step-By-Step

1. Close all open sketches and begin a new sketch.

2. Trace a point.
    - Construct a point.
    - With the point selected, choose Trace Point from the Display menu.
    - Drag the point around the sketch plane and observe the locus.

    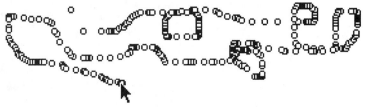

    When you release the mouse button to end the drag, the traced outlines of the point change to a continuous line showing the path the point has followed:

    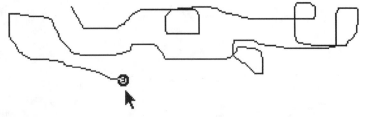

3. Use the trace feature and animate one circle's center around the circumference of another circle.
    - Undo to remove the point (and any other objects you may have created).
    - Draw a circle, dragging straight down so the point that defines the radius is directly below the center of the circle.

- Construct a new point anywhere on the circle. Select this new point, and then select the point which defines the radius of the circle. (Both points are on the circumference of the circle.)

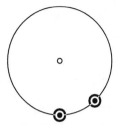

- Construct a second circle by choosing Circle By Center+Point from the Construct menu.
- With the second circle still selected, choose Trace Circle from the Display menu.
- Select the center of the second circle and select the first circle itself. You should have only two objects selected: a point and a circle.

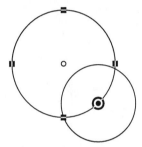

- Hold down Option (to bypass the options in the Path Match dialog box) and choose Animate from the Display menu.

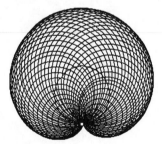

Click anywhere in the sketch plane to stop the animation.

Further Play

A. Experiment with several sample sketches that use tracing and/or animation in interesting ways:

Look in the Trig and Conic Sections folder within the Sample Sketches folder to find Ellipse/Hyperbola Tracer, Sin/Cosine Tracer, and Tangent Tracer.

Look in the Presentation Sketches folder to find Life's Highway and Bogus Cosmos.

Some of these sketches contain an Animate button that you can double-click as a shortcut to start the animation. Some were saved with the Animate button selected, so the animation starts automatically as soon as you open the sketch.

After starting an animation, click anywhere in the sketch plane to stop the animation.

Questions

1. How can you get a moving object to leave a trail behind?

2. How can you skip the Path Match dialog box?

Answers

1. Select the object, choose Trace from the Display menu, then move or animate the object.

2. Select points and paths in order (all points for the first path, the first path, all points for the second path, the second path, and so on). Hold down Option while choosing Animate from the Display menu.

Tour 16: Graphing and Locus Construction

In this tour you'll use Sketchpad to plot a graph of a geometric relationship. You'll also construct a locus of a plotted point.

Free Play

Experiment with Sketchpad to learn about every task listed in Free Play, using the numbered steps if you need more guidance. Then go to the Further Play section of the tour. Finally, check to see if you understand everything by answering the questions.

The idea of this tour is to find the relationship between the side length of a constant perimeter rectangle and its area, then to determine the side length for which the rectangle has maximum area.

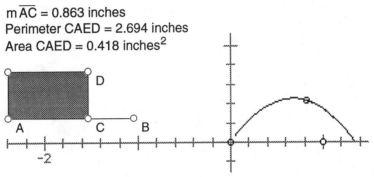

$m \overline{AC} = 0.863$ inches
Perimeter CAED = 2.694 inches
Area CAED = 0.418 inches^2

✔ Construct a rectangle whose perimeter remains constant as you change the length of one side.

✔ Measure the length of one side of the rectangle and the rectangle's area.

✔ Plot side length versus area and construct a locus of the plotted point as the side length changes.

Step-By-Step

1. Starting with a new sketch, construct a rectangle whose side length can be changed without changing the rectangle's perimeter.

    - With the Segment Tool, draw a segment, approximately horizontal. This segment's length will be half the perimeter of the rectangle.

    - With the Point tool, place a point on the segment.

    - Hide the original segment and connect the three points with two segments.

    - With the Label tool, label the three points.

    - Through points A and C, construct perpendiculars to segment AC.

- With the Circle tool, draw a circle with center at point *C* and radius control point at point *B*.

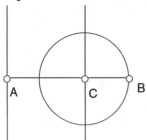

- Where the circle intersects the perpendicular line, construct a point and label it *D*.
- Through point *D*, construct a line parallel to segment *AC*.
- Construct the fourth vertex of the rectangle.

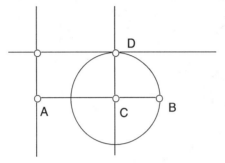

- Hide all the lines and the circle.
- With the Segment Tool, draw the sides of the rectangle.
- Select the four points of the rectangle and choose Polygon Interior from the Construct menu.

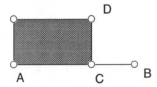

Drag point *C* and convince yourself that the perimeter of the rectangle stays constant while the area changes.

2. Measure the length of side *AC* and the perimeter and area of the rectangle.
   - Select segment *AC* and choose Length from the Measure menu.
   - Select the rectangle's interior and choose Perimeter from the Measure menu.
   - Select the rectangle's interior and choose Area from the Measure menu.

   m $\overline{AC}$ = 0.863 inches
   Perimeter CAED = 2.694 inches
   Area CAED = 0.418 inches^2

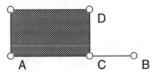

Again, drag point *C* and observe that the perimeter remains constant while the area changes.

3. Plot a point with the rectangle's side length as an *x*-coordinate and its area as a *y*-coordinate.

   - Select the length measurement. With the Shift key down, select the area measurement.

   - Choose Plot as (x,y) in the Graph menu.

     An *x-y* coordinate system appears with a point at the origin, a point at (1, 0), and a point corresponding to the ordered pair of measurements.

     Drag point *C* and observe how the plotted point moves.

4. Construct the locus of the plotted point determined by the motion of point *C* along its path.

   - Select the plotted point and Shift-select point *C*.

   - Choose Locus from the Construct menu.

     The result is a curve representing the areas for different locations of point *C* along its segment.

   - Drag point *B*. Notice how the curve changes as a different range of areas are possible.

   - Drag point *C* so the plotted point moves to the top of the locus. What does the rectangle look like and what can you conclude about the length of the sides?

Further Play

A. Try other locus constructions. For example, find the locus of the midpoint of a line segment where one end of the segment is constructed on a circle.

B. Do the tracing tour with locus construction instead of animation.

C. Construct the locus of a polynomial using the *x*-coordinate of a point on the *x*-axis and a polynomial expression for the *y*-coordinate.

Questions

1. How do you plot a point from measurements?

2. Do the units matter when you are using measurements to plot points?

3. What do you have to select to construct a locus?

Answers

1. To plot a point from measurements, first select the measurement for the *x*-coordinate and then Shift-select the measurement for the *y*-coordinate. Choose Plot as (x,y) in the Graph menu to plot the point.

2. Units have no affect on plotting points in a graph.

3. To construct a locus, first select the object whose locus you want. Then select the point that drives the locus. This point must be constrained to lie on a path. Finally, choose Locus from the Construct menu.

Sketches

What Are Sketches?

Sketches are visual, geometric drawings you create with Sketchpad, like that shown below.

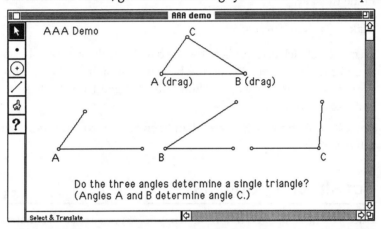

↪ Teachers can prepare sketches in advance so that students can explore a particular concept.

When you create sketches, you draw and combine objects—points, circles, segments, rays, and lines—to construct figures and to investigate geometric principles. You can also just have fun drawing interesting geometric figures and constructing animated "machines."

Sketches are visual, while scripts, the other half of Sketchpad, are verbal. This chapter gives a functional overview of sketches. The Command Reference and Toolbox Reference chapters describe every command and every tool, giving step-by-step instructions on how to use the command or tool.

Opening Sketches

When you start Sketchpad, a new, empty sketch appears. You can start drawing on the blank sketch or you can open an existing sketch. To open an existing sketch, choose Open from the File menu and when the dialog box appears, specify which sketch you want. You can start a new sketch at any time by choosing New Sketch from the File menu.

The Active Sketch

You can have more than one sketch open at a time in Sketchpad. The top sketch is the *active* one (the title bar has stripes). Inactive sketches (and scripts) show a title bar without stripes. In the following illustration, the sketch named Conic Sections is active and the Untitled sketch is inactive.

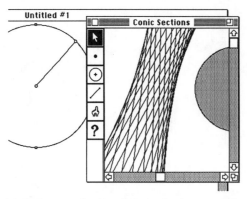

You can use the size box in the lower right corner to drag the sketch window to a different size so that you can see more than one sketch or script at a time. Even though you can see more than one sketch or script, only the one on top is active—the one showing the stripes in the title bar.

Making a sketch active

To make a sketch active, click the title bar. Actually, you can click anywhere in the window to make it active, but clicking might select a tool or start a drawing, depending on where the pointer is when you click. Therefore, it's a good idea to click the title bar when you want to make a window active.

You can also choose the name of an open sketch from the Work menu to make it the active sketch.

Constructing Objects

Points, straight objects, and circles are the building blocks of geometry. From them, you can construct angles, polygons, and other geometric figures.

Once you have opened a new sketch, you're ready to start constructing *objects*. Objects are the building blocks for geometric drawings; you can use them individually or combine them to make figures. An object is a single unit: a point, a circle, or a straight object (segment, ray, or line). Captions and measurements are also objects, but they are discussed in Adding Text on page 110.

You can create objects with the drawing tools in the Toolbox or with the commands in the Construct menu.

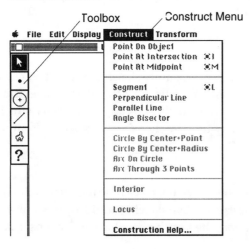

Drawing Tools

The drawing tools are equivalent to Euclid's tools: a point, a straightedge, and a collapsible compass. These tools are the building blocks of geometric explorations, giving you the primary tools you need.

Point	The Point tool creates points: free points, points on other objects, and points at intersections. Points that are constructed on another object always remain on that object, even when you alter the object. A point at an intersection remains at the intersection, even when the intersection moves. (You can create midpoints with a command on the Construct menu.)
Compass	The Compass tool creates a circle from the center point and radius you designate. This tool acts like a collapsible compass in that it does not hold its setting between uses. With the Compass tool you can also place points that define circles either in space or on other objects.
Straightedge	The Segment, Ray, and Line tools create straight objects with two endpoints, one endpoint, and no endpoints, respectively. With the Straightedge tool you can also place points that define straight objects either in space or on other objects.

Other objects such as polygon interiors can be created from commands on the Construct menu, as described later in this chapter.

Using the tools

Once you know what you want to construct, use the procedure given below.

1. Choose the drawing tool you want to use.

2. Move the pointer into the sketch plane.

   The pointer takes on a shape representing the tool you selected.

3. Click to create points; drag to create circles and straight objects.

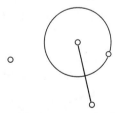

The tool you use stays in effect until you select a different one. The active, or current, tool is highlighted in the Toolbox. For the two tools that have a palette of tools (the Selection Arrow tools and the Straightedge tools), the last selected tool appears in the Toolbox. You can press on the tool to display the palette, then drag to select a different tool within the palette.

Selection Indicators

In some Macintosh programs, selected segments display indicators at the segment's endpoints. Rays and lines do not have two endpoints, however, and so in Sketchpad, straight object indicators divide the visible portion of the selected object into thirds.

Each object you draw is *selected* until you draw or select another object. This "selection" indicates the focus of action if you specify a transformation or a new characteristic.

Black, solid squares on circles and straight objects indicate selection. For points, selection is indicated by a bold circle surrounding the point.

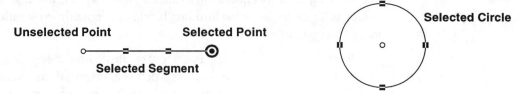

When you construct another object, that object is selected and the previous one is deselected. You'll learn more about selection later in this chapter.

Parents and Children

Geometric objects are often related. For instance, in a triangle the vertices and the edges are related objects. When you use one object to create another object, the original object is known as the parent and the second object as the child.

The relationships among objects are important, because changes you make in one often affect others. For example, if you create a triangle, each segment is determined by two points; in other words, the segment is the child of the two points it connects. Each point is a parent of two segments in the triangle. By definition, if you move either a vertex point or a segment, all the related points and segments move with it.

In the illustration below, point C is a parent of segments k and m. If you drag point C to a new location, segments k and m follow along.

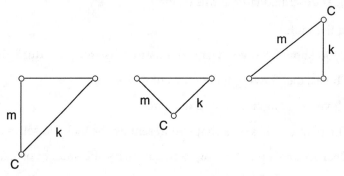

Likewise, if you drag segment m, points A and C move with it.

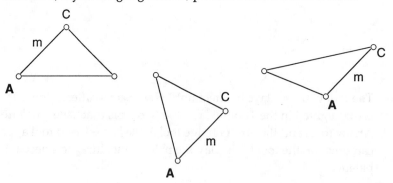

Construct Commands

If a command is not enabled in the Construct menu, it's because the proper objects have not been selected to give unambiguous meaning to the new object the command creates.

The tools in the Toolbox allow you to construct objects freehand, while the commands in the Construct menu enable you to create more specific or exact objects. For example, you can use the Construct menu to construct a circle with its center point at the vertex of a triangle, using the length of a particular segment as the radius of the circle.

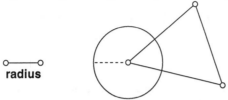

radius

Using tools, you could position the circle at the vertex of the triangle, but there is no way you could use the length of the segment to set the radius of the circle without moving the segment.

The Construct commands require certain objects to exist and be selected in order for each command to be enabled. The Command Reference chapter lists the prerequisite objects for each command. If those prerequisite objects are not selected, the command isn't available on the menu. For example, if you want to construct a segment perpendicular to another segment and through a specific point, you must have constructed and selected a segment and a point. The key to knowing the prerequisite for a particular construction is to consider what geometric objects uniquely determine the object you want to construct.

If you want help with prerequisites while you are using Sketchpad, you can use the Construction Help command in the Construct menu.

Dynamic Geometry

Your ability to change objects smoothly and dynamically is the most important feature of Sketchpad. The major principle of dynamic geometry is that whenever you make a change to an object, Sketchpad maintains the mathematical relationships between the object and its parents and children. This section focuses on how you construct these mathematical relationships and on how you make changes to objects in Sketchpad.

Selection

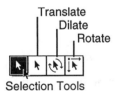

Translate
Dilate
Rotate

Selection Tools

As you have already learned, an object must be selected before it can be changed. Once the object is selected you can move it, rotate it, dilate it, reflect it, hide it, and change the color or thickness of its lines. You can even get rid of it. How do you select an object you constructed previously? The first tool in the Toolbox is the Selection Arrow tool. Actually, three Selection Arrow tools are on the Selection Arrow tool palette. All three tools select objects in the manner described in this section, and each tool also transforms selected objects by dragging. Transformations (translate, rotate, or dilate) are discussed in the next section of this chapter. For now, consider the basic Selection Arrow tool, which is called just a Selection Arrow tool here, but can be any of the specific three Selection Arrow tools.

Selecting one object

1. Choose a Selection Arrow tool in the Toolbox.

2. Click an object you want to select in the sketch plane.

    The objects display selection indicators—circles for points and solid squares for straight objects and circles.

    All objects are selected in this illustration.

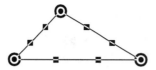

If you want to select an object while you are using another tool, hold down the Option key to temporarily activate the current Selection Arrow tool.

Deselecting objects

To deselect one or more selected objects, select another object or click in an empty space with a Selection Arrow tool.

Selecting all objects

You can choose Select All from the Edit menu to select all objects.

Selecting all objects of a particular type

The Select All command has some special features. If the Selection Arrow tool is the active tool, then Select All selects every object. If the Point tool is active, then the command reads Select All Points. By choosing a drawing tool first, you can create a filter for the Select All command, which comes in very handy when you have complicated constructions.

Selecting several objects by clicking

1. Choose a Selection Arrow tool.

2. Click the first object you want to select.

3. Hold down the Shift key.

4. Click any additional objects you want to select.

   Each object you click is selected.

5. Release Shift.

Selecting several objects with a selection marquee

You can drag a selection *marquee* (a rectangle that resembles a theater marquee) around a group of objects to select them. All objects that lie within or intersect the marquee are selected.

1. Choose a Selection Arrow tool.

2. Visualize a rectangle that contains or intersects all the objects you want to select.

You can start a selection marquee from any corner and drag diagonally.

3. Move the pointer to empty space near the upper left corner of the imaginary rectangle.

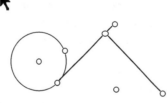

4. Press and hold down the mouse button.

For your convenience, Sketchpad will not select any coordinate axes that are showing in your sketch with the marquee. This helps you select segments that may be collinear to, or points that may be on, an axis without selecting the axis itself. If you want to select a coordinate axis, you'll have to click it with the Selection Arrow Tool rather than with the selection marquee.

5. Drag the mouse down and to the right until the selection marquee surrounds the objects.

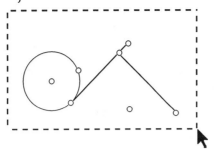

6. Release the mouse button.

    All objects are selected.

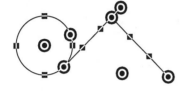

Deselecting an object from a group of selected objects

When you have a group of selected objects, you may want to deselect one (or more) of them without deselecting the others.

1. Hold down Shift. ˙

2. Click the object(s) you want to deselect.

Selecting parents and children

You can get information about the parents and the children of a selected object with the Object Information tool.

You may want to select the parents or children of one or more objects. The directions are the same for selecting parents and children.

1. Select the object for which you want to select the parents or the children.

2. Choose Select Parents (or Select Children) from the Edit menu.

    The original object is deselected and the parents (or children) of the object are selected.

By using these commands you can readily see which objects are the parents and which are the children.

Selecting coincident objects

Sometimes you construct objects that are coincident. For example, a segment lies on top of a ray, or a line might be overlapped by a polygon interior. You can select either of the objects. For example, if a segment lies on top of a ray, follow the steps below.

1. Select the segment with a Selection Arrow tool.

    The segment is selected.

2. Click again in the same location.

    The ray is selected. Repeated clicks cycle through the selection of coincident objects.

The Tool Status box names the object about to be selected by a mouse click. After you have clicked, the position of the selection indicators is often a clue as to what got selected. Finally, the Object Information tool (see below) can list the currently selected objects.

Object Information Tool

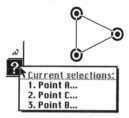

The Object Information tool displays a list of the current selections in the order of selection. You can choose an object from this pop-up menu to see an Object Information dialog box about the object's characteristics and get further information about objects which are geometrically related to it. Additionally, you can click on an object with this tool to see a summary balloon, and double-click an object to see its Object Information dialog box.

Transformation

Once an object is selected, you can transform it. You can use both tools and commands to translate, rotate, and dilate the object or objects.

Transformation Tools

You can use the Selection Arrow tools to transform as well as select objects, dynamically transforming the selections. If you want to specify exact quantities for a transformation, you must use the Transform menu commands.

Translate	Moves the selection as you drag.
Rotate	As you drag the object, rotates the selection around a point you've marked previously as the center.
Dilate	As you drag the object, enlarges or shrinks the selection relative to a point you've marked previously as the center.

Moving an object

Translating an object to a new location is the simplest of the transformations.

1. Select the object to be moved.

2. Then move the Selection Arrow tool near the selected object.

   The drag arrow appears.

3. Press and hold down the mouse button and drag the object to its new location.

   You can see the translation of the selected object(s) and the parents and the children.

4. When the object is where you want it, release the mouse button.

Rotating and dilating

Before you can rotate or dilate an object, you have to mark the center of transformation. Then select the objects to be rotated or dilated and drag them. A dilation enlarges or shrinks a figure along lines that extend to the center of dilation.

Mathematically speaking, a translation doesn't change a figure's size or orientation.

It is not strictly true that you must mark a center before rotating or dilating. If there is at least one unselected point in your sketch, Sketchpad will mark a center for you. (But it may not be the center you wanted.)

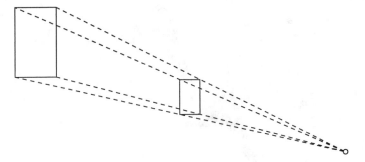

1. If necessary, create the point that will be the center of transformation.

2. Select the point. It's most efficient to use the Rotate or Dilate tool for this selection so that the active tool is ready when you start the transformation

A useful shortcut for marking a center is to double-click on a point with the Selection Arrow tool.

3. Choose Mark Center from the Transform menu.

4. Then move the Selection Arrow near the selected object.

   The drag arrow appears.

5. Press and hold down the mouse button and drag the object. As you drag it, you will see the transformation of the selected objects and the parents and the children.

6. When the transformation suits you, release the mouse button.

Transformation Commands

The commands on the Transform menu allow you to construct the images of selected objects under some geometric transformation. (Translation, rotation, dilation, and reflection are geometric transformations.)

To use the transformation commands, you must select the object(s) to be transformed, and you must have previously marked a center of transformation if you want to rotate or dilate the selection. If you want to reflect the selection, first mark the mirror line.

Transformation tools and commands are discussed in detail in the Command Reference and Toolbox Reference chapters of this manual.

Transformations by Dynamic Quantities

Translating by Marked Vector

Dragging an object with the Translate tool can be thought of as a freehand translation. You move an object from one place to another without changing its size, shape, or direction. Translation by a marked vector, however, enables you to construct a fully dynamic translated image instead of moving the object itself.

To translate by marked vector, you must first mark two points as a vector in the Transform menu. Select two points and choose Mark Vector in the Transform menu. Then select an object to translate and choose Translate in the Transform menu. Click the button By Marked Vector in the Translate dialog box.

If you choose By Polar Vector or By Rectangular Vector in the Translate dialog box, your transformation won't be dynamic. The image and pre-image will always remain the same fixed distance apart.

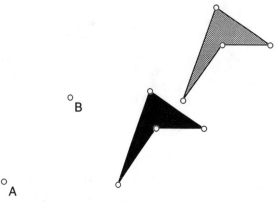

The light polygon is the image of the black polygon, translated by the vector from point *A* to point *B*.

When you translate by a marked vector, Sketchpad constructs the translated image of your selection, translated by the distance and direction defined by the two points you marked as vector. If you now move the vector points, the translated image will move correspondingly.

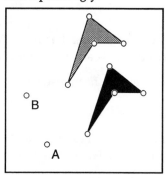 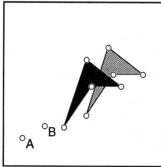 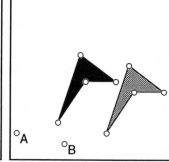

Selecting points C-A-B in order will mark a counterclockwise angle with vertex A. (Selecting in the opposite order would mark a clockwise angle.)

If you choose By Fixed Angle, your rotation won't be dynamic. The image will always be rotated from the pre-image by the fixed angle.

Rotating by Marked Angle

Freehand rotation of an object itself is possible with the Rotate tool. However, by rotating by a marked angle, you can construct a fully dynamic rotated image. To rotate by a marked angle, you must mark an angle *by* which and a center *around* which to rotate. Select three points and choose Mark Angle in the Transform menu. Select one point and choose Mark Center in the Transform menu. Select the object or objects to be rotated and choose Rotate in the Transform menu. Click the button By Marked Angle in the Rotate dialog box. Do Tour 13: Dynamic and Custom Transformations on page 79 to practice.

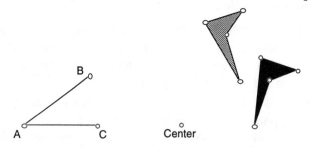

The light polygon is the image of the dark polygon, rotated by angle *CAB*.

When you rotate by a marked angle, Sketchpad constructs the rotated image of your selection, rotated by the angle that is defined by the three points you marked. If you now move the angle points, the rotated image will move to correspond to the new angle.

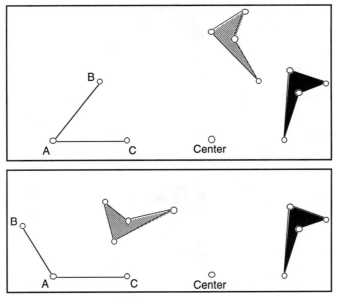

Dilating by Marked Ratio

Freehand dilation of an object itself is possible with the Dilate tool. However, by dilating by a marked ratio you can construct a fully dynamic dilated image.

To dilate by a marked ratio, you must mark a ratio *by* which and a center *toward* or *away from* which to dilate. To mark a ratio, select two segments in order: numerator, then denominator in the scale factor. Then choose Mark Ratio in the Transform menu. To mark a center, select a point and choose Mark Center in the Transform menu. Select an object or objects to be dilated and choose Dilate in the Transform menu. Click By Marked Ratio in the Dilate dialog box. Do Tour 13: Dynamic and Custom Transformations on page 79 to practice using a marked ratio.

Selecting first a shorter segment and then a longer one will result in a scale factor less than one. In this example, j was selected first, so the scale factor will be j/k. Dilated images will be smaller than their pre-images, because j is shorter than k.

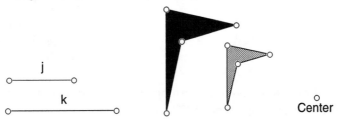

The light polygon is the image of the dark polygon, dilated by a ratio of j/k.

If you choose By Fixed Ratio, your dilation won't be fully dynamic. The image will always be proportional to the pre-image by the same fixed scale factor.

When you dilate by a marked ratio, Sketchpad constructs the dilated image of your selection, dilated by the scale factor defined by the two segment lengths you marked as ratio. If you now change the ratio segments' lengths, the dilated image will shrink or stretch to correspond to the new ratio.

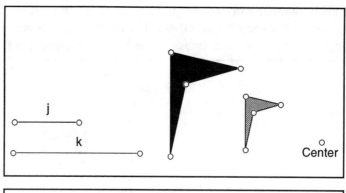

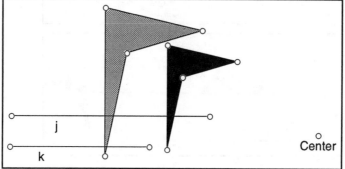

Transforming by Marked Measurements

You can translate, rotate, or dilate by amounts defined by measurements or calculations. For example, to construct a line segment whose length is the same as the circumference of a circle, you measure the circumference of the circle, mark the measurement as a distance to be used in translation, and then translate a point by that distance. As the radius of the circle changes, the length of the line segment changes correspondingly.

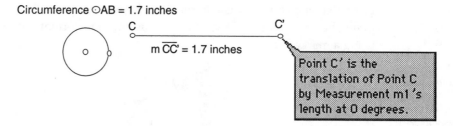

For more information on transforming by measured quantities, see the Command Reference section beginning on page 177.

Custom Transformations

A custom transformation is a sequence of one or more transformations. The basic steps to defining a custom transformation are given below.

- Transform an object one or more times.

- Hide any intermediate objects or format them as you wish them to appear when you apply your transformation.

- Select the pre-image and the final image.

- Choose Define Transformation in the Transform menu. Name your transformation. It will appear in the Transform menu. You can apply it on up to thirty objects at a time.

Do Tour 13: Dynamic and Custom Transformations on page 79 to practice using a custom transformation.

In this example, the dark polygon was reflected about the segment, then the reflection was translated by the marked vector from point *A* to point *C*.

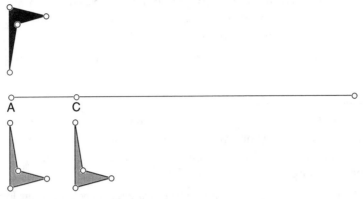

The first image (the reflection) was hidden and a custom transformation (a glide reflection) was defined by the original polygon and the second image. The glide reflection was applied to the transformed polygon interior several times to create the pattern shown below.

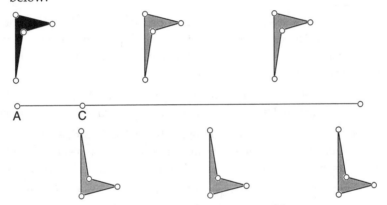

Custom transformations and scripts (a philosophical aside)

Custom transformations are sequences of transformational steps that you define and then apply to new objects. Scripts, described in the next chapter, are sequences of constructions—they may be transformational constructions—that you record, then play back on new objects. What's the difference? When should you use a custom transformation and when should you use a script?

Scripts are much more powerful than custom transformations. With scripting, you can describe—in geometric language—any set of relationships between sets of objects. Custom transformations are, comparatively, quite limited. They describe only the fixed relationship between an object and some transformed image of that same object.

However, *because* they are more limited you may find custom transformations to be more convenient than scripts in many cases (especially if you are focusing on transformation geometry!). Imagine the relationship between an object and its dynamically rotated and dilated image. In addition to the image and the pre-image, three points determine the angle of rotation, a fourth the center of rotation, and two segments are used to determine dilation's dynamic ratio. If you wrote a script to describe this set of relationships, it would require you to specify (as Givens) four points and two segments—six objects!—in addition to the pre-image of the transformation. Every time you played this script, you would have to select seven objects in your sketch to match the script's Givens.

Custom transformations allow you to factor out most of this work. When you define a custom transformation, Sketchpad remembers all those quantities except for the pre-image, which you provide when you apply the transformation. In many transformational, tessellation, and tiling activities, you'll find yourself using the same angles, ratios, mirrors, and vectors on different pre-images. In these cases, custom transformations allow you to focus on the *transformation*—the relationship between image and pre-image—instead of on all the secondary intermediate details.

For further discussion of scripts, see the Scripts chapter beginning on page 123.

Cut, Copy, and Paste

You can use the Cut, Copy, and Paste commands from the Edit menu to transfer constructions from one area to another in a sketch, to another sketch, or even to another application. (Many of the images in this manual were copied from Sketchpad and pasted into a word processing application.)

Cutting removes not only the selected objects but their children as well.

Both cutting and copying allow you to transfer objects to other locations, but cutting removes the selection from the original location, while copying leaves it in its original location. When you use either Cut or Copy, the selected objects go on the Macintosh Clipboard.

Clipboard

☞ You can use Sketchpad as a personal productivity tool to make graphics that you can paste into other applications, like a word processor. It's very useful for creating attractive worksheets or tests.

The Clipboard is a temporary electronic holding place (a buffer) that contains the last selection that was cut or copied. Objects on the Clipboard always retain their geometric relationships, even when you copy two objects that are related by a third, hidden object—the hidden object is copied as well.

If you copy two objects that are related by a third object that you explicitly do not copy, the two objects are no longer related on the Clipboard or after you paste them.

When rays and lines are cut or copied to the Clipboard, an arrowhead appears on the straight objects where no endpoint exists. When you paste into a sketch, the rays and lines are reinstated. If you paste to a different application, the arrowheads remain.

When you choose the Paste command from the Edit menu, the contents of the Clipboard appear in the active sketch and stay on the Clipboard until you cut or copy something else. The Clipboard is cleared when you turn off the computer.

Displaying the contents of the Clipboard

If it's been some time since you cut or copied anything, you may not remember what is on the Clipboard. In that case, choose Show Clipboard from the Edit menu. Choose Hide Clipboard or click the close box to return to your sketch.

Pasting to a different application

1. Select the objects you want to paste.

2. Cut or copy the selection.

3. Start the new application.

4. Open the document you want to paste into.

5. Choose Paste from the Edit menu.

   The objects appear in the document (assuming the application allows you to paste graphics).

Using color when pasting to a different application

Most graphics applications don't import color images from the Clipboard. Consequently, when you paste colored Sketchpad objects, they appear in limited color, or in black and white, in the other application. If the application accepts color images, hold down the Shift key while choosing Cut or Copy from the Edit menu to copy the full color specification to the Clipboard along with the objects.

Pasting graphics from a different application

Using the Paste command, it is possible to enhance sketches with graphics created in other applications. You may want to paste graphics into your sketch as illustrations, or as backgrounds for geometric investigations. See the Edit portion of the Command Reference chapter for more information.

Undo and Redo

Use Undo to remove unwanted objects from your sketch. Avoid using the Delete key whenever possible!

The Undo command provides a way of reversing unwanted steps by undoing your last action. You can choose Undo (and Redo) an unlimited number of times, undoing all the way back to an empty sketch (or the last saved sketch). This is particularly useful if you move an object and decide after you release the mouse button that you really should leave it in the original location. When this happens, choose Undo from the Edit menu. Unlimited Undo is also handy when you have constructed a figure that doesn't work out quite right. You can Undo back to the beginning of the figure, regardless of how many steps are involved.

If you do use Delete, be aware that it deletes not only the selected objects, but also their children. If you wish to delete only the selected objects, hold down Option while pressing Delete.

Undo has another function in Sketchpad. If you are familiar with other Macintosh programs, you may have developed the habit of clearing the work area by choosing Select All, then pressing the Delete key or choosing the Clear command. This is not a recommended practice in Sketchpad because Sketchpad keeps a history of all events since the last time you saved. Deleting or clearing objects you have created makes the history longer because the history would have to list the deleting and the clearing. Deleting and clearing can also break parent-child relationships. Instead of deleting or clearing, you should use the Undo command to remove unwanted objects whenever possible.

⚮ Unlimited Undo and Redo enables you and your students to review and discuss steps in a construction.

You can hold down Option while choosing Undo to undo everything since the last save, or you can repeatedly choose the Undo command to trace back the construction one step at a time.

Undo and Redo retrace the steps for creating, moving, hiding, and changing objects.

Using Undo to create a step-by-step visual explanation

⌘Z is a useful shortcut for choosing the Undo command from the menu.

One way to create a step-by-step visual explanation is to undo back to the beginning of an interesting construction and then choose Redo to step through a visual explanation of the construction. Be careful not to add a step in the middle of the process, however, because if you do, the rest of your undo history will be lost.

Action Buttons

Action buttons allow you to consolidate the process of showing and hiding groups of objects, and animating designated points along designated paths, into single buttons that you can later use to repeat the action. You may want to postpone reading about action buttons until you are familiar with the operation of the Show, Hide, and Animate commands in the Display menu.

An action button acts like any other object—you can select, move, hide, and show it; you can change its label or its label's text style; you can delete it. Some action buttons have geometric relationships to other objects. (In Sketchpad terminology, they are the children of the other objects.)

More importantly, action buttons have actions, which Sketchpad performs when you double-click them with a Selection Arrow. Buttons can perform any of the actions given here.

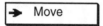

These buttons move points in your sketch, just as you do when you translate points with the Selection Arrow tool. More specifically, a Move button causes points to move from wherever they exist in the sketch to precise destinations, specified by other points in the sketch. (After the move, each moved point will be *coincident* with its destination point.) You can control the speed with which the points move, or you can have them move instantaneously.

Once you've created a Move button, you can hide the destination points of the moved points, allowing viewers to focus on the moving points.

Move buttons are the children of both the moving points and these moving objects' destination points.

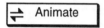

These buttons cause one or more points to move along predesignated paths, just like the Animate command in the Display menu. If you encapsulate an animation into a button, however, you can repeat it again and again by simply double-clicking the button. You don't have to go through the Path Match dialog box associated with the Display menu's Animate command.

Once you have created an Animate button, you can hide the paths of the animated points. Viewers can focus on the animated objects rather than on the motionless objects that serve as paths. You can even hide the animated points, though the animated results will only be visible if the points affect the position of other (showing) objects.

Animate buttons are the children of the points and the paths of the animation.

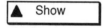

These buttons cause one or more hidden objects to become visible. Show buttons are the children of the objects they show.

| △ Hide |

These buttons cause one or more showing objects to be hidden. Hide buttons are the children of the objects they hide.

You can use Show and Hide buttons in pairs to reveal selected portions of a geometric construction that would be too complex if you showed all hidden objects simultaneously. In a single sketch, for instance, you could construct the medians, altitudes, and bisectors of a single triangle, and then use Show and Hide buttons to reveal them selectively. Show and Hide buttons can also be used with captions and measurements.

| ◁)) Play Sound |

∞ *If your students submit sketches to you as in-class assignments, use a microphone to record your comments on their work directly into their sketches.*

These buttons play back prerecorded sounds. You'll only be able to hear the sounds if the volume of your Macintosh is turned up in the Control Panel desk accessory.

Certain Macintoshes, such as the LC, IIsi, and Quadra, come with microphones. You can also buy add-on microphones from third-party distributors. If you have a microphone, Sketchpad will let you record Play Sound buttons directly into a sketch. Use Play Sound buttons to explain the geometric principles demonstrated by your sketch.

Play Sound buttons are not the children of any other objects. (In Sketchpad terminology, they are free objects.)

| ▣ "Fractal Triangle" |

These buttons play QuickTime movies in a movie window. You will not be able to view the movies unless QuickTime is installed. QuickTime is a multimedia system extension available from Apple Computer, Inc. (See your Apple dealer for more information.)

You can enhance your sketch with any QuickTime movie you choose. You may want to use movies to provide "real-world" tie-ins to geometric investigations, for example, or to demonstrate and explain three-dimensional corollaries of the two-dimensional geometry presented in your sketch.

Sketchpad can also generate QuickTime movies, as explained under "Film Button" in the Command Reference chapter.

Movie buttons are not the children of any other objects. (In Sketchpad terminology, they are free objects.)

| ••• Sequence |

These buttons perform sequences of the above actions. Double-clicking a Sequence button is equivalent to double-clicking a series of action buttons, one after the other.

By creating individual action buttons and then sequencing them with Sequence buttons, you can create complete presentations. A single Sequence button can demonstrate the construction of a triangle's medians (by showing them with Show buttons, one after the other) while verbally explaining the construction (with a Play Sound button), and then animate the triangle's vertices (with an Animate button) to demonstrate that the medians always concur in a single point.

Sequence buttons are the children of the action buttons they sequence.

Creating action buttons

Create action buttons with commands in the Action Button submenu of the Edit menu, as described in the Command Reference chapter. You may have to select certain prerequisite objects before these commands become available.

Performing actions

There are a number of ways you can perform an action represented by an action button. The easiest, of course, is to double-click the button with the Selection Arrow tool. Alternately, you can select an action button, then follow the procedure given below.

- Choose Do Button from the Action Button submenu. This is identical to double-clicking the button.

- Choose Film Button from the Action Button submenu. This performs the action, and creates a QuickTime or PICS movie of the button's animation, movement, or sequenced action. See the Command Reference chapter for more details on movie generation.

Use action sketches to create entirely self-sufficient geometric presentations.

- Save your sketch with the action button (and *only* the action button) selected. This creates an *action sketch*, which will automatically perform that action whenever you—or another user—reopens it.

Adding Text

Sketchpad provides four types of text: labels, captions, measurements, and tables. You can display or edit all four types. Use the Text tool to display labels and create captions. Use the Measure menu commands to measure objects. You can also use the Text tool to edit the text in labels, captions, measurements, and tables, or use commands in the Display menu. Using the Text Font and Text Style cascading menus in the Display menu, you can control the text characteristics of any visible text—captions, measurements, labels, and tables.

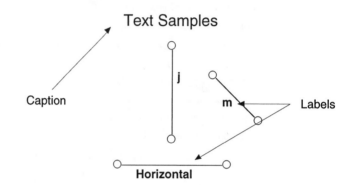

Labels

Every object has a label, and you can use the Text tool in the Toolbox to display and hide these labels. When you construct an object, it appears without its label showing. (You can use Preferences in the Display menu to change this and automatically display new objects with their labels showing.)

Displaying object labels with the Text tool

1. Choose the Text tool.

2. Move the tip of the pointed finger to any object until the hand turns black. Click the object to display its label.

    You can move the label by dragging it. Move the pointed finger to the label until the letter *A* appears in the hand. Drag the label.

Once a label appears, it can be hidden by clicking the object again with the Text tool.

You can use the Relabel Options command in the Display menu to change the way Sketchpad assigns labels to new objects. (See "Label Options and Relabeling" on page 163.)

You may find that descriptive labels are more useful than the letters and the numbers that Sketchpad assigns. You might want to change the label of point *B* to something like `Orthocenter`. You can change any label by double-clicking the label with the Text tool. (Again, look for the letter *A* in the hand. This indicates that the tool is pointing at a label that can be edited.) You can use as many as 32 characters in a label.

If you want to label an object while using another tool, hold down the ⌘ key to invoke the Text tool temporarily.

Unlike captions and measurements, labels are not text objects. They are actually part of the geometric objects they describe. You can show and hide labels and move them around the periphery of the object. You can't copy, delete, or transform labels unless you copy, delete, or transform their objects.

Captions

☞ Have your students use captions to include their name and the date on the sketch they hand in.

You can also add text to your drawing to name parts, to give the sketch a title or an identification, or to provide instructions.

Creating captions with the Text tool

1. Choose the Text tool.

☞ If you are using an overhead display, click Style and specify 14 pt boldface text to create text that is readable from a distance.

2. Move the pointer to a blank area in the sketch plane where you want the caption to begin.

3. Press and hold down the mouse button and drag.

   As you drag, you establish the corners of a rectangle in which to display the caption. The caption may be as wide as you want, although its height will be determined by how much text the caption contains. When the caption marquee is the size you want, release the mouse button. An I-beam appears at the top of the blank caption.

4. Type the text you want as a caption. Sketchpad automatically wraps lines at the right margin of the caption's marquee.

5. When you are done typing your caption, click anywhere outside the caption's marquee. You have now completed the caption.

   You can change the font, font size, and formatting using the Text Style and Text Font commands in the Display menu. You can also change the shape of the caption's rectangle, as described in the Toolbox Reference chapter.

Measurements

The Measure commands and the prerequisites for each measurement are in the Command Reference chapter.

A measurement includes text that describes some measured quantity of an object or objects. The measurement changes when you change the object. For example, if you measure the length of a segment, the measurement changes when you change the length of the segment (by dragging the endpoint, for instance).

m $\overline{AB}$ = 1.2 inches

m $\overline{CD}$ = 1.4 inches

A○————————○B   C○————————○D

When you create measurements of selected objects, Sketchpad uses the label of the object to describe the measurement. In the example above, for instance, it described 1.2 inches as " m $\overline{AB}$." If you rename j to be base, the label text will change to " m base = 1.2 inches."

If you edit the text of a calculated measurement, you can use the Object Information tool to see the original formula used in the calculation.

To edit the text of a measurement, double-click the measurement with the Text tool. In the resulting dialog, you can switch the measurement to Text Format and change the text to be something more informative, such as, The length of the hypotenuse is 1.2 inches. If you do edit the measurement text, the label in the measurement will no longer update if you change the label of the measured object.

Tables

You can create tables in Sketchpad by measuring geometric quantities in your sketch (using the Measure menu and perhaps the calculator), and then using the Tabulate command to compile these measurements into a table.

Tables are composed of *entries*, each of which contains the values of your measurements at the moment you added that entry to the table. (Tables start with only one entry and contain the measured values at the moment you created the table.) As you manipulate your construction and change the measurements, you can add new entries at any time.

AC = 1.21 inches
BC = 0.60 inches
AC/BC = 2.00

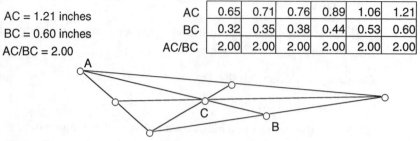

AC	0.65	0.71	0.76	0.89	1.06	1.21
BC	0.32	0.35	0.38	0.44	0.53	0.60
AC/BC	2.00	2.00	2.00	2.00	2.00	2.00

Tables allow you to investigate constant and changing numeric relationships in a sketch. In the above illustration, three measures involving the centroid of a triangle have been tabulated on the right. You can see that while the distances *AC* and *BC* change over time, the ratio of these distances remains constant.

Creating tables

1. Select measures to tabulate. Choose Tabulate from the Measure menu.

2. To add an entry to an existing table, select the table and choose Add Entry from the Measure menu, or double-click the table with a Selection Arrow.

   You can also edit a table's labels, change its text format, and choose whether its entries are displayed horizontally or vertically. You can copy a table from Sketchpad and paste it into a spreadsheet application to chart or to pursue further numerical or graphical investigations with its data. Data points may be plotted within Sketchpad itself using Plot Table Data... as described on page 199. Tour 6 provides a tutorial introduction to tables, and the Command Reference chapter describes the Tabulate, Flip Direction, and Add Entry commands of the Measure menu.

Analytic Geometry and Graphs

In Sketchpad you can display the coordinates of points and the equations of lines and circles. Coordinates may be rectangular or polar, and there are two forms of equations for lines and two for circles. Coordinate values and equation parameters may be used in computations, allowing you to investigate analytic geometry theorems and derivations.

You can display the coordinate system as a pair of axes, with or without grid points. The origin and unit length for a coordinate system may be changed dynamically. You can plot measurement values and construct graphs of geometric relationships that respond dynamically to changes you make in the geometry.

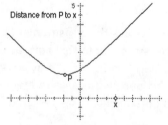

The above graph shows the relationship between position on a horizontal line (the *x*-axis) and distance to a point *P*. As the *P* is dragged, the curve changes dynamically.

For an introduction to Sketchpad's analytic geometry capabilities, try Tour 10: Coordinates and Equations on page 68. To get started with graphing with Sketchpad, go through Tour 16: Graphing and Locus Construction on page 89. The Command Reference has details on analytic geometry computations in the sections describing the Coordinates and Equation commands in the Measure menu (beginning on page 192) and the section describing the Calculator (beginning on page 192). A detailed description of the commands in the Graph menu begins on page 197.

Changing Text Characteristics

You can choose any font or font size you have installed on your computer. You can alter the text appearance by choosing bold, italic, underline, or other formatting characteristics, and you can specify different sizes of text. There are three ways to change how the text looks.

Text Tool
Use this tool to change the characteristics of individual labels and measurements. You can also change and edit text with this tool. Double-click a label or a measurement to display the editing dialog box, then make the changes as you want.

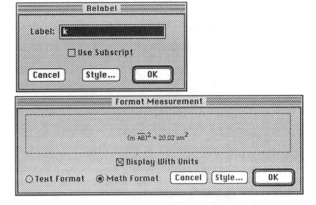

To change the appearance of captions, use the I-beam inside the caption marquee to highlight text you want to change. Select other fonts, font sizes, or formatting from the Type Style or Type Font submenus in the Display menu.

Text Style
After selecting the label, measure, or caption with a Selection Arrow tool, use the Text Style submenu in the Display menu to change the size or formatting of all selected text and subsequent text in the current document.

Text Font
After selecting the label, measure, or caption with the Selection Arrow tool, use the Text Font stripes in the Display menu to reassign the font of all selected text and subsequent text in the current document.

Preferences
Use this command in the Display menu to set the text characteristics for subsequent text in the current document and all new documents. When you quit from Sketchpad, the characteristics are saved and will be in effect when you start the program again.

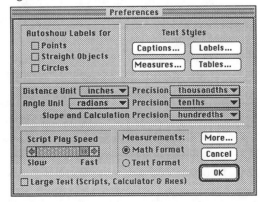

A label belongs to an object and stays with the object when you move, hide, or delete the object. Captions, measurements, and tables are objects on their own. You can select, hide, and delete captions, measurements, and tables. You can transform text objects with the Selection Arrow tools, but you cannot use the commands on the Transform menu with text objects.

Details on using the Text tool, the Text Style and Text Font submenus, and Preferences dialog box are in the Command Reference and Toolbox Reference chapters.

Setting the Display

Use the commands on the Display menu to add visual interest and animation to your constructions. You can add color and shades, trace loci, and animate points on paths. You can also change the appearance of text.

Visual Enhancements

If you have a color monitor, you can specify the color of any object. Colors can highlight your geometric explorations.

Regardless of your monitor, you can specify thick, thin, or dashed lines for circles and straight objects, and shades of gray for circle and polygon interiors.

Animation

Animations are created from objects that move along a path. Since parents and children often move and stretch together, you can set up animations and add traces to illustrate many different mathematical principles.

For example, as shown above, you can trace a segment as its endpoint animates along another segment.

Details on how to use the Animate command are in the Display Menu section of the Command Reference chapter.

Calculations

You can use the Calculate command in the Measure menu to perform calculations. For example, if you want to prove that the area of a circle equals πr^2, you could display the measurement for both the radius and the area of a circle, then use the calculator dialog box to verify the relationship.

Radius $\odot$AB = 0.29 inches
Area $\odot$AB = 0.27 inches^2
$\pi \cdot$(Radius $\odot$AB)^2 = 0.27 inches^2

For more information about performing calculations see Measure Menu on page 189.

The calculator's Function pop-up menu also has a number of trigonometric and transcendental functions. To calculate the value of a function, choose the function from the pop-up menu, enter the function's *argument* (either a constant or a calculated value), and click the close-parenthesis key to indicate the end of the argument. Thus, to compute the sine of an angle, enter the expression Sin[Angle(ABC)]. The functions given below are available.

sin	trigonometric sine
cos	trigonometric cosine
tan	trigonometric tangent
arcsin	trigonometric arcsine
arccos	trigonometric arccosine
arctan	trigonometric arctangent
abs	absolute value
sqrt	square root
ln	natural logarithm
log	base 10 logarithm
round	the nearest integer
trunc	the integer rounded toward zero
signum	the sign of the number, -1 if $x < 0$, 0 if $x = 0$, 1 if $x > 0$

Note: If the argument of sin[], cos[], or tan[] does not have the units of an angle, its value will be interpreted with the angle current units. Thus sin[90°] = 1 regardless of current angle units; sin [90] = 0 if the current angle unit is degrees, but 0.894 if the current angle unit is radians. Sin[90 inches^2] is the same as sin [90] because the units are not angle units and so are ignored. Use the Preferences command in the Display menu to set the current angle unit.

Preserved Units

Units are preserved across calculations. When you add two lengths together, your calculated result is also expressed as a length. If you multiply two lengths, your result is expressed as an area (a square length), and so forth. You can use calculated units to help verify that an expression you've computed is what you intended. For instance, if you are trying to compute an area and your result is in cubic units, your calculated expression must be wrong, because area is measured with *square* units, not *cubic* units.

Accuracy and Precision

In mathematics, *accuracy* refers to the closeness of an estimated value to the actual "ideal" value being estimated. *Precision* refers to the degree of trust you can put in the estimate.

The accuracy of Sketchpad's measurements and calculations is determined by the full computational power of your Macintosh. (Initial computations are usually accurate to 19 significant digits.) Values derived from these values will be less accurate, because any error in the accuracy compounds across calculations. You'll find that error compounds much less quickly in Euclidean constructions (and the measurements derived from them) than in non-Euclidean ones. Euclidean constructions—those performed with the compass and straightedge, or with the Construct menu—can be computed exactly. Non-Euclidean constructions, such as those found in the Transform menu using fixed quantities, involve mathematical identities that Sketchpad can only approximate, and therefore cannot be computed exactly. (Note that transformations by dynamic quantities inherit the accuracy—either Euclidean or non-Euclidean—of the marked dynamic quantity.)

The precision of displayed measurements is determined by your choice in the Preferences dialog box. Sketchpad rounds calculated values to your chosen precision, which may be to the nearest unit, or tenth, hundredth, or thousandth of a unit.

Functions
sin[
cos[
tan[
arcsin[
arccos[
arctan[
sqrt[
ln[
log[
round[
trunc[

Function pop-up menu

Be careful to avoid confusing accuracy with precision. If you are displaying precision to the nearest tenth, Sketchpad can accurately represent the equation of two lengths that measure 1.3 as 1.3 + 1.3 = 2.6. If you are rounding each value to the nearest unit, however, the equation seems nonsensical: 1 + 1 = 3.

Make Script

The Make Script command in the Work menu allows you to make a script from a sketch. Scripts are verbal descriptions of relations between objects, so you can only make a script from a sketch if you have selected objects that relate to one another (as parents or children).

When you make a script from a sketch, you are not putting the actual geometric figures into a script. Sketchpad analyzes the objects and their relationships and converts the process into words in a script. The eldest parents become the Givens of the script, and the steps of the script describe the construction of the parent's descendants. This function is described in the Scripts chapter.

Saving and Closing

While you are working, it is a good idea to save your sketch often. What appears on the screen is protected only when saved to disk. If there is a blackout or someone accidentally unplugs your computer, you will lose everything you did since the last time you saved.

You name your sketch when you save it the first time. That name must be unique in the folder to which you are saving. It is important to give your sketches and scripts different names because the same name can't exist twice in the same folder. If you happen to choose a name that is already used, you are asked if you want to replace the file that is already on the disk. Therefore, if you are saving a script named Sine Demo and you have a sketch also named Sine Demo, you will lose the sketch if you tell Sketchpad to replace the existing file. *Be careful that you don't replace a file you want to keep.*

When you have finished working on a particular sketch, you should close it to make room in the computer's memory for more sketches.

Saving and the Undo History

The only caution about saving often is that each time you save, the Undo history is erased. That is good if you want to free some memory (see the General Issues chapter for more information on memory management). However, if you were trying to create a step-by-step visual explanation, you would lose your Undo history when you save. It's a good idea to save often, especially when you are creating something complex. But if saving removes the Undo history, how can you create a step-by-step visual explanation and save often?

Here's a solution to this dilemma. When the construction is as you want it, save it, close the document, then reopen it. When you open a document, the Open dialog box includes a checkbox to Include Work. This is a streamlined Undo history which Sketchpad creates for you to use for step-by-step visual explanations. The sequence of the Undo history may not be the same as the construction process you used to create the figures.

Networked Collaboration

Networked collaboration is only possible if all shared computers are running System 7.0 or higher of the Macintosh operating system.

If you are using a network operating under System 7.0 or higher of the Macintosh operating system, Sketchpad can provide collaborative support for your classroom.

With students at different computers, starting any computer investigation that uses existing documents can be tedious work. Class time is wasted while you ensure that every student has opened the correct files and is ready to start. Sketchpad's *document sharing* allows you to open shared sketches and scripts instantly on any (or every) station on a network. See Share Documents in the Command Reference chapter for more information.

With *demonstrations*, you can demonstrate your work in a sketch—the actual steps of a construction, the measurements, motions, and labels—to any group of other Sketchpad users.

⌖ Using networked collaboration, you can start all your students on an investigation simultaneously, the can work together, or they can demonstrate to a computer with an overhead projection device.

While the sketch is being demonstrated, you retain control of it—viewers can watch, but cannot interfere. When you're finished, however, the demonstrated copy remains on each viewer's desktop for him or her to review, embellish, and enhance independently. As a teacher, you can begin investigations with demonstrations, setting up a problem to study for the entire class. Then cut them loose, allowing pairs of students working at computers to pursue your initial work on their own. After that, they can demonstrate to each other and back to you. In that any Sketchpad can have multiple demonstrations active (incoming *and* outgoing), you can even use demonstrations to track the work of four or five independent study groups simultaneously!

Program Linking

Sketchpad's demonstrations and document sharing rely on the operating system's ability to link programs together. If you wish to use demonstrations in your class, you'll have to set up your network so that individual copies of Sketchpad can be linked together. This section describes a procedure for doing this, which you'll have to repeat for every Macintosh in your classroom. (If this seems like a long process, don't worry! You'll only have to do this once, not every time you wish to demonstrate.)

Program linking is fully described in the *Macintosh Network Reference Manual*, which came with your copy of System 7.0 or higher. You should read this manual to understand that the procedure given here describes only one of a number of possibilities for configuring your network. In particular, the method given assumes no hierarchy or secrecy in your classroom. Every user will be given full access to program linking on other users' computers. If you wish to use passwords for different users to protect programs from being linked unintentionally, you'll have to refer to the *Macintosh Network Reference Manual*.

Indicate that Sketchpad can be linked across the network

1. At the Finder desktop, select the Sketchpad icon.

2. Choose Sharing from the File menu.

    At this point, your Macintosh may warn you that applications cannot be shared unless program linking is started from the Sharing Setup control panel. If this is the case, your Macintosh will open Sharing Setup for you so you can start program linking. Once it's started, select the Sketchpad icon and choose Sharing again.

    A dialog box appears.

3. Click the Allow Remote Program Linking check box so that it's checked.

    This copy of Sketchpad is now ready to link to programs across the network. Next, you'll want to authorize Guests to link to programs on this Macintosh. Guests do not require passwords. By linking computers via generic guest users, you also save yourself the work of authorizing each real user (your students and colleagues) to link to this Macintosh.

Link your computers across the network

1. Choose Control Panels from the Apple menu.

    A folder appears, showing all of the control panels installed on your Macintosh.

2. Locate the Users & Groups control panel and double-click it.

    The Users & Groups control panel opens.

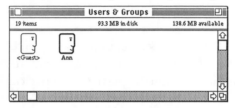

3. Double-click the <Guest> user icon.

    Information for the generic guest user appears.

4. Click the "Allow guests to link to programs on this Macintosh" check box so that it's checked.

5. Close the <Guest> window and save any changes your Macintosh asks you to.

You've now authorized any user on the network to connect to programs on this Macintosh as a guest. The first time you connect to another Macintosh (either to demonstrate or to share documents), you'll be asked for a user name and a password with which to connect to that computer. Simply click the Guest button and you will not be required to supply a password.

Demonstrations

A demonstration is a process in which one person's work in a sketch window is viewed as it happens in copies of the window on other people's computers. The person controlling the sketch is the *demonstrator;* the other participants are *viewers*.

The demonstrator initiates the demonstration by choosing viewers from a list of all Sketchpad users on the network. Potential viewers are notified that the demonstrator wishes to send a demonstration, and Sketchpad gives them the opportunity to accept or refuse the demonstration. If no viewers accept, no demonstration occurs.

If one or more viewers accept, the demonstration begins. Copies of the demonstrator's sketch window appear on the viewers' screens. However, only the demonstrator's copy has a Toolbox because only the demonstrator can alter the contents of the sketch. Viewers can continue to work in other sketches and scripts if they choose, but they will not be able to alter the demonstrator's sketch while the demonstration is in process. As the demonstrator constructs and manipulates geometric objects, his or her actions are duplicated on the viewers' screens across the classroom.

In the following illustration, Adam is demonstrating his Equilateral sketch to Kelvin and Joan (who is working on a script called Circle Shearer at the same time.)

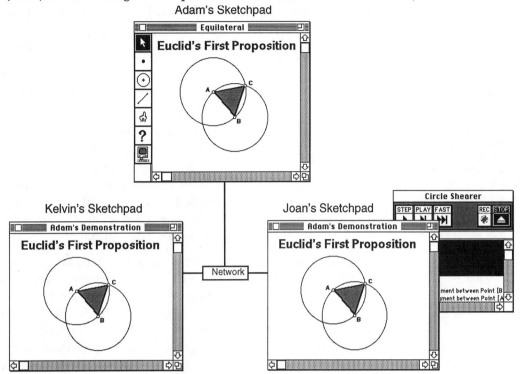

When the demonstrator stops the demonstration, it is stopped on all viewers' screens simultaneously. Alternately, viewers can individually stop an incoming demonstration, which doesn't stop the demonstrator from continuing to demonstrate to other viewers. The demonstration is over when the demonstrator stops it or when all viewers have stopped viewing it.

When the demonstration stops, the viewers' copies regain Toolboxes. Each viewer now has a personal copy of the demonstrator's sketch. Each copy is now a normal sketch that viewers can save and close or work on further. (They can even undo and redo the demonstrator's work step-by-step to review it and later demonstrate it to new viewers of their own.)

Starting a Demonstration

To start a demonstration, use Demonstrate To from the Display menu as explained in the Command Reference chapter. Sketchpad will present a list of all other computers that are using Sketchpad on your network. (If Sketchpad warns you that no one else is using it, and you know that to be false, make sure you've set up your network as described Program Linking.)

If you have a network consisting of different models of Macintosh computers, keep in mind that not everyone's screen may be as big as yours. If one of your viewers has a screen that's smaller than your sketch window, Sketchpad will shrink your sketch (on your computer and on your viewers') to fit everybody's screen.

Working While Demonstrating

Sketches currently demonstrated across the network display a new tool in their Toolbox: the Viewer tool. You can use this tool to keep track of which viewers are following your demonstration, and to inspect other facts about them. See the Tool Reference chapter for more information about this tool.

As you demonstrate a sketch, you'll work much as you normally do. Draw objects with the freehand tools or construct them with the table—almost every action you take is reflected on viewers' screens across the network. There are a few exceptions, however, with which you'll become familiar as you start demonstrating.

Dragging	The network is not fast enough to show every intermediate stage as you drag objects from one location to another. On viewers' screens, your objects will move only when you release the mouse.
Scrolling	Because viewers may have screens that are different from yours in size, and because they may independently resize your demonstration window, scrolling does not have meaning across a network. Instead, viewers can scroll about your sketch on their own. Be sure to warn your viewers if you start working in a portion of your sketch scrolled far from the portion visible when you began the demonstration.
Animating	Animation (as well as the Move action button described in the Command Reference chapter) works fine in a demonstration, and can be used to reveal many interesting properties of a demonstrated construction. However, viewers will only "see" your animations if their copy of your demonstrated sketch is foremost on their desktop. Because Sketchpad's animation requires most of a computer's available processing power, Sketchpad won't animate your demonstration for a viewer if the viewer is working on some other document or application.

You can simulate a continuous transformation by moving your objects in small steps, rather than in one smooth mouse motion.

Ending a Demonstration

Eventually, you will want to stop your demonstration. Choose Stop Demonstration from the Display menu, and the Viewer tool will vanish from your sketch, indicating that your demonstration is over. Across the network, Toolboxes will reappear on viewers' copies of your sketch, indicating that each viewer now "owns" a personal copy of your work.

If for some reason you don't want viewers to retain your work for further exploration, you can *cancel* the demonstration, which causes copies of your demonstration window to be closed on all viewers' computers (except your own, of course). To cancel a demonstration, hold down Option and choose Cancel Demonstration from the Display menu.

Viewing a Demonstration

If you accept a demonstration, you become one of the demonstrator's viewers. The demonstrator remains in control of the sketch for the course of the demonstration, so you'll notice that there's no Toolbox in the window. Additionally, the Edit, Display, Construct, Transform, and Measure menus are dimmed when the incoming demonstration is foremost.

You can still scroll the sketch with the scroll bars or resize it with the size box in the lower-right corner. You can also continue to work in other sketch or script windows on your desktop. (Click on other windows to make them active.)

☞ Use summary balloons to follow the demonstrator's logic if he or she is not explaining it to the class as the demonstration proceeds.

If an incoming demonstration sketch is active, you can investigate its geometry by clicking on visible objects. When you click on an object in a demonstration, Sketchpad presents a *summary balloon*, describing how the object was constructed. (Summary balloons are shown with the Object Information tool, described in the Tool Reference chapter. The Information tool is always active in an incoming demonstration.)

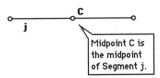

Midpoint C is the midpoint of Segment j.

You can stop an incoming demonstration at any time either by closing the window, or by pressing the period key (.) while holding down the ⌘ key when the window is active. If you close the window, of course, you won't be able to manipulate its contents. If you type ⌘ period, however, you'll cancel the demonstration without losing its window. After that, you'll be able to work with the sketch.

Scripts

What Are Scripts?

Scripts are verbal recordings of geometric constructions of objects and their relationships to one another. When you play a script, it constructs the figures in a sketch.

Another way to say this is that the eldest ancestors become the Givens of the script and the steps of the script describe the construction of the offspring.

Each script is based on certain *Givens,* objects which are required to reconstruct the figures described in the script. A script describes a procedure for constructing a figure (one or more objects) based on the Givens.

You create a script by constructing an example in a sketch. The basic steps are given below.

- Start a new script.

- Press the REC button in the script window to begin recording the script.

- In a sketch, construct the geometric figures.

  Sketchpad renders each object constructed as the appropriate Givens and Steps and writes the information in the script.

- Press the STOP button in the script window to end the script.

  The script not only describes the construction you just did, but it can also be replayed to create an equivalent construction from new Givens in the same sketch or in any other sketch.

For a simple example, suppose you create a script that draws a triangle from three points and then creates a midpoint on each side of the triangle. The script for the triangle and midpoints might be as shown below.

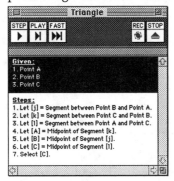

In order to play this script, you must select three points in a sketch. When played, the script draws a figure in the active sketch.

When you play the script, Sketchpad temporarily substitutes the three selected points for the Givens in the script, then carries out the steps of the script. The figure appears in the sketch with the vertices of the triangle at the points you selected. From then on, unless you choose to play it again, the sketch has no actual relationship with the script. You can use a script in as many sketches as you want or as many times as you want in a single sketch.

Once you play the script to create the triangle, you can drag points and segments around to observe that this construction acts exactly like the one you originally drew. In addition, if you select the three midpoints and play the script again, a new triangle will be constructed with vertices at the original midpoints.

This chapter describes creating and using scripts, and assumes that you already understand how to use sketches.

Script Window

The Script window has controls that are like the controls of a tape recorder.

You can use these buttons to record, to stop a recording or a playback, and to play back a recording with certain options. (These are explained in detail later in this chapter.) You simply click the buttons to use them.

This window works like other Macintosh windows, as described in The Basics chapter. You can move it and size it so that you can see as much of the sketch or more of the script as you need. When you want to make a script or a sketch window active, click the title bar rather than within the work area.

Opening a Script

You can open scripts that have been saved using the File menu.

Open Command   When you use the Open command in the File menu, the list box contains all the documents in the current folder. If you have a mixture of sketches and scripts in a folder, you can't tell which is which unless their names make the distinction. Of course, if you organized the sketch files and the script files into separate, well-labeled folders, there is no problem.

Creating Scripts

There are two ways to start a new script.

- Choose New Script from the File menu and record a construction from scratch.

- Select all the objects in a construction for which you want to create a script. Then choose Make Script from the Work menu. This automatically creates a new script with a complete construction description.

The Make Script command allows you to script a construction even if you forgot to turn on the recorder before starting the construction.

The first method creates (or activates) an empty script window. The second method creates a new script of an existing construction. This is particularly useful if you have already constructed something that would make a good script, but you didn't record the construction.

Recording a script

When you use the File menu to create a new script, you must record the construction in the script window by constructing the objects in a sketch window. Sketchpad acts like an analytical stenographer, converting the objects you draw (in a sketch) into words (in a script) that describe the constructed relationships between the objects.

1. Select New Script from the File menu.

   A new script window opens and becomes the active window.

2. Click the REC button.

   The top sketch becomes active, and the script window moves behind the sketch window.

3. Proceed with your construction.

4. If you can see the STOP button, click it. If you cannot see the STOP button, you can choose the script name (probably Script #1) from the Work menu to bring it to the top. Then click the STOP button.

When you are recording a construction, you may want to resize the sketch and script windows so that they do not overlap and so that you can see the steps recorded in the script.

Using Make Script

Another method for creating a script does not require a script window at the beginning. Additionally, it doesn't record the construction exactly as you did it, but rather looks at the entire set of objects and interprets the construction in the simplest manner possible. The final result is the same as if you had recorded the construction, but the order of the process may be different.

1. Select all the object(s) for which you want a construction script.

2. Choose Make Script from the Work menu.

   A new script window opens and the construction is interpreted and recorded.

If you want your script to end with some object(s) selected, or you want to continue recording new steps into the recently made script, see Make Script in the Work Menu section of the Command Reference chapter.

Setting Up the Givens

The names of the Givens in your script come from the actual labels of the objects in your sketch. You can use this to very good advantage by choosing names that help you—and others who will use your script—figure out what roles each given is supposed to play in the construction. For example, if a particular given point is supposed to be the center of a circle and another point is supposed to determine the radius, you could label them `center` and `radius`.

You can judiciously control which objects become the Givens by controlling when you click the REC button.

To determine more precisely which objects will become the Givens, think your construction through before beginning the recording of a script. Imagine, for example, that you want a script to construct the midpoint of a segment. (This is simplistic for the sake of discussion—you never would need to do this because midpoints are available in the Construct menu.) If you begin recording before drawing the segment, then your script will have two points for Givens because the first recorded construction was a segment with two endpoints. If, however, you begin recording after drawing the segment and then construct the midpoint, the script will have only one Given: the segment. The choice of Givens is up to you. In this example, you can choose either one segment or two endpoints, depending on when you begin recording.

What Isn't Recorded

Scripts record abstract geometric constructions, not specific locations of objects. In other words, scripts don't record dragging actions. They record transformations only when the transformed image is constructed as a separate object from the pre-image.

Scripts record measurements but not captions.

Using Labels

Objects in a script are general and abstract. Objects in a sketch are specific and concrete. For example, in the Triangle script shown at the beginning of this chapter, the three vertex labels represent the vertices of *any* triangle. The vertices in a Triangle sketch, however, are only the vertices of that specific triangle. Think of the script as the formula (or equation) for the triangle, and the script labels as the variables of the formula. When you play the script, you temporarily assign values, derived from a sketch, to these variables.

The object labels in a script are in brackets to indicate that they are placeholders for real objects in the sketch. For example, in the Triangle script, the first step showed three variables: *j*, *B*, and *A*.

> 1. Let [j] = Segment between Point B and Point A.

You may want to give the segment *j* a name to describe its purpose or function in the script. Possibly you can call the segment `tangent` because it represents a segment tangent to a circle. While recording, you can edit the label of the tangent segment in the sketch with the Text tool.

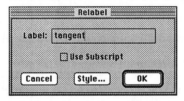

When you read the script, the word *tangent* is not in brackets because it is no longer a variable. When you play the script, the segment will also be labeled tangent when it appears.

Stopping the Recording

When you have completed the construction you want to record, press the STOP button. When you stop the recording, the script records the characteristics of all the objects in it: their color, shade, line thickness, and whether or not they are hidden. When the script replays, the constructed objects have the same characteristics as those recorded.

When you stop the recording, the script records this information about each object.

- The display characteristics (color, shade, and line weight)

- Whether it is hidden or visible

- Whether the label is showing

- The actual labels of objects you specified in the label-editing dialog box

- Whether the object is selected or not

During playback, all objects are created with these characteristics. Since the script does not create Givens, their characteristics are not changed when the script plays back.

Comments

You can add a comments to a script to describe the script. For example, you might add a comment to provide important information about creating and selecting the objects to be matched with the Givens. The first line of a comment is used as the name of a Script Tool. Comments appear directly in the script window and will be saved with your script.

Creating or editing a comment

∞ *Teachers can add comments to scripts to provide visual explanations and discuss the mathematics of a construction. Students can write comments explaining their work and hand in scripts as assignments.*

1. Move the pointer to the *comment bar*: the double lines just over the Givens. It will become a double-headed arrow.

2. Click and drag the double-headed arrow downward until you have an opening big enough to write your comment.

   Another way to make the comment pane visible is to use the Show Comments command in the Edit menu.

3. Type your comment.

You may resize the comment pane—or close it entirely—by dragging the comment bar up and down. If a script's comment area is closed but comments have been entered for that script, the comment bar will appear shaded gray.

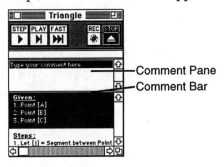

Saving Scripts

Scripts can be saved, just like any document information. When the script is the active window, choose Save or Save As from the File menu. It is important to give your scripts and sketches different names because the same name can't exist twice in a folder. Another strategy for avoiding name conflicts is to keep your scripts and sketches in separate folders. You can save a script as text using the Save As Text checkbox that appears in the Save As dialog box as described on page 140.

Playing Scripts

Once you have created a script, you can play it back to construct the objects it describes. Here is the general process for playing a script.

1. Open the script and a sketch.

2. In the sketch, create and select objects to match the Givens in the script.

3. Click a playback button in the script.

   The objects described by the script appear in the sketch. The process of playback depends on which playback button you have clicked.

You can select one of three playback buttons.

PLAY	Plays the script from beginning to end. All hidden objects remain displayed until the last step of the script, then they disappear. The script window remains on top. You can set the speed for the play-back using the Preferences command in the Display menu.
FAST	Replays the script very quickly, so fast you probably can't follow the construction. Hidden objects remain hidden throughout the playback. The sketch window remains on top. Use this option if you are more interested in the result than in the process.
	This playback option is particularly useful when the script is long, such as the sample script to create a snowflake.
STEP	Steps through the playback, one instruction at a time. You must press the STEP button to proceed to the next step in the script. You can step through part of the construction and then click the PLAY or FAST button to finish the script. Use this option if you want to follow the script closely or you want to investigate the construc-tion in the sketch while the script plays. For example, after one step finishes, you can measure or move objects in the sketch and then proceed to the next step.

Givens

The Givens are the eldest ancestors of the objects created by the steps in the script—or the "independent parameters" of a construction. They appear in the highlighted section at the top of the script.

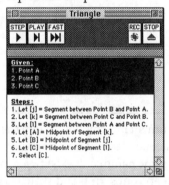

You must create and select objects in the sketch that match those listed in the Given section of the script before you can play the script. Be sure to select sketch objects in the same order they appear in the Givens. Once you make the selections in the sketch, you can proceed with playing the script.

You can select more objects than you have Givens, but if you select fewer, or the wrong type of objects, a warning message describes your error.

The list of selections shown by the Object Information tool can help you verify that you have selected the appropriate number and types of objects to match the script's Givens.

Finding Matched Objects

While recording or stepping through a script, you may lose track of which object in your sketch refers to a particular Given or step in the script. Matching script and sketch objects do not always have the same labels because one script can be played in many sketches, and one sketch can record many scripts. Use the following procedure to display the matching objects.

1. In the script, move the pointer over the Given or the Step you are interested in.

2. Press and hold the mouse button.

The matching object in the sketch flashes and the label for the matching sketch object replaces the Given or Step text you are pressing in the script.

3. Release the mouse button.

The sketch object stops flashing and the script returns to normal.

Stopping the Playback

If you clicked the PLAY or STEP button, you can pause the playback by clicking the STOP button in the script. Click the PLAY, FAST, or STEP buttons to resume playback.

Recursive Scripting

In Sketchpad, scripts support full recursion, allowing you to define self-similar fractals and other recursive or iterative constructions.

Recursion in General

Review for a moment the concept of recursion. Recursion involves a definition—of an object, a procedure, or in Sketchpad's case, a geometric construction—which is stated *in terms of itself*. While this is thought to be bad form when defining words in English (You don't say: "Well, a dog is—uh—a form of dog-like creature."), recursive definitions allow you to capture an aspect of the infinite in mathematics.

Engineers use the term feedback *to describe an essentially recursive phenomenon. Audio feedback—the screaming of a microphone—occurs when a microphone picks up as input the sound which it is amplifying as output. The (already amplified) input is further amplified as output, which then returns as new input. The feedback noise emitted by the speaker is defined in terms of itself.*

Consider the (nonmathematical) example of a picture containing a picture of itself. While you don't encounter such images every day, they can occur in a variety of situations: when gazing into a pair of opposing parallel mirrors, for instance, or when filming a television that is simultaneously displaying the image being filmed. This image can only be defined in terms of itself: the picture contains the picture. Which picture? The picture of the picture of the picture of the picture, and so forth. We say the picture is defined *recursively*.

Recursion allows us to elegantly phrase certain mathematical definitions. The factorial function $n!$ is equal to the product of all whole numbers between 1 and n. for instance, 5! is $5 \times 4 \times 3 \times 2 \times 1 = 120$. We can define the factorial function recursively.

$$
\begin{array}{llll}
n! & = 1 & \text{if } n \le 1 & \textit{terminal condition} \\
& = n\,(n-1)! & \text{if } n > 1 & \textit{recursive relation}
\end{array}
$$

By this definition, 5! = 5(4!). We have defined the factorial function for $n = 5$ in terms of the same factorial function for $n = 4$. To evaluate 5!, we must recursively evaluate 4!, then 3!, then 2!, until we reach 1!, which the definition's *terminal condition* tells us is 1. Thus,

$$
\begin{array}{lllllll}
5! & = & 5(4!) \\
& & 4! & = & 4(3!) \\
& & & & 3! & = & 3(2!) \\
& & & & & & 2! & = & 2(1!) \\
& & & & & & & = & 2(1) \\
& & & & & & & = & 2 \\
& & & & & = & 3(2) \\
& & & & & = & 6 \\
& & & = & 4(6) \\
& & & = & 24 \\
& = & 5(24) \\
& = & 120
\end{array}
$$

The terminal condition in this example prevents the factorial function from recursing to infinity. In the case of the picture containing a picture of itself, it might seem like nothing prevents the image from continuing to infinity. While this is theoretically true, in practice there is an implicit terminal condition. In the opposing parallel mirrors, one can only see to the limits of your vision. Eyesight provides a terminal condition. In the audio microphone's feedback, the maximum output of the amplifier limits the potentially infinite process. If you attempt to draw a picture containing a picture of itself, you give up when the picture within the picture within the picture becomes so small no one could see it anyway. In this instance, human exhaustion provides a terminal condition!

Recursion in Sketchpad

Sketchpad's scripts can be defined, recorded, with infinite recursion. When you play them back, you'll provide a terminal condition to determine how many "pictures within pictures" to construct before deciding you've gone far enough. If you didn't specify this *depth of recursion*, the script would never stop playing.

A recursive step in a script is an instruction—at the point that step is reached during playback—to play the entire script on new objects before continuing to the next step. The entire script played back at this step includes, of course, the recursive step, and when it is reached, the entire script is played again at *that* step. Recursively, you have a script inside a step inside a script inside a step, to whatever depth of recursion you've chosen.

LOOP button

A recursive step in a script constructs a part of a figure that is defined by the figure itself. This recursion can yield a figure with self-similarity—the figure looks the same viewed at different scales, or "powers of magnification." Fractal guru Benoit Mandlebrot points to a quote from Jonathan Swift to describe self-similarity: "So, Nat'ralists observe, a Flea/Hath smaller Fleas that on him prey,/And these have smaller Fleas to bite 'em,/And so proceed ad infinitum." The Koch curve is an example of a self-similar figure created by a recursive procedure. It is briefly described here to illustrate these concepts. Tour 12: Recursive Scripts on page 75 takes you step-by-step through recording a script to construct this figure.

Start with a segment and divide it into thirds.

On the middle third, build an equilateral "bump" so that you now have four equal segments. This is stage 1 of the curve, and is the figure that will define subsequent stages of the final figure.

Now apply this procedure recursively to the segments created by the procedure itself. That is, divide each segment into thirds and erect an equilateral bump on it. You'll have a stage 2 curve.

Apply the procedure again to all the segments in the figure to create a stage 3 curve, and so on.

To record a recursive script, you'll use the LOOP button, which replaces the PLAY button on the script deck when you are recording a script. Think of LOOP as the ability to record a PLAY of the current script into itself. Just as with PLAY, you'll select objects to correspond to the script's Givens and then click LOOP. Use objects that you've created earlier in the script to define the script in terms of itself. When you click LOOP, Sketchpad adds the recursive step to your script.

You'll want to try a few examples of recursive scripts, recording them and playing them back. In addition to Tour 12, in which you can learn how to construct the Koch curve, the Sample Activities: Creating a Fractal introduces you to another recursive script, the Sierpinski Gasket. Try both of these activities to get a feel for the LOOP button, recursive steps, and depth of recursion. There are also many recursive scripts in the Sample Scripts folder that came on Disk 2 of Sketchpad.

Notes on Recording Recursive Scripts

When you loop, the objects you select to match the script's Givens *must* be objects you've constructed previously in the script. Otherwise, the recursion is not well defined (the script is not defined in terms of itself).

Also note that when you record a recursive step, you fix the number of given objects in the script. Normally, as you construct while recording, Sketchpad continues adding script Givens to describe any previously unknown objects. When you include a recursive step in your script, however, you specify a fixed number of objects to match the number of Givens listed in your script at that moment. Though you can continue recording steps that do not alter the number of Givens, you cannot add a step that would create new Givens, because then your recursive step would no longer sufficiently match the script's Givens. If you attempt to record such a step, Sketchpad will warn you and stop your script's recording.

Notes on Playing Recursive Scripts

When you begin playing a recursive script, Sketchpad asks you to specify a depth of recursion. It also estimates the total number of objects the script will create at the specified depth.

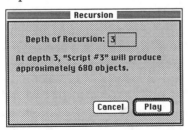

Depth 0 instructs Sketchpad to play the script but to ignore the recursive steps. Depth 1 indicates that a recursive step should recurse once, but that the recursed script should not recurse further. Depth 2 indicates that the script can recurse twice, but not further, and so forth. You may specify any depth you choose, provided there's enough available memory for the total number of objects that depth would create.

You might want to try increasing Sketchpad's available memory if you intend to work with complex recursive constructions. See the General Issues chapter for more information.

If you STEP or PLAY through a script (as opposed to using FAST), you'll notice a Depth Gauge in the script's status bar. The indicator is expressed as a fraction in which the numerator is the depth of the current step and the denominator is the maximum depth of recursion you specified in the Recursion dialog box. For instance, "<Depth: 1/3>" indicates that the current step is in the first recursion in a script that will recurse three levels "deep."

What Can Go Wrong?

A number of things can go wrong when you are playing scripts. The first, and simplest, is that you have not specified enough or the right type of selections for the Givens in the script. You should be aware of the following possibilities.

Insufficient Constructions

When you play back a script and the construction is not what you expected, it's time for some detective work. For example, what if while you are creating a script you draw a right triangle? You might expect the script to create a right triangle when you play it back, but actually there isn't anything in the script to force subsequent triangles to be right triangles; it's just that your original triangle happened to be a right triangle. The type of triangle created depends on the placement of the points in the sketch, not the definition in the script.

With a little effort, however, you can construct a right triangle that would always play back as a right triangle.

1. Draw one side of the triangle from point *A* to point *B*.

2. Construct a perpendicular to this side passing through point *B*.

3. Choose any point *C* on the perpendicular.

4. Connect point *C* with segments to point *A* and point *B*.

5. Hide the perpendicular.

You can observe that this construction will always be a right triangle by dragging the various components and observing that it always includes a 90° angle.

Ambiguous Constructions

Having scripts turn out differently than you expect can be frustrating, but it can also be educational. In general, you can count on Sketchpad to execute your script precisely; however, precise execution can reveal that your script was geometrically ambiguous. Tracking down the ambiguity can help you develop more robust scripts and can lead to a more sophisticated understanding of geometry.

The following example illustrates a typical ambiguous script. Suppose you are attempting to square the edges of a triangle. You might begin by recording a script while squaring one edge. With a segment as a Given, the script would build a square on that segment.

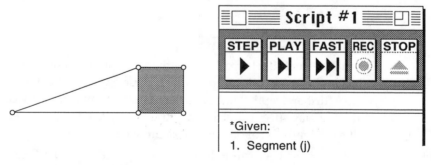

If you intend to use this script to square the other two sides of the triangle, you might find that when you select another segment on the triangle, the script produces the first figure shown below.

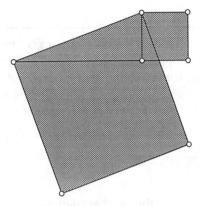

rather than what you wanted.

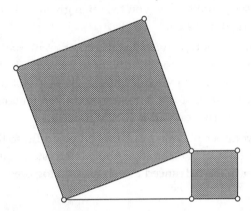

To understand what went wrong, you can Undo the second square and step through the script to see that Sketchpad did exactly what you recorded. The one segment (the script's Given) implies two possible positions for a square. In other words, the script does not include enough information to distinguish between a square hanging down from a segment and a square that goes up.

In order to uniquely determine a single square, you must specify more than a single edge as givens. Here are some ways to write a "better" square script.

- Choose as Givens a segment edge and a point that determines on which side of the edge the square is constructed.

- Choose a nonvertical segment edge and build a square that is always above (or always below) the segment.

  (Hint: Use the Translate command.)

- Choose an ordered pair of adjacent vertices and construct a square so that the segment between the first vertex and the second vertex always follows the perimeter of the square in a constant direction (clockwise or counterclockwise).

  (Hint: Rotate a segment by a fixed angle around one endpoint as a center.)

Script Tools

Another way to add scripts as commands is to save them in a common folder on your disk. Then inform Sketchpad that this folder is your Script Tools Folder by using the Advanced Preferences dialog box. Sketchpad lists all scripts that it finds in this folder in a pop-up menu available under the Script Tool portion of the sketch toolbox.

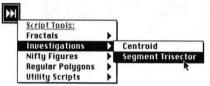

Press the mouse on the Script Tool to see the list of available tools. Choose a script from this list to use it. Instead of requiring that you select objects to match all givens ahead of time, scripts that are used as script tools allow you to match givens interactively by pointing to existing or new objects in your sketch.

You can create your own geometry environment using a combination of script tools and configuration of Geometry menus through Advanced Preferences. Suppose, for example, you want to create an environment for exploring the geometry of the Poincaré disk. You could remove the Construct, Transform, Measure, and Graph menus from the menu bar, and add script tools for construction within the Poincaré disk.

Sketchpad remembers your Script Tools Folder when you quit, so the same tools will be available the next time you start Sketchpad. If you want to stop using these tools, choose Clear Script Tools Folder in the Advanced Preferences dialog box.

More About Scripts

Scripts in the Work Menu

Scripts allow you to expand the Sketchpad commands into complex actions that are readily available from the Work menu. When a script opens, it automatically appears in the Work menu. In this way you can create commands to perform complex constructions that are specific to the work you do. All you have to do is select the appropriate objects in a sketch, then hold down the Option key while choosing the script name from the Work menu. The script automatically executes the construction.

For example, you may be working on something that requires you to construct various regular polygons. If you have regular polygon scripts in a folder, you can choose Open from the File menu, open the folder, and click Open All to open all of the scripts. Then each of the scripts is available from the Work menu.

Scripts Within Scripts

You can play other scripts while recording a script to create complex constructions. For example, the "Magnificent Nick" script included with the samples has more than 150 steps. The author, "magnificent" Nicholas Jackiw, created it by repeating a smaller script, which projected a single ray of light to its shadow many times to create multiple shadows. By playing one script into another recording script, you can use some scripts as building blocks to create others scripts of virtually unlimited complexity.

Command Reference

Sketchpad understands a few additional commands which are not available through any menu. See the Advanced Applications chapter for more information.

Organized by the order of the menus on the sketch menu bar, this chapter describes every menu command. The menus displayed in the menu bar operate on the foremost or active window. When the sketch window is active, you'll see the sketch menu bar.

| ⚏ File Edit Display Construct Transform Measure Graph Work | **Sketch Menu Bar** |

When a script, desk accessory, or Clipboard window is active, some of the menus will be dimmed because the sketch commands cannot operate on those kinds of windows.

The Apple menu is described in the *Macintosh User's Guide.*

File Menu

The File menu contains commands for opening, saving, and using sketch and script documents. Many of these commands are common to other Macintosh programs and are described in more detail in the *Macintosh User's Guide.*

New Sketch

Opens a new, empty sketch. The new sketch window appears on top of all other windows and is the active window.

The new sketch is untitled until you name it by saving it.

⌘N is the keyboard shortcut for this command.

New Script

Opens a new script window on top of all other windows.

The new script is untitled until you name it by saving it.

Open...

Opens an existing sketch or script. You can use the Open All button to open every document in the current folder.

1. Choose Open from the File menu.

   The Open dialog box displays the names of sketches and scripts in the current folder.

↩ Arrange all your documents for a lesson in one folder, then have the students use Open All.

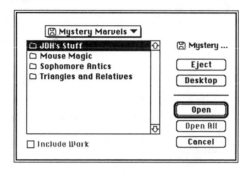

You can double-click the name of the document rather than clicking the Open button.

2. Click the name of the sketch or script you want to use in the list box.

3. Click Open.

   ⌘O is the keyboard shortcut for Open.

Opening every document in a folder

The Open All option is particularly useful when you have a group of exercises saved in one folder or when you have a group of scripts you want to appear on the Work menu.

1. Choose Open from the File menu.

2. Open the folder that contains the files you want to open.

3. Click the Open All button.

   Every script and sketch opens.

Including the construction history

Normally when you open a sketch, it appears in the form in which you last saved it. If you would like to undo the construction step by step to examine its composition, you can click the Include Work check box in the Open dialog box. The steps may not be the same steps you used to create the figures in the sketch but they still logically describe the relationships which make up the construction.

Displaying the names of documents from a different folder

The Open dialog box lists all the files in the current folder. If you want to select a different folder at a higher level than your current folder, you can click the disk drive icon to move up one level.

Disk Drive Icon

Folder Icon

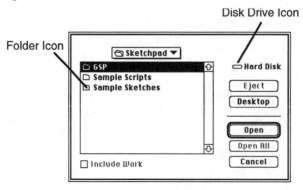

To move down one level into a folder, double-click the folder icon in the list box. See *Getting Started With Your Macintosh* for more information on using this dialog box.

Using Sketchpad with both Macintosh and Microsoft Windows

If you use Sketchpad on both a Macintosh and on a PC with Microsoft Windows, you can open sketches and scripts you create in one version with the other version. (Your work is portable.) However, because the DOS disk format used by a PC is different from the Macintosh disk format, you'll need a file exchange tool such as the PC Exchange control panel.

Older Macintosh computers may have a similar tool called Apple File Exchange. We will only explain use of PC Exchange here, so refer to the documentation that came with your Macintosh for details on using Apple File Exchange.

PC Exchange can be found on the system disks that accompany your Macintosh. These tools require a Mac with a floppy disk drive compatible with high density disks (although the disk you use need not be a high density disk). Older Macintoshes such as the Mac Plus, some Mac II's, and some Mac SE's may not have this capability. Your PC will also need a 3.5-inch disk drive.

Opening Macintosh files in Microsoft Windows

1. Make sure the PC Exchange control panel is installed and has been turned on.

PCDisk

2. Insert a DOS formatted disk in the floppy disk drive. (If you do not have a DOS formatted disk, you can format one using the Erase Disk command in the Finder's Special menu.)

3. From Sketchpad, save the Macintosh document on the DOS disk with a name of no more than 8 characters followed by **.gsp** if it is a sketch (for example **MySketch.gsp**) or **.gss** if it is a script (for example **MyScript.gss**).

4. Insert the disk into a computer running the Windows version of Sketchpad. Choose Open from the File menu, select the proper drive and open the file.

Opening Windows files on a Macintosh

1. On the computer running the Windows version of Sketchpad, save or copy your file or files to a DOS formatted 3.5-inch floppy disk. Eject the disk and take it to your Macintosh.

2. On the Macintosh, open the PC Exchange control panel, which should have been installed on your hard disk as part of the system software. If this is the first time you have attempted to open Windows Sketchpad files on your Macintosh, you will need to configure the control panel to automatically recognize Sketchpad files. You do that by using the Add button in the control panel to specify the appropriate DOS suffix, application program, and document type, as shown below.

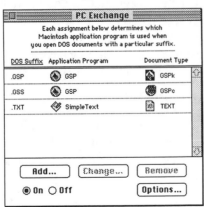

3. Insert the DOS disk into the floppy drive. The files on the floppy disk should appear as normal Macintosh files with their correct finder icons.

4. You can drag the Windows Sketchpad files onto your hard disk if you wish. You can open the files directly from the DOS disk.

5. If you wish, use the Save As command from the File menu to save the Windows Sketchpad files on your Macintosh disk. You may want to rename them.

For more information on Microsoft Windows files, see the Advanced Applications chapter.

Save

Saves the current sketch or script, whichever is active. The sketch or script remains open, but the program pauses while it writes the information onto the disk. Once the saving process is complete, you can continue work.

Save often. What is on the screen is really only so many electrons until it is written on a disk. If someone trips on your power cord and you have not saved your work, you will lose it.

If you choose Save for a sketch or a script that has not been previously saved, the Save As dialog box appears.

Saving releases the Undo history, as described in the Undo section of this chapter.

⌘S is the keyboard shortcut for Save.

Save As...

Names and saves the active sketch or script.

1. Choose Save As from the File menu.

    The Save As dialog box appears with the name entry box highlighted.

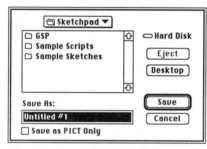

2. Double-click the folder where the sketch or the script will be saved.

3. Type a name for the sketch or the script. The name must be unique in the folder you have selected.

You can press Return after typing the file name rather than clicking the Save button.

4. Click the Save button.

The document is saved with the name you entered. If another document in that folder has the name you specified, you are asked if you want to replace the document. Before clicking Yes, be certain you will not write over a document you want to keep. For example, if you want to save a script named Triangle and you already have a sketch named Triangle in the current folder, replacing the existing file will replace the old sketch with the new script.

Saving a sketch or a script with a different name

If you want to save a sketch or a script with a different name from the name by which you originally saved it, choose Save As from the File menu. When you complete the dialog box, the current sketch or script is given the new name, while the original remains on the disk as it was when you last saved it.

Saving a script as a text file

If you want to use a script in a word processor, you can save it as a text file.

1. Make the script the top, active window.

2. Choose Save As from the File menu.

3. Click the Save As TEXT Only check box.

4. Click the Save button.

   A warning appears to tell you that the file you create is not a script file and cannot be opened as a script file. You should save the script as text if you want to use it as a text file; however, if you want to use the file as a script, you must also save it as a script file.

5. Click OK.

   The script is saved as text.

Saving a sketch as a PICT file

PICT is a graphic format understood by many drawing programs. When you save a sketch as PICT, a warning appears to tell you that the file you create is not a sketch file and cannot be opened as one. Sketchpad itself cannot open PICT files, but you can open PICT files with other drawing programs to enhance printed images of your constructions beyond Sketchpad's own graphic ability.

If you want to save the current sketch as a PICT file, choose Save As from the File menu. Then click the Save As PICT check box in the dialog.

Saving a sketch or a script on a different disk

You can save the current sketch or script on a different disk.

1. Choose Save As from the File menu.

2. If you are working on a floppy disk, click the Eject button and insert the new disk into the disk drive.

   If you are working on a hard disk, insert the new floppy disk into the disk drive.

3. If you wish, enter a new name for the sketch or script. Since this is a different disk, the document can have the same name as the original, in which case you need only click the Save button.

Close

The Close Box

Closes the current sketch or script, whichever window is active. If you have done any work since you last saved, Sketchpad gives you the opportunity to save.

The keyboard shortcut for Close is ⌘W. You can also click the close box at the left of the title bar to close the document.

Page Setup...

Allows you to specify the size of paper, the orientation of the drawing, and other printing options.

1. Choose Page Setup from the File menu.

   The Page Setup dialog box appears.

This dialog box is typical for a laser printer.

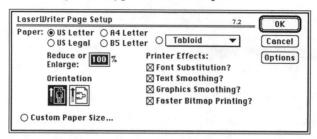

This dialog box is typical for an ImageWriter printer.

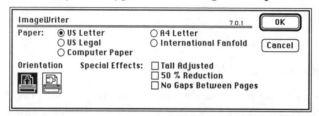

2. Set the options you want. Click the Help button if you want more information about the LaserWriter page setup. If you use an ImageWriter printer, be sure to check the Tall Adjusted check box. This guarantees that the horizontal and vertical proportions of your printed sketch are the same as those you see on screen.

3. Click OK.

The page is set up for the printer you specified with Chooser from the Apple menu.

Print Preview... /Print Options...

When a sketch is the active window, Print Preview appears on the File menu and provides a miniature picture of how your sketch or script will look when it is printed. After looking at the preview, you may want to make changes to this drawing, or you may want to make some changes in Page Setup, such as changing the orientation of the image on the paper.

Previewing sketches

The Print Preview dialog box lists the name of the sketch, the number of visible objects, the total number of objects, and how much memory is used by the sketch.

1. Choose Print Preview from the File menu.

    The Print Preview dialog box appears.

Lines and rays go on forever in the sketch plane. When lines or rays are on a printed page, or when you cut or copy lines or rays to the Clipboard, they appear with arrowheads to indicate that they are not segments. (You can eliminate the arrowheads using the Preferences command.)

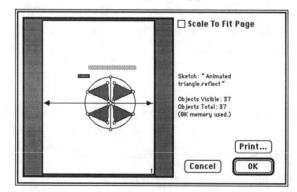

Text in the Print Preview graphic is displayed as a gray area rather than as actual text.

2. Click Scale To Fit Page if you want. This option resizes the sketch to fill one printed page exactly, regardless of how large or small it was originally. This scaling only changes the image visually; any measured quantities in your sketch will print the values as you measured them in the window, not the values as scaled on the printed page. Also be aware that not all printers can scale text as well as they can scale graphics. You may have to adjust your captions manually to get the best results.

3. Click OK to return to the sketch or click Print to print the image as it appears. Click Cancel to dismiss the dialog box.

Previewing scripts

When a script is the active window, the Print Preview command becomes Print Options on the File menu.

You can use the Print Options dialog box to specify how the script will appear when it is printed. You can click the check boxes to indicate which script components are printed.

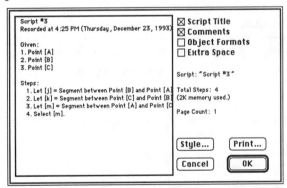

1. If necessary, click the title bar of the script you want to print to make it active.

2. Choose Print Options from the File menu.

   The beginning of the script is displayed in the dialog box.

3. Click any of the options (Script Title, Comments, Object Formats, or Extra Space) you want to include in the printed version of your script.

   The effects of each option are demonstrated in the display area on the left.

4. To specify text characteristics, click the Style button and select the characteristics you want.

5. Click the Print button.

   The script is printed as it is illustrated. (If you click OK instead of Print, your settings are saved, and you return to the script without printing.)

Print...

Sends the current sketch or script to the printer, using the specifications set in Page Setup and Print Preview/Print Options.

1. Choose Print from the File menu.

   The Print dialog box appears.

   The dialog box below is for a LaserWriter printer.

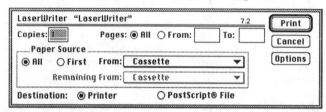

   If you print in Draft mode on an ImageWriter, only the text in a sketch will be printed. To print the objects, you'll have to choose Faster or Best mode.

2. Set the options you want. If you have a LaserWriter, you can get help with the print options by clicking the Help button.

   You can print any or all pages and specify the number of copies.

3. Click OK.

   The sketch or the script goes to the printer. You can stop the printing in progress by pressing the ⌘ key and the period key simultaneously (⌘.).

Share Documents...

Opens saved sketch and script documents on other computers running Sketchpad on a network. This command only appears if you are running System 7 or higher.

1. Choose Share Documents from the File menu.

   The network users dialog box displays the names of every computer running Sketchpad in your current AppleTalk zone.

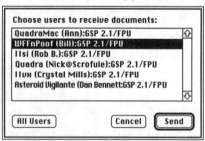

If your network has more than one zone, and you would like to share documents with users in other zones, press the Option key while choosing Share Documents. Sketchpad users in all zones will be listed.

2. Click the machine names of the users with whom you wish to share documents.

   To select a user, click his or her machine name. To deselect a name, click it while pressing the ⌘ key. You can click and drag to select multiple names simultaneously, or you can click All Users to share documents with everyone appearing in the list.

3. Click Send (if you haven't already clicked All Users).

The standard Open dialog box appears, showing you all the documents on your hard disk and on any volumes you are sharing.

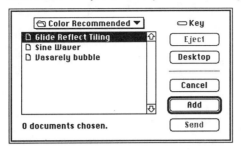

4. Select a document to share, and click Add.

   To share more than one document, continue to locate documents and click Add.

5. Click Send when you have chosen all the documents you wish to share.

   If this is the first time you are linking to these computers, you may have to connect to them as a Guest or a Registered User. See the *Macintosh Networking Reference* that came with System 7 for more details.

   The documents open on the chosen users' screens.

Troubleshooting Shared Documents

If a Macintosh does not appear in the network viewers dialog box, make sure that it is correctly set up for program linking. Program linking is described at length in your *Macintosh Networking Reference*. In brief, a machine must be running System 7, it must be connected to your network, and Program Linking must be started in the Sharing Setup control panel. In addition, make sure that Program Linking is allowed for the user who will send documents in the Users & Groups control panel.

Keep in mind that Sketchpad shares only the *location* of your chosen documents, not the *contents* of them. This means that a document cannot be shared with users unless those users could open the document themselves (with the Open command). On a file server or shared volume to which all of your users have access, store documents you wish to send. If a user cannot open shared documents, you'll be notified with an alert reminding you to first share them in the Finder. See your *Macintosh Networking Reference* manual for information about sharing files and folders from the Finder.

Quit

Quits from Sketchpad. If any sketches or scripts are open and have not been saved, Sketchpad gives you the opportunity to save them.

The keyboard shortcut for Quit is ⌘Q.

Edit Menu

The Edit menu contains commands for undoing and redoing Sketchpad activities, for using the Clipboard, for selecting objects, and for showing and hiding the Clipboard. The Edit menu also allows you to create action buttons, to select geometric objects, and to control the visibility of the Toolbox, script comments, and Clipboard. The menu shown below is typical for an active sketch.

```
┌─Edit──────────────┐
│ Undo          ⌘Z  │
│ Redo          ⌘R  │
├───────────────────┤
│ Cut           ⌘H  │
│ Copy          ⌘C  │
│ Paste         ⌘U  │
│ Clear             │
├───────────────────┤
│ Action Button   ▶ │
├───────────────────┤
│ Select All    ⌘A  │
│ Select Parents ⌘U │
│ Select Children ⌘D│
├───────────────────┤
│ Hide Toolbox      │
│ Show Clipboard    │
├───────────────────┤
│ Create Publisher… │
└───────────────────┘
```

Undo

A quick way to obtain an empty sketch is to Undo All by holding down Option while you choose Undo All from the Edit menu.

This command allows you to undo any action that affects objects, their creation, or their location. Sketchpad stores each action in a list, an Undo history. You can undo actions back to the last time you saved or, if you have not saved, to the beginning of the sketch. (This is different from most other programs, which let you undo only the most recent action.) If you hold down Option before pulling down the menu, the command becomes Undo All.

When you pull down the Edit menu in Sketchpad, you'll notice that the Undo command changes, depending on the last action you performed. It might be Undo Delete Segment or Undo Point. If you undo something you want back, you can choose Redo.

The keyboard shortcut for Undo is ⌘Z and for Undo All is Option-Z.

Creating a step-by-step visual explanation with Undo and Redo

↬ You can use Undo and Redo together to review work or discuss a construction sequence with students.

1. Complete a construction.

2. Choose Undo repeatedly to return to the beginning of the process or use Undo All.

   You can use the keyboard shortcut ⌘Z to go back one step at a time or Option-Z to return to the sketch at the last save or the beginning of the work session.

3. Use Redo (⌘R) to proceed one step at a time through your construction, explaining as you go. Do not perform any other action during this Redo sequence, or the Undo history will be changed.

Redo

This command allows you to redo the last undone action. Sketchpad maintains an Undo history. You can undo back to the beginning and use Redo to trace your steps forward again. If you hold down Option before pulling down the menu, the command becomes Redo All. See the Undo section for a description of using Undo and Redo for explaining constructions.

The keyboard shortcut for Redo is ⌘R and for Redo All is Option-R.

Cut

The Clipboard is a buffer, a temporary storage place that holds the last selection that was cut or copied.

The Cut command removes the selection from the sketch and places it on the Clipboard. Only the last selection that was cut or copied is on the Clipboard. When you cut objects, any visible and hidden children of the selected objects are cut also. By holding down the

Option key while you choose Cut, you can cut just the selection, leaving the children in place.

You can use Cut to move a selection to a different sketch. If you just want to move a selection within a sketch, you can use the Translate tool or Translate in the Transform menu.

Arrowheads replace the infinite ends of a line or a ray in the Clipboard, but the entire line or ray reappears when you paste it back into a sketch. If you paste into a different application, the arrowheads remain on lines and on rays. (You can also turn off arrowheads with the Preferences command.)

The keyboard shortcut for the Cut command is ⌘X.

Cutting and pasting objects into another sketch

When you cut or copy an object, its parents are not cut or copied with it unless they are selected too.

1. Select the objects you want to place into another sketch.

2. Choose Cut from the Edit menu.

   The selected objects disappear from the current sketch and go onto the Clipboard.

3. Open the sketch you want to paste into or bring that sketch to the top by clicking its title bar or by selecting it from the Work menu.

The difference between the Cut and Copy commands is that when you cut a selection, you remove the selected objects from the sketch, and when you copy, the selected objects remain in the sketch.

4. Choose Paste from the Edit menu.

   The selected objects appear in the new sketch in the same position they occupied when they were cut from the original sketch. The objects remain selected so that you can move them if you wish.

Copy

The Copy command places the selected objects onto the Clipboard without removing them from the sketch. Only the last selection cut or copied is on the Clipboard. Unlike Cut, the Copy command does not copy children of the selected objects onto the Clipboard.

If you just want to move a selection within a sketch, you can use the Selection Arrow tool or Translate in the Transform menu.

Arrowheads replace the infinite ends of a line or a ray in the Clipboard, but the entire line or ray reappears when you paste it back into a sketch. If you paste into a different application, the arrowheads remain on lines and on rays.

The keyboard shortcut for the Copy command is ⌘C.

Copying and pasting objects into another sketch

When you cut or copy an object, its parents are not cut or copied with it unless they are selected too.

1. Select the objects you want to place in another sketch.

2. Choose Copy from the Edit menu.

   The selected objects remain in the current sketch and also go to the Clipboard.

3. Open the sketch you want to paste into or bring that sketch to the top by clicking its title bar or by selecting it from the Work menu.

4. Choose Paste from the Edit menu.

   The selected objects appear in the new sketch in the same position they occupied when they were copied from the original sketch. The objects remain selected so that you can move them if you want.

   Note that the copied objects are completely independent of the original objects. Changes in the original objects do not affect the copies, and vice versa.

Copying the picture of a trace

When a trace of an object is visible in the active sketch, you may copy a picture of it to the Clipboard to paste into another application. The Copy command changes to Copy Trace when a trace is showing. When you choose Copy Trace, you will be asked whether to copy just the trace or the trace along with all other objects in your sketch.

Because some traces are very large, Copy Trace may create a very large picture on the Clipboard. If you want to copy a picture of only one portion of the trace, arrange your sketch window (through scrolling and resizing) so that only the desired portion of the trace is visible. Then choose Copy Trace while holding down the Option key. This will trim the copied picture so that it only contains the portion of the trace currently visible in the sketch window.

See Trace described on page 165 for more information on traces. For more information on copying objects to paste into other applications, see Pasting into Other Applications in the next section.

Paste

This command pastes the contents of the Clipboard into the current sketch. If the paste is applied to a different sketch than that from which the clipboard objects came, they will be pasted in the same position as they had when they were cut or copied. Otherwise they will be pasted in a position offset down and to the right of the original objects.

The keyboard shortcut for the Paste command is ⌘V.

Pasting into Other Applications

When you Cut or Copy sketch objects to the Clipboard, Sketchpad puts them onto the Clipboard in a wide variety of data formats. When you then Paste these objects into another application, multiple formats allow the other application to choose its preferred representation of your objects.

The exact data format Sketchpad puts onto the Clipboard depends on what you've cut or copied:

↬ This wide variety of formats allow you to use Sketchpad with a suite of applications. Create assignments and handouts in a word-processor using graphics created in Sketchpad. Conduct numeric investigations with your class using spreadsheets to examine Sketchpad-tabulated data.

- When you copy only a single caption, Sketchpad puts unformatted text onto the Clipboard. This text can be pasted into word processors, where it can be further edited and reformatted.

- When you copy one or more measurements, Sketchpad puts unformatted text that describes the measurements onto the Clipboard, one measurement per line.

- When you copy only a single table, Sketchpad puts the table's data onto the Clipboard as text, one line for each row in the table, with tabs separating data columns. This format can be pasted into most spreadsheet and data-graphing applications.

- When you copy a single sound-playing action button, Sketchpad puts the sound onto the Clipboard as raw sound data ("snd" format). Sound data can be pasted into advanced sound-editing and multi-media presentation applications.

- When you copy anything else, Sketchpad puts a picture of all your copied objects onto the Clipboard. Pictures can be pasted into most drawing and word-processing applications.

Of course, Sketchpad objects are also stored on the Clipboard as Sketchpad objects. When you paste objects into a sketch instead of into another application, they reappear exactly as they appeared when you first cut or copied them.

Preserving color in objects cut for export

Color stays in effect when you work inside Sketchpad, regardless of how you cut your objects. Many applications do not understand full color images, so when you paste to another application, Sketchpad sends a "simple" color image that other programs are more likely to understand. If you plan to paste to an application that understands full color images, hold down Shift while choosing Copy from the Edit menu. Sketchpad will place a full color image of your selection onto the Clipboard.

Pasting from Other Applications

You can paste pictures and text copied from other applications into Sketchpad. When you are editing a caption, choosing Paste inserts any text on the Clipboard into the current caption. If there is a picture (either a painting or a drawing) on the Clipboard, you can paste it into your sketch as an imported picture. (The text of the Paste command changes to Paste Picture when a picture is on the Clipboard.) You may want to use pictures to illustrate and embellish your sketches or to provide backgrounds for geometric investigations.

How the imported picture behaves in Sketchpad depends on your selections at the time you choose Paste.

- If you have selected a single point, the picture is pasted into Sketchpad with its top left corner at the selected point. If you move or animate the point, the pasted picture moves with it. You can use the Selection Arrow tool to resize the picture by selecting it and dragging the resize handle that appears at the object's bottom right corner.

- If you have selected two points, the picture is pasted into the rectangle determined by the two points. If you move or animate the points, the pasted picture moves and shrinks or stretches so as to remain within the rectangle determined by the two points.

- With any other selections, or with no selection, the picture is pasted as a free object. Free objects do not depend on any other object in the sketch, but you can move or resize them with the Selection Arrow tool.

You can also paste sounds from other applications into Sketchpad. See the description of the Sound command in the Action Button submenu of the Edit menu for more information.

Clear

The Clear command removes selected objects and their children from the sketch without placing them on the Clipboard. Hold down the Option key to clear only the selected objects and not their children. This action appears in the Undo list, so you can use Undo to retrieve any cleared objects. Using this command is equivalent to pressing the Delete key.

To save memory and to maintain parent-child relationships, use Undo All rather than this command to remove all objects from a sketch.

Action Buttons

This submenu creates and manipulates action buttons, which are powerful shortcuts for complex sequences of Sketchpad actions.

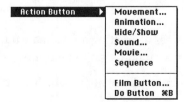

With action buttons, you can prepare sketches with simple point-and-click interfaces for other users to explore—even if the sketches contain elaborate animations or multiple levels of significant objects. You'll also create action buttons to access Sketchpad's powerful multi-media capabilities.

Movement...

This command creates a Move button that moves one or more points to specified destinations in your sketch.

1. Select a point to move and a second point at the desired destination of the first point.

2. If you wish to move more than one point simultaneously, continue selecting pairs of points (one to move and the other at the location to which the first should be moved).

3. Choose Movement from the Action Button submenu.

    The Movement Speed dialog box appears.

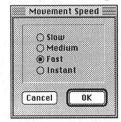

Slow, Medium, and Fast speeds are all relative. When you double-click an Instant Move button, however, all of the button's moved points leap to their destinations in a single motion.

Choose a speed with which to move your point(s).

If you move multiple points simultaneously, Sketchpad times all points so they arrive at their destinations at the same moment. In this case, the speed you choose applies to the point that has to move the greatest distance.

If you hold the Option key down while choosing Movement, Sketchpad will skip the Movement Speed dialog and create your movement button immediately, using fast speed for the movement.

4. Click OK.

    Sketchpad creates a Move button with a default label. You can change this label to something more meaningful by double-clicking on the button with the Text tool.

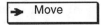

5. Double-click the button to move its parental points to their destinations.

    Clicking the mouse while the movement is taking place will cause the points to complete their movement instantly.

Take a look at the sample sketch entitled THE "Δ" that comes with Sketchpad. It is an example of how movement can be effectively used in a presentation sketch.

If a point is constrained and cannot move to its destination, it will move as close as it can to its destination.

Impossible movements

While you can always move one point to its destination, sometimes it may be impossible to move two points to two separate destinations, if the two points are geometrically related to each other. Sketchpad will warn you if you attempt to create a Movement button that contradicts the geometric relationships between your points.

Animation...

Creates an Animate button. The process of creating an Animate button is the same as starting a direct animation with the Display menu's Animate command.

1. Select a point and a path (segment or circle) along which to animate it.

2. If you wish to animate more than one point simultaneously, continue selecting points and paths. You may animate up to ten points simultaneously.

3. Choose Animation from the Action Button submenu.

   The Path Match dialog appears.

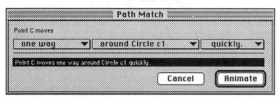

You can bypass the Path Match dialog by pressing Option while choosing Animation from the Action Button submenu. Sketchpad will create an Animate button in which points are matched to paths in the order in which you select them.

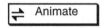

4. Choose a direction, a path, and a speed for each animated point, as explained later in this chapter.

5. Click Animate.

   Sketchpad creates an Animate button labeled Animate. You can change this label to something more meaningful by double-clicking on the button with the Text tool.

6. Double-click this button to view your animation. To stop the animation, wait for it to complete (if you chose "once" for any of the point matches) or click the mouse button until the animation stops.

Impossible animations

A point cannot be animated along a path if that point determines the position of the path geometrically. Also, it may not be possible to animate two or more points along separate paths if the points are geometrically related to each other. Sketchpad will warn you if you attempt to create an animation that contradicts the geometric relationships you've created in your sketch.

Hide/Show

Creates two action buttons. One will hide the selected objects, the other will show them once they've been hidden.

1. Select the objects whose visibility you wish to control through buttons.

2. Choose Hide/Show from the Action Button submenu.

   Sketchpad creates a Show button and a Hide button. You can change their labels by double-clicking on the buttons with the Text tool.

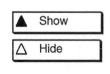

3. Double-click these buttons to toggle the visibility of your previously selected objects.

Sketchpad always creates these buttons in pairs, under the assumption that if you want a button to hide something, you'll probably want a button to bring it back. (Otherwise, just choose Hide Objects from the Display menu to hide them instantaneously.) If for some reason you want only a Hide button, or only a Show button, simply delete the other button.

Sound...

Recorded or pasted sounds require large amounts of memory to store. You may want to increase the amount of memory available to the Sketchpad application before working with sound. (See the "General Issues" chapter or your Macintosh Owner's Guide for more information.)

Creates a Sound button containing a microphone-recorded sound. It will only be available if you have a microphone attached to your Macintosh.

1. Choose Sound from the Action Button submenu.

The recording dialog box appears.

2. Click Record to begin recording sound.

3. Speak into your microphone. The length of sound you can record is determined by available memory.

   The memory indicator gradually fills to indicate the length of sound already recorded.

4. Click Stop when you've finished recording the sound you want.

5. Click Save.

   Sketchpad creates a Sound button labeled Play Sound. You can change this label to something more meaningful by double-clicking on the button with the Text tool.

6. Double-click the button to play your recorded sound.

Importing sounds from other applications

If there is not enough available memory to open all the sounds when reopening a saved sketch containing sound buttons, Sketchpad will open a window containing all of your geometric objects without sounds attached to sound buttons. This way you can work on or explore a sketch even in low-memory situations.

If you do not have a built-in microphone, or if you want to use a sound you have recorded elsewhere, you can still create Sound buttons by importing sounds from other applications. ResEdit, HyperCard, and a variety of multimedia applications allow you to work with sounds.

1. Select the sound in some other application.

2. Choose Copy from the Edit menu.

   The other application puts a copy of the sound onto the Clipboard.

3. Open or switch to the Sketchpad application.

4. Hold down Option.

5. Choose Paste Sound from the Action Button submenu. Paste Sound is only available when there is a sound on the Clipboard and you are pressing Option.

   Sketchpad creates an action button containing your pasted sound.

Movie...

You may find it useful to place a movie inside a sketch when the movie shows something you are modeling with Sketchpad.

Creates an action button to play a QuickTime movie. The command will only be available if QuickTime is installed in your System Folder. QuickTime can only be installed on color-capable Macintoshes.

1. Choose Movie from the Action Button submenu.

The Open dialog box appears, displaying any QuickTime movies in the current folder.

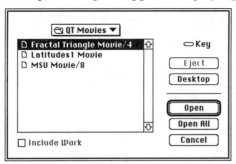

2. Select the name of the QuickTime movie to play.

3. Click Open.

Sketchpad creates a Movie button with the same name as the QuickTime movie file. You can change the label by double-clicking on the button with the Text tool.

4. Double-click the button at any time to view the movie. To stop viewing the movie, click the movie window's close box (in its upper left corner).

Movies and memory

QuickTime movies tend to be extremely large in memory size and disk space. This has two ramifications. First, you may want to increase the amount of memory available to Sketchpad before playing movies. To do this, refer to the General Issues chapter or to your *Macintosh Owner's Guide*.

Second, because movie files are often hundreds of times the size of sketch documents, Sketchpad stores only the *location* of your movie file (and not its *contents*) when you create a Movie button. If you move or delete the movie file from the folder or the disk in which it is stored, your Movie button will no longer be able to play the movie. In this case, a message will be displayed when you double-click the Movie button.

Sequence

Creates an action button that sequences the actions of other selected buttons. Sequence buttons are useful in creating presentation sketches. The sample sketch Hypercubethat comes with Sketchpad shows one example of how to use sequence buttons.

1. Select two or more action buttons in the order you wish them to be sequenced.

2. Choose Sequence from the Action Button submenu.

Sketchpad creates a Sequence button labeled Sequence. You can change the label to something more meaningful with the Text tool.

3. Double-click the Sequence button to perform each of the previously selected actions in turn.

You may want to hide the Sequence button's parents (the buttons that it sequences) if they are only cluttering your sketch. These buttons do not have to be showing in order for the Sequence button to use them.

Timing a sequence

If you create a lengthy sequence of action buttons, you may want to insert pauses between some of the sequenced actions. For instance, you might want to delay momentarily after showing some objects (with a Show button) before beginning to move them (with an Animate button).

To add a delay after an action button that is used in a sequence, follow these steps.

1. Choose the Object Information tool from the Toolbox.

2. Double-click the action button.

   The Object Information dialog box appears.

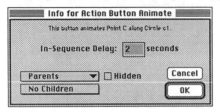

3. Enter the number of seconds you wish to pause after performing this action.

4. Click OK.

   Now when you perform a sequence containing this action, Sketchpad will pause for the specified in-sequence delay.

Note that if you sequence animations that do not stop by themselves, you will have to explicitly stop the animation by pressing the mouse button, or the sequence will stall when it reaches the never-ending animation.

While playing a sequence, pressing the mouse button will advance the sequence.

- It will instantly move any noninstant movement to its destination and advance to the next sequenced action.

- It will interrupt any animation action and advance to the next sequenced action.

Overlapping sound and action is not available on all Macintoshes. If your Macintosh cannot overlap sound with action, From Sound Start will not appear in the Object Information dialog box.

- It will skip any in-sequence delay.

When you add a delay to Sound buttons, you can also choose whether to time the delay from the start of the sound or from its end. (Click the From Sound Start check box in the Object Information dialog box.) If you time from the sound's start and your delay is less than the length of the sound, Sketchpad will continue playing the sound through the next actions in the sequence. This way you can overlap sounds with actions to create sound effects or "running commentary."

Film Button

PICS is a data format used by movies before QuickTime was invented. A number of other multimedia applications can play PICS movies, but Sketchpad itself cannot. Use QuickTime if you're creating movies with Sketchpad to be played back in Sketchpad.

Creates a QuickTime or PICS movie of the selected button's action. Use this command to make movies of Sketchpad animations or action sequences.

1. Select the action button to film. You can only make movies based on Animate, Move, or Sequence buttons. (Sound, Show, and Hide buttons cause instantaneous actions instead of continuous ones, so they make dull movies.)

2. Resize your sketch window so that it frames the area you wish to film. When creating movies, Sketchpad uses the sketch window frame as the movie's viewfinder.

3. Choose Film Button from the Action Button submenu.

The Save dialog box appears.

Remember that movie files take up lots of space on your hard disk! Make sure you have plenty of available disk space before filming any movies. If you film an animation that does not stop by itself, you will have to explicitly stop it (by clicking the mouse button), or the movie will film forever, gradually filling up all available disk space!

If QuickTime is installed, two radio buttons allow you to choose between PICS and QuickTime movies. (Otherwise, PICS movies are created by default.)

If you choose QuickTime, an Options dialog box allows you to configure the standard QuickTime choices.

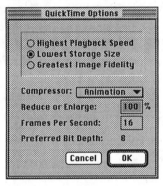

These alternatives include:

Optimization	Choose among Highest Playback Speed, Lowest Storage Size, and Greatest Image Fidelity. QuickTime will choose the best available compression technique for your optimization goal.
Compressor	Choose among the available compressors. In almost all cases, if you do not have special-purpose compression hardware, the Animation compressor works best.
Reduce or Enlarge	Enter a scaling factor other than 100 percent if you wish to resize your movie. QuickTime movies work best when relatively small (about two square inches).
Frames Per Second	Enter the desired playback speed—the higher the frame rate, the faster the motion on playback. You can create movies that play faster or slower than Sketchpad's movie-making animation by raising or by lowering this value. The maximum frame rate is 32 per second.

If you want to film a movie without first creating an Animate button, you can choose to film directly with the Animate command. After completing the Path Match dialog, press and hold down Option before clicking Animate. You will then be allowed to set up a PICS or QuickTime movie as described above.

Preferred Depth	This number indicates the bit-depth of your monitor, which in turn reflects the number of colors your monitor is capable of displaying (1 bit = 2 colors, 2 bits = 4 colors, 4 bits = 16 colors, and so on). A movie created at a given bit-depth can be played back at any depth, but will be smoothest at the same depth in which it was recorded. If you have a color or grayscale monitor, you can change this value with the Monitors control panel.

4. Type the name of a new file in which to save your movie.

5. Click Save.

    Sketchpad begins filming the movie, starting the button's animation or sequence. As the animation or the sequence continues, Sketchpad saves each frame into the movie file. When the action stops, Sketchpad closes the movie file.

Do Button

You can perform any action button by double-clicking it with the Selection Arrow tool, rather than selecting it and choosing Do Button.

Performs the action associated with the selected button. Do Button is only available if you have selected a single action button.

The action performed depends upon the selected button: objects may be moved or animated; sounds or movies played or entire multimedia sequences initiated.

The keyboard shortcut for Do Button is ⌘B.

Select All

This command selects every object in the sketch plane. The current drawing or text tool (Point, Circle, Segment, Ray, Line, or Text) acts as a filter with the Select All command. If a drawing tool or the Text tool is active, Sketchpad limits the Select All command to selecting all objects of the type created by the tool. For example, if the Point tool is the current tool, then Select All will read Select All Points. If the Selection Arrow tool is active, Select All will select all types of objects.

Use the Selection Arrow tool to select individual objects or groups of objects.

The keyboard shortcut for Select All is ⌘A. This shortcut also works with the current tool as a filter.

Select Parents

If dragging an object does not give you the behavior you want, try selecting the object's parents and dragging them instead.

If you use ⌘U repeatedly, you can eventually select the parents from which your entire figure was constructed (unless they are hidden).

This command selects the parents of the selected object(s). The parents of an object are the objects from which it was created. In the example below, the centerpoint of the circle and the point on the circumference are the parents of the circle. The circle is the child of those parents.

Parents   **Child**

If the object has no parents, it remains selected. If the object's parents are hidden, the object's parents' parents are selected. If all parents up the family tree are hidden, the object is deselected. The keyboard shortcut for Select Parents is ⌘U. (U is a mnemonic for *up*.)

Select Children

This command selects the children of the selected object(s). The children of an object are the objects created from it. For example, the child of a point could be a circle, or a segment, or even a circle and a segment.

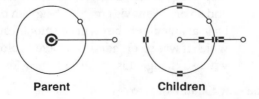

Parent   **Children**

If the object's children are hidden, the object's children's children are selected. If all children down the family tree are hidden, the object is deselected. Use the Object Information tool to explore an object's parents and children.

The keyboard shortcut for Select Children is ⌘D. (D is a mnemonic for *down*.)

Hide/Show Toolbox

Toggles between hiding and displaying the Toolbox in the active sketch. Hiding the toolbox can be useful when you are ready to distribute a presentation sketch and you want all space in the sketch available for objects. When the Toolbox is visible, the command is Hide Toolbox. This command is only available when a sketch is foremost.

Selecting Tools from the Keyboard

If you want to use your keyboard to select a tool, you can use the Spacebar and the Up and Down Arrow keys.

Up or Down Arrow	Moves up and down through the Toolbox, respectively.
Spacebar	Cycles to the right through the Straightedge tools.
Shift and Spacebar	Cycles to the right through the Selection tools.

For example, when the Compass tool is active, pressing the Up Arrow makes the Point tool active.

Keyboard access to tools is available whether the Toolbox is visible or not.

Show Clipboard

When you choose this command, a window appears showing the contents of the Clipboard. Click the close box to remove the Clipboard window.

According to the preference you have set, arrowheads may or may not replace the infinite ends of a line or ray in the Clipboard. Even if your preference is for arrowheads, the entire line or ray reappears when you paste it back into a sketch. If you paste into a different application, the arrowheads remain on lines and rays.

Create Publisher... /Publisher Options...

Publishes the selected objects in the current sketch to an edition. It is only available if you are using System 7 or higher of the Macintosh operating systems.

Under System 7 and higher versions, certain applications support Subscribe and Publish, a powerful form of dynamic data exchange. Subscribe and Publish is described at length in your *Macintosh System 7 Reference*. Briefly, one application *publishes* data to an *edition*, which is a special file that updates automatically when you save the published data. Other applications can then *subscribe* to this edition, and subscribers update whenever the edition changes. You'll use Sketchpad on the publishing side of things. With it you can publish geometric drawings, which you then subscribe to, for instance, in a classroom handout you prepare in a word processor. If you subsequently change the published sketch, the word processor document will automatically update to reflect the changes.

To publish a portion of the current sketch, follow these steps.

1. Select the object(s) you wish to publish.

2. Choose Create Publisher from the Edit menu.

You'll be asked to choose a name and a location for the edition, which is a special file containing the dynamically-updating data. A preview of your selected objects appears on the left.

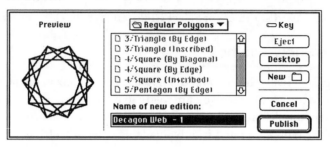

3. Type a name for the edition.

4. Click Publish.

    Sketchpad creates the edition file. In your sketch, a gray border appears around the published objects.

    This border is your publisher. As you move and manipulate the objects, the publisher will stretch and grow to surround them. Whenever you resave your sketch, the published edition will automatically update to reflect the current position of your published objects.

Removing a publisher

Publishers—the gray rectangles—act like any other object in Sketchpad. Thus, to remove a publisher, simply select it by clicking, and then press the Delete or Backspace key. You can also remove a publisher by using the Publisher Options dialog box described later in this chapter.

Moving a bound publisher

Publishers are geometrically bound to the objects they publish. In Sketchpad terminology, the publisher is the child of the published parents. As long as this relationship is intact, moving the publisher by dragging it with a Select arrow will move the publisher's parents as well.

Creating a free publisher

To create a free publisher, hold down the Option key before pulling down the Edit menu and choosing Create Publisher.

Sometimes it is useful to publish a portion of your sketch that is determined by a rectangle whose bounds are controlled by you rather than by selected objects. To do this, you need a free publisher. A free publisher is simply an arbitrary rectangle, which you can move and resize as you choose. When you save the document, Sketchpad will publish (to your edition) the objects or portion of objects that intersect the publisher's rectangle.

Moving a free publisher

To relocate a free publisher—one that is no longer related to geometric objects—click and drag it with the Select arrow, just as you would move another object in Sketchpad.

Resizing a free publisher

To change the area of a publisher's rectangle, you'll need to resize it.

1. Select the publisher. Make sure that only the publisher is selected.

   Four black handles appear on the publisher's corners, indicating that it is selected.

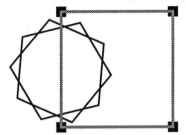

2. Click and drag one of the publisher's resize handles.

3. Release the mouse. The publisher resizes to its new position.

Contents of a published edition

The contents of a bound publisher's edition depend upon the objects published. Editions obey the same rules for data export as the Clipboard. (See Pasting into Other Applications described on page 148.) You can subscribe to published editions

- as pictures, in painting and drawing programs, and most word processors, spreadsheets, and other applications;

- as tabulated numeric data in a spreadsheet if you publish a table;

- as unformatted text in a word processor if you publish a caption or a group of measures.

Bound publishers publish *only their parents*—only those objects that were selected when you chose Create Publisher. Even if other objects intersect the bound publisher's rectangles, they are not published to the edition.

Free publishers publish all the objects that intersect their rectangle at the moment the sketch is saved. If no objects intersect a free publisher's rectangles, it will be empty.

Publisher Options allows you to configure a publisher's edition. This command only appears if you are using System 7 and have selected a single publisher. It replaces the Create Publisher command in the Edit menu.

1. Select a publisher by clicking on its gray border.

2. Choose Publisher Options from the Edit menu.

You can also access the Publisher Options dialog box by double-clicking the publisher border with a Select arrow.

The Publisher Options dialog box appears.

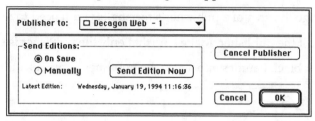

3. Choose your options by clicking them.

Send Edition Now   Updates the published file with the present contents of this publisher.

On Save   Sets Sketchpad to automatically update the edition of this publisher whenever you save the sketch. This is the default for new publishers.

Manually   Prevents Sketchpad from updating the edition whenever you save. If you choose to send editions manually, the edition will only be updated when you click Send Editions Now.

Cancel Publisher   Removes the publisher. You can also remove a publisher by selecting it in Sketchpad and pressing Delete or Backspace.

4. Click OK or Cancel to dismiss the Publisher Options dialog box.

Display Menu

The commands in the Display menu control the appearance of your sketch. The commands displaying indicators have submenus providing further choices. The following menu is typical for an active sketch.

✐ When using Sketchpad with an overhead projector display, use thick lines for greater visibility.

Line Weight

This command sets the weight for selected and subsequently created segments, rays, lines, and circles. If you want to change only the selected objects, not the setting for future objects, hold down Option while choosing the command.

The choices on the submenu are Thick Lines, Thin Lines, and Dashed Lines. This command doesn't affect points or interiors of polygons and circles.

Changing the line weight of existing objects

1. Select the objects to be changed.

2. Choose the line weight you want from the submenu.

Color

This command is available if your system has a color monitor. It sets the color of selected and subsequent points, segments, rays, lines, circles, and interiors. If you want to change only the selected objects without changing the setting for future objects, hold down Option while choosing the command.

The choices are black, red, magenta, blue, cyan, green, and yellow.

Changing the color of existing objects

1. Select the objects to be changed.

2. Choose the color you want from the submenu.

Shade

This command sets the shade of selected and subsequent interiors (polygon, circle, sector, and arc segment). If you want to change only the selected objects and not change the setting for future objects, hold down Option while choosing the command.

For color monitors, the shade represents the saturation of the object's color. For monochrome monitors, the shade represents a shade of gray. All shades except 100 percent saturation, whether color or gray, are translucent and the shades of overlapping objects blend.

Changing the shade of existing interiors

1. Select the objects to be changed.

2. Choose the shade you want from the submenu.

Text Style

This command changes the size or format of any text object. Text objects include captions, measures, tables, action buttons, and the visible labels of labeled objects.

Changing the font size of existing objects

1. Select the objects to be changed.

2. Choose a new size from the Text Style submenu.

    All selected text reappears in the new size.

    You can also increase or decrease the size of selected text by typing the greater-than sign (>) to increase or the less-than sign (<) to decrease while pressing the ⌘ key.

Adding text formatting to existing objects

1. Select the objects to be changed.

2. Choose a format to add from the Text Style submenu. Available formats include those shown here.

Boldface	Outline
Italic	<u>Underline</u>
Condensed	Extended

Removing text formatting from existing objects

1. Select the objects to be changed.

2. A check mark appears beside the format in the Text Style submenu. Choose the format to remove the check mark from the submenu, which removes the formatting of the text.

Setting Future Font Sizes and Styles

When you choose a size or a style from the submenu, Sketchpad uses that style for new objects of the same kind. Thus, if you set a caption to be 24 pt and some point labels to appear in boldface, new captions you create will also be 24 pt and new object labels will also be boldface.

You can reset selected text's formatting without affecting the format of future text by pressing Option while choosing from the Text Style submenu.

If you choose a font size or a style when no objects are selected, you set the size or format for future captions.

You can also permanently change the default text styles for captions, labels, tables, and measurements with the Preferences command in the Display menu.

Text Font

This command changes the font of selected text objects. Text objects include captions, measures, tables, action buttons, and the visible labels of selected objects.

Changing the font of existing objects

1. Select the objects to be changed.

2. Choose the new font from the Text Font submenu.

   All selected text reappears in the new font.

Setting Future Text Fonts

When you choose a font from the submenu, Sketchpad uses that style for new objects of the same kind. Thus, if you set a caption to appear in the Geneva font and some segment labels to appear in Chicago, new captions you create will also be in Geneva and new object labels will also be in Chicago.

You can reset the selected text's font without affecting the font setting of future text by pressing Option while choosing from the Text Font submenu.

If you choose a font when no objects are selected, you set the font for future captions.

Hide

Hides the selected objects. Use this command to hide objects without altering their geometric role in your construction. Hidden objects do not appear on the screen, but they continue to affect the figures in your sketch. You should hide objects that are important in determining a result but which visually detract from the result.

The keyboard shortcut for this command is ⌘H.

Show All Hidden

When a script is played back, all hidden objects appear (except during Fast Play) until after the last step of the script and then all objects marked as hidden in the script are simultaneously hidden.

This command displays and selects all objects that have been hidden. If you want to show only a few objects, use this procedure.

Displaying one object from a group that has been hidden

1. Choose Show All Hidden from the Display menu.

   All hidden objects appear and are selected.

2. Choose the Selection Arrow tool or hold down Option while a drawing tool is in effect.

3. Hold down Shift and click the objects you want to display.

    The objects are deselected.

4. Choose Hide Objects from the Display menu.

    All the objects still selected are rehidden.

You can also selectively hide and display objects by navigating through the parents and children network in the Object Information dialog box, which appears when you double-click the Object Information tool on an object.

Show/Hide Labels

This command toggles between displaying and hiding the labels of selected objects. If you have selected only objects whose labels are showing, the menu choice will be Hide Labels. If you have selected a group of objects, some but not all of which have labels showing, the menu selection is Show Labels.

The keyboard shortcut for this command is ⌘K.

Label Options and Relabeling

This command changes depending on what you have selected. If you have no objects selected, it appears as Label Options, allowing you to set how Sketchpad labels each of the kinds of objects. If you have a single object selected, the command is Relabel and has the same function as double-clicking on an existing label with the text tool (see page 211). If you have more than one object selected, then the command is Relabel Objects and will allow you to relabel the selected objects in a sequence.

The keyboard shortcut for setting label options and relabelling objects is ⌘/.

Setting Label Options

1. Make sure you have nothing selected.

2. Choose Label Options from the Display menu. This should bring up the dialog box shown below.

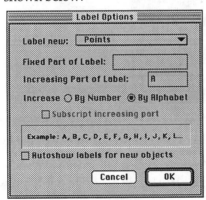

3. The pop-up menu near the top lets you choose among different kinds of objects: points, straight objects, circles, arcs, and interiors. For each choice, you can set the labeling options for new objects of that kind.

4. Sketchpad can assign new object labels based on both a fixed part and an increasing part. The default labels for circles, for example, use "c" as the fixed part and integers for the increasing part, yielding "c1, c2, c3, . . ." as the sequence of labels assigned to new circles in a blank sketch. Points, on the other hand, by default do not use a fixed

part for their labels, and use uppercase letters for their increasing part, as in "A, B, C, . . .". Type the fixed part of the new labels, if any, you wish to use; for example, type P as the fixed part of new labels for points.

5. A labeling scheme must have an increasing part for the labels. It can be an integer, starting with whatever integer you specify, or it can be an upper- or lowercase letter starting with the letter you specify. For example, type   5 as the first number in an increasing sequence "P5, P6, P7, . . .".

6. The By Number option should be automatically selected for you when you type in a number as the increasing part of the label. Choosing the By Alphabet option will set the increasing part of the labels to "A."

7. Choose "Subscript increasing part" so that the labels appear with the fixed part normal and the increasing part subscripted. The example portion of the dialog box shows you what to expect for new objects.

> Example: P5, P6, P7, P8, P9, P10, P11...

New objects are assigned labels as they are created, not when you first show their labels.

8. Checking Autoshow labels for new objects will cause new objects to show their labels as they are created. If this option is not checked, labels for new objects will remain hidden.

Relabeling a series of objects

Relabeling a sequence of objects can help make sketches match figures you're duplicating from a geometry textbook. To change the vertices of a square to T_1, T_2, T_3, T_4, for example, select the vertices and relabel with a fixed part of T and a subscripted increasing part starting at 1.

It sometimes happens that you have a series of objects already created that you would like to relabel in a sequence.

1. Select the objects you wish to relabel in the order you wish the labels to appear.

2. Choose Relabel Objects from the Display menu. (If all the objects are of the same type, the command will reflect that type, as in Relabel Points, for example.)

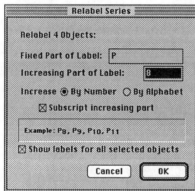

3. As with Setting Label Options described on page 163, you can set the fixed part and the increasing part of the label, and choose to subscript the increasing part or not.

4. If you want the labels to show, click on the "Show labels" check box; otherwise, objects that are not showing their labels will continue not to show their labels.

Relabeling a single object

With a single object selected, this command appears as Relabel Point (or Segment or Arc or whatever type of object is selected). The command then has the same effect as double-clicking on the object with the text tool. (See page 211.)

Trace

Allows you to trace the path of a dragged or an animated object. When the checkmark (✓) appears in front of the command, the Trace feature is in effect for the objects currently selected. Choose the command again to turn off the Trace and remove the checkmark. If you select a different object to trace, you must turn the trace feature on for that object.

Tracing

The Trace command varies depending on your current selection—Trace Point, Trace Segment, etc. Measures, captions, and pictures cannot be traced.

1. Select the objects to be traced when dragged or animated.

2. Choose Trace from the Display menu.

    The checkmark (✓) displays beside the Trace command in the menu.

3. Drag or animate the objects or the parents of the object.

    The trace appears in the sketch plane.

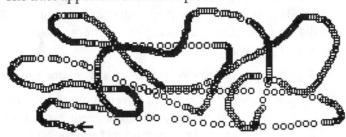

4. When you finish dragging or animating, the trace of any point that was traced becomes a single continuous trace instead of overlapping outlines. (You can control whether this happens. See the Object Information tool's description in the Toolbox Reference chapter.)

To learn how to construct a dynamically variable trace, see Locus described on page 175.

The trace disappears when you click the mouse anywhere in the sketch plane. If you want to print the trace, you must print before you click in the sketch.

The keyboard shortcut for this command is ⌘T. If you want to copy a picture of the trace to the Clipboard to paste into another program, such as a drawing application or a word processor, choose Copy Trace from the Edit menu while the trace is still showing.

Animate...

When you choose a ray, line, or coordinate axes as an animation path, Sketchpad animates along only a portion of the path's infinite length. If this portion isn't to your liking, you can animate along any other portion by first drawing a segment collinear to the ray or line, and then animating

This command moves selected points along specified paths. The point you select need not be constructed on the path, because the animation will start with a leap to the path unless the point is constrained. As many as ten points can be animated simultaneously on as many as ten paths. Paths may be straight or curved objects, including axes, circles, arcs, point loci, polygon interiors, sectors and arc segments. (Animation on a polygon, sector, or arc segment moves the point along the perimeter of that interior.)

Clicking the mouse button stops the animation.

For example, the endpoint of a segment can be animated along the circumference of a circle.

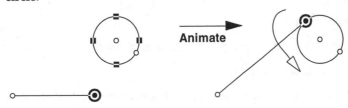

Animating a point along a path

∞ Animation works nicely with the Trace command. For example, construct a segment and its perpendicular bisector. Trace the perpendicular bisector while animating one endpoint of the original segment along a new segment. Replace the segment path with a circle and try animating along it. Animate along the circular path with the nonanimated endpoint of the original segment in the interior of the circle.

1. Select one or more points to be animated.

2. Select one or more segments or circles for the point(s) to travel.

3. Choose Animate from the Display menu.

   The Path Match dialog box appears. Each selected point appears in a list of animation statements at the bottom of the dialog.

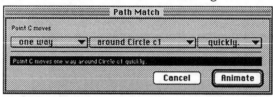

4. Click the statement in the list naming the point you wish to animate. (If you only selected one point, this statement will already be chosen.) Three pop-up menus appear at the top of the dialog, allowing you to choose the type of motion, the path, and the speed for that point.

5. Change the type of motion, if you want. There are three choices.

   One Way The point travels continuously in one direction along the path. If the path is a segment, when the point reaches one endpoint, it resumes travel from the other.

   Bidirectionally The point travels continuously back and forth along the path. When it reaches one endpoint, it reverses direction toward the other. If the path is a circle, the endpoint is considered to be the rightmost point of the circle.

   Once The point travels one way along the path. Once it has completely traveled the length of the path, the animation stops.

   If the path is a circle, the default direction is one-way. If the path is a segment, the default setting is bidirectional.

6. You can change the path along which the point will travel if you want.

   The paths listed are those objects you selected before choosing Animate.

7. You can change the speed of movement if you want.

8. Click the Animate button when you have set the choices correctly for all points.

9. Animation stops when you click the mouse button.

Bypassing the Path Match dialog box

If you select points and paths in the appropriate order, you can bypass the Path Match dialog box and animate all pairs at fast speed in the default direction (one way for circle paths, bidirectionally for segments).

1. Select all points that will travel the same path.

2. Select the path.

3. Select all points that will travel a second path.

4. Select the second path.

5. Continue selecting points and paths in order until all are selected.

6. Hold down Option and choose Animate from the Display menu.

Filming an animation

You can create a movie file that contains your animation in either QuickTime or PICS format. Select points and paths as described above and choose Animate. Make any corrections to the default settings in the Path Match dialog. Then hold down the Option key. The Animate button in the Path Match dialog will rename to Movie. While holding down the Option key, click this button. You'll be asked to choose a movie file and any movie options as discussed with the Film Button command earlier in this chapter.

Preferences...

Establishes settings for the current and subsequent sessions of Sketchpad. The command brings up the Preferences dialog box. The More button in this dialog box brings up a set of less often used preferences.

The Main Preferences Dialog Box

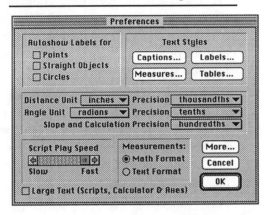

Autoshow Labels   When this option is checked, Sketchpad automatically displays labels for newly created points, straight objects, and circles.

Units and Precision   These pop-up menus allow you to set the units and precision for distance measurements and angles. You can display distance units as inches, centimeters, or pixels. You can display angle units as degrees, directed degrees, or radians.

☞ For class demonstrations, you may want to check Autoshow Labels for Points so that your constructions conform to textbook labeling conventions.

- Degrees have magnitude but no direction, and range between 0 and 180. In degrees, any angle *XYZ* is equal to the reverse angle *ZYX*.

- Directed degrees have both magnitude and direction, and range from −180 to +180. If the direction from the first point (on the initial side of the angle) to the third point (on the terminal side) is clockwise, the angle is negative. If this direction is counterclockwise, the angle is positive. In directed degrees, any angle *XYZ* is equal to the negative of the reverse angle *ZYX*.

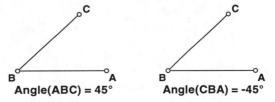

Measure of Angles with Directed Degree Units

Remember that Sketchpad's accuracy is greater than its displayed precision. Most calculations are performed to 19 significant digits. Using the calculator, you can multiply a displayed value by some power of ten to observe its value to more decimal places. For instance, if you have set the Calculation Precision pop-up menu to display precision to the hundredths, $\pi = 3.14$, but $1000\pi = 3141.59$.

Use 12 or 14 pt size if you are displaying Sketchpad with an overhead projector. Otherwise, you'll probably want a smaller size.

- Radians have both magnitude and direction, and range from -3.14159 ($-\pi$) to +3.14159 ($+\pi$). In radians, any angle XYZ is equal to the negative of the reverse angle ZYX. When an angle of 90° is displayed in units of radians and with precision of hundredths, Sketchpad displays 1.57.

Slopes have no units, and the units of calculations depend on the nature of the calculation. You can set the precision for slopes and calculations from the pop-up menu.

Sketchpad can display distances, angles, or calculated values rounded to the nearest thousandth of a unit. This precision may be useful in certain numerical investigations, such as exploring trigonometric identities or approximating π.

Text Styles

Click these buttons to choose the font, font size, and text format for various sketchpad objects.

When you set a text style for captions, labels, measurements, or tables from the Preferences dialog box, as opposed to the Display menu, Sketchpad remembers the text style even after you quit the program. The next time you use Sketchpad, the preferred text style will still be in effect.

Script Play Speed

Drag the slider to set the relative speed for the playback of scripts. This only affects the speed when you choose Play on a script's deck. If you choose Fast, Sketchpad will play the script at maximum speed, regardless of this setting. Likewise, if you choose Step, Sketchpad will play only one step of the script, regardless of this setting.

Measurements

Measurements and calculations have a default display format which you may set by clicking on either Math Format or Text Format. Math Format assigns measurements and calculations with angle markers, segment markers, true fractions and other mathematical conventions. Text Format shows measurements and calculations in pure text form.

Large Text

Setting this preference will cause Sketchpad to use larger type than usual for displaying text in the calculator, scripts, and on the coordinate system axes. (This is particular useful for classroom demonstrations.)

The Advanced Preferences Dialog Box

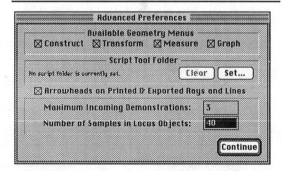

If you want to prevent students from changing settings you've made to Advanced Preferences, see the description of the Protect command in the Advanced Applications chapter.

Available Geometry Menus

The check boxes indicate which of the menus are available. You can use this preference to simplify the program for beginners or to restrict student's available commands to a limited set.

Script Tool Folder You can set a folder to be the one that Sketchpad looks in for scripts to be used as tools. (See Script Tools described on page 134 for more information.) To set or change the folder containing tools, press the Set button and choose a folder. Pressing the Clear button will cause there to be no special folder for script tools and will remove the script tool from Sketchpad's toolbar.

Arrowheads on Printed and Exported Rays & Lines

When this option is checked, Sketchpad puts arrowheads on all lines and rays when you print a sketch, copy and paste objects to another application, or publish editions containing lines and rays. When this option is not checked, Sketchpad doesn't include arrowheads on these objects, and instead draws them simply as long segments.

Note that the setting of this option doesn't affect the way lines and rays appear on the screen in Sketchpad. Because they are infinitely long, lines and rays appear on the screen without endpoints or arrowheads.

Maximum Incoming Demonstrations This preference is only available under System 7. You can use it to limit the number of simultaneous demonstrations you can receive from other Sketchpad users on your System 7

Any Sketchpad on the network can receive up to ten incoming demonstrations simultaneously, each displayed in its own window. However, you may find it difficult to follow ten different demonstrations simultaneously. If another user attempts to send you a demonstration when you are already viewing the maximum number you prefer, that viewer will be warned that you are accepting no further demonstrations.

You can refuse all incoming demonstrations by setting this value to 0.

You can explicitly terminate an active incoming demonstration by either closing its window or by pressing the period key (.) while pressing the ⌘ key.

If you set Maximum Incoming Demonstrations to a value less than the number of current incoming demonstrations (assuming other users are demonstrating to you when you set it), Sketchpad will not prematurely terminate these incoming demonstrations. It will, however, prevent any new demonstrations from arriving until the current number is less than your preferred maximum.

Number of Samples in Locus Objects

When you construct a locus object with Sketchpad, you specify an object whose locus you want and a point constrained to lie on a path such as a segment or a circle. (For more information, see Locus described on page 175.) The locus is constructed by sampling a certain number of positions of the point on the path. The number of positions is determined with this preference setting.

The larger the number of samples, the smoother the locus you will get, but the slower your sketch will respond to dragging.

Demonstrate To...

This command commences a networked demonstration of your current sketch. It only appears if you are running System 7.

If your network has more than one zone, and you would like to demonstrate to users in other zones, press Option while choosing Demonstrate To and Sketchpad users in all zones will be listed.

1. Choose Demonstrate To from the Display menu.

    The network users dialog box displays the names of every computer running Sketchpad in your current AppleTalk zone.

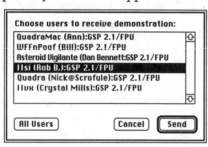

2. Click the machine names of the users with whom you wish to share documents. To select a user, click on his or her machine name. To deselect a name, click on it while pressing the ⌘ key. You can click and drag to select multiple names simultaneously.

    Alternately, click the All Users button to select and send your demonstration to every machine appearing in the list.

3. Click Send (if you didn't click All Users already).

    If this is the first time you are linking to these computers, you may have to connect to them as a Guest or Registered User. See the *Macintosh Networking Reference* that came with System 7 for more details.

    Demonstrations of your sketch will appear on all the chosen users' screens. The Viewer tool will appear in your sketch's Toolbox, indicating that this sketch is currently being viewed across the network.

    If any of the computers to which you demonstrate has a smaller screen than your demonstrated sketch, your sketch will shrink to that size before the demonstration commences. Sketchpad shrinks your sketch to remind you that not all viewers can see as much of your sketch's contents as you can.

Troubleshooting Demonstrations

Make sure that any Macintosh you wish to demonstrate to is set up for program linking. Program linking is described at length in your *Macintosh Networking Reference* manual. In brief, a machine must be running System 7, it must be connected to your network, and program linking must be started in the Sharing Setup control panel. In addition, make sure that program linking is allowed for the user who will demonstrate in the Users & Groups control panel.

⤴ In a classroom setting, you will find it easiest to set up each machine so that Guest users can link to its programs.

Each Sketchpad user can limit the maximum number of incoming demonstrations in the Preferences dialog box. Sketchpad will warn you if a user to whom you attempt to demonstrate is already receiving his or her maximum number of incoming demonstrations.

Don't forget to stop or cancel your demonstration when you're finished.

Stop Demonstration

Finishes the networked demonstration of your current sketch. This command is only available if you are demonstrating the current sketch.

Choose Stop Demonstration from the Display menu.

The Viewer tool disappears from your sketch, indicating the sketch is no longer being viewed across the network. On your viewers' computers, a Toolbox appears in the demonstration window. The viewers can now manipulate and explore the sketch themselves.

Cancel Demonstration

If for some reason you do not wish to leave copies of your demonstrated sketch on viewers' computers, you may cancel your demonstration instead. This will close the demonstrated window on all viewers' machines (though not on your own). To cancel a demonstration, hold down Option and choose Cancel Demonstration from the Display menu.

Construct Menu

The Construct menu embodies compass and straightedge geometry. Most of the commands on this menu are short-cuts for constructions that you can accomplish with the drawing tools.

The commands on the Construct menu allow you to construct objects that are related to other objects.

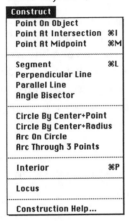

```
Construct
Point On Object
Point At Intersection    ⌘I
Point At Midpoint        ⌘M

Segment                  ⌘L
Perpendicular Line
Parallel Line
Angle Bisector

Circle By Center+Point
Circle By Center+Radius
Arc On Circle
Arc Through 3 Points

Interior                 ⌘P

Locus

Construction Help...
```

Prerequisites

If you think about what you need mathematically to construct the objects on this menu, the prerequisites will become obvious.

The objects needed for a construction, and on which the construction is based, are called the prerequisites of a construction. The prerequisites must be selected in the sketch before you can choose the construction from the menu. For instance, the prerequisites for constructing a segment are two points. You must have two points selected to be able to choose Segment from the Construct menu. When nothing is selected, all commands in the Construct menu are unavailable except Construction Help.

If you think you have the correct prerequisites for a construction, yet its command remains unavailable, use Construction Help in the Construct menu. It will tell you the prerequisites for the construction you want to make. You can check for further errors by pressing the mouse button on the Object Information tool. This will display a menu of all currently selected objects.

The prerequisites for each command appear in this section as well as at the end of the Quick Reference guide.

Point on Object

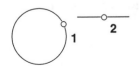

Creates a point placed randomly on the selected object(s). You can drag the constructed point, but it always stays on the object on which it was created.

You can also create a point on an object by using tools from the Toolbox. You can click on the object with the Point tool to make a point, or you can use the Compass or Straightedge tool to draw a circle, segment, ray, or line that begins or ends on the object.

Prerequisite: One or more straight objects, circles, arcs, polygon interiors, arc segments, or arc sectors. (Points on an interior are fixed to the perimeter of that interior.)

Point at Intersection

Arcs may intersect at zero, one, or two points. If two arcs are currently intersecting at just one point, Sketchpad will construct that point. Otherwise both points of intersection will be constructed.

Creates a point at the intersection of the two selected objects. If the intersection is in two places, as with a segment intersecting a circle, two points appear. The point always remains at the intersection even when you drag the objects. You cannot create a point at the intersection of three selected objects. Select only two of the objects and then choose the Point At Intersection command.

If the objects do not intersect, a message alerts you and you have the opportunity to construct an intersection point in case the objects intersect in the future.

The keyboard shortcut is ⌘I.

You can also create an intersection point by using tools from the Toolbox. You can click on the intersection with the Selection Arrow tool or the Point tool, or you can use the Compass or Straightedge tool to draw a circle, a segment, a ray, or a line which begins or ends at the intersection. As you move the tool over an intersection, the Tool Status box changes to read, "point at intersection" to indicate that clicking will construct the point.

Prerequisite: Two objects, each of which is a straight object, circle, or arc.

Point at Midpoint

Creates a point at the midpoint of the selected segment(s). When you change the length of the segment, the midpoint moves accordingly.

The keyboard shortcut is ⌘M.

Prerequisite: One or more segments.

Segment/Ray/Line

Remember that you set this command to Segment, Ray, or Line by choosing the appropriate tool from the Straightedge palette in your sketch's Toolbox.

Creates a segment, a ray, or a line through the selected points. The current Straightedge tool in the Toolbox determines which command is available on the Construct menu. If the current tool is the Ray, the first selected point is the endpoint of the ray.

You can choose Segment, Ray, or Line with more than two points selected. Sketchpad will construct straight objects between pairs of points in the order you select them and a final straight object between the first and last selected points. You can use Segment to create the polygonal edges of the same polygon you would create by selecting points and constructing the Polygon Interior.

Remember that the order of points you select is important:

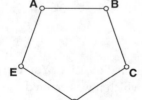

Segment command after selecting (in order) points *A, B, C, D,* and *E*

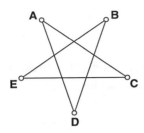

Segment command after selecting (in order) points *A*, *C*, *E*, *B*, and *D*

You can also create a segment, a ray, or a line with the Straightedge tool.

The keyboard shortcut is ⌘L.

Prerequisite: Two or more points. If you are drawing a ray, select the endpoint of the ray first.

Perpendicular Line

Creates a line perpendicular to the selected segment, ray, or line, passing through the selected point.

You can construct multiple perpendiculars simultaneously, either by selecting one point and multiple straight objects, or by selecting one straight object and multiple points.

If you select one point and multiple straight objects, Sketchpad will construct lines passing through the point perpendicular to each straight object. If you select one straight object and multiple points, Sketchpad will construct lines perpendicular to the straight object passing through each point. Selecting a segment with its endpoints will result in the construction of two perpendicular lines through the endpoints.

Prerequisite: One point and one or more straight objects, or one straight object and one or more points.

Parallel Line

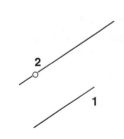

Creates a line or lines parallel to a selected segment, ray, or line, passing through the selected point. You can construct multiple parallels simultaneously, either by selecting one point and multiple straight objects, or by selecting one straight object and multiple points.

If you select one point and multiple straight objects, Sketchpad will construct lines passing through the point parallel to each straight object. If you select one straight object and multiple points, Sketchpad will construct lines parallel to the straight object passing through each point.

Prerequisite: One point and one or more straight objects, or one straight object and one or more points.

Angle Bisector

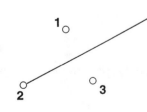

Creates a ray bisecting the angle determined by three selected points. The order of selection determines the angle, with the second point determining the vertex. The ray begins at the vertex of the angle.

Prerequisite: Three points. Select the vertex second.

Circle By Center + Point

Creates a circle with the first selected point at its center and the second selected point on its circumference.

You can also create a circle from two points with the Compass tool.

Prerequisite: Two points. Select the center first.

Circle By Center + Radius

Creates a circle with the selected point at the center of the circle and a radius the same length as the selected segment. When you change the length of the segment, the radius of the circle changes accordingly.

Prerequisite: One point and one segment.

Arc on Circle

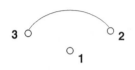

Constructs an arc on a circle. If a circle and two points are selected, the two points must both lie on the circumference of the circle, and the arc extends counter-clockwise around the circle from the first selected point to the second. If three points are selected, the second and third points must be equi-distant from the first, and the arc uses the first selected point as its center and extends counter-clockwise about this center point, from the second selected point to the third. (For a variation on this construction, see Arc By Center and 2 Points described on page 220.)

Prerequisite: A circle and two points on the circle's circumference, or three points with the second and third points equi-distant from the first.

Arc Through 3 Points

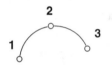

Creates an arc passing through the selected points in the order selected.

Prerequisite: Three points.

Polygon Interior

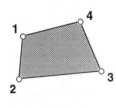

Creates a filled polygon with selected points as vertices. The order of selection determines how the vertices connect. Select the points in clockwise or counterclockwise order to create a non-self-intersecting polygon. The fill is determined by the setting for color and for shade on the Display menu. When the interior is selected, the fill flashes.

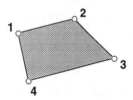 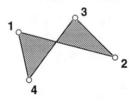

The keyboard shortcut is ⌘P.

Prerequisite: At least three and no more than thirty points.

Circle Interior

Fills the selected circle or circles with the shade and the color set on the Display menu. When the interior is selected, the fill flashes.

Prerequisite: One or more circles.

Arc Sector Interior

Fills the sector defined by the selected arc or arcs with the shade and the color set on the Display menu. When the sector is selected, the fill flashes.

Prerequisite: One or more arcs.

1

Arc Segment Interior

Fills the segment defined by the selected arc or arcs with the shade and the color set on the Display menu. When the segment is selected, the fill flashes.

Prerequisite: One or more arcs.

Locus

It may be helpful to think of the locus as a function, f(x), and the driver as the function variable, x. First select the f(x) and then the x.

Constructs a dynamic locus of an object. Select the object whose locus you wish to construct and a point (the driver point) constructed to lie on a path. A path can be a segment, ray, line, graph axis, circle, arc, polygon interior, arc segment, or arc sector. If the locus object is a point, the result will be a continuous curve stitched together from sampled locations of the point as the driver point moves along its path. Otherwise the locus will be a set of images of the locus object.

The left illustration below shows a possible selection for constructing a locus—a circle and its center, where the latter is constructed to lie on a second (dashed) circle. The resulting locus is shown at right.

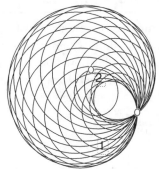

A constructed locus looks similar to the trace of an object. But a trace disappears after your next action, and a locus persists, responding dynamically to dragging in the sketch. In addition, the operations you can perform on a constructed locus include the following.

- You can change its appearance using commands in the Display menu.
- You can construct a point on a point locus.
- You can get information about the locus using the Object Information tool and use the information dialog box to change the number of samples in the locus.

The larger the number of samples used to construct a locus, the slower it will respond to dragging in the sketch. For faster response, reduce the number of samples.

The default number of sampled locations of the driver point used in constructing a locus can be set using Advanced Preferences (see page 168).

When the locus object is a point, the constructed locus is normally a continuous line. You can control whether the locus of a point is continuous or discrete by double-clicking on the locus with the Object Information tool. The resulting dialog box allows you to change the number of samples used in the construction of the locus and whether the locus is continuous or discrete.

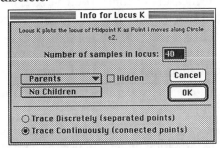

Normally the driver point must be constructed to lie on a path. But you can specify a path for a free (unconstrained) driver point by selecting the desired path as third prerequisite and then holding down the Option key as you choose the Locus command from the Construct menu.

Prerequisite: An object whose locus you wish to construct, followed by a point constructed to lie on a path. The locus object may be any geometrical object except an interior.

Construction Help...

The Help dialog box describes the objects you must select to make each construction command available.

1. Choose Construction Help from the Construct menu.

2. Move the pointer to the command you want.

3. Click the mouse button.

    The prerequisites display in a box beside the command.

Transform Menu

This menu implements transformational geometry in Sketchpad. The Translate, Rotate, Dilate, and Reflect commands apply geometric transformations to selected objects. Marking commands allow you to designate geometric objects, relationships, or measurements which determine the transformations. You can also define your own transformations by combining translations, rotations, dilations, and reflections.

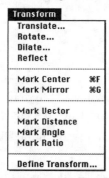

Of the four transformations, translation and rotation are called "rigid motion" transformations. Geometrically, a translation or a rotation can be achieved by translating or rotating the plane itself. A dilation requires stretching or shrinking the plane. An object needs to come out of the plane or the plane itself needs to be turned over for an object to be reflected. Thus, dilations and reflections are not rigid motion transformations.

Mark Center and Mark Mirror designate geometric objects that help define the transformation to be applied. Rotation and dilation require a center, so you must first mark a center to enable these two commands. Similarly, reflection requires a mirror, so you must mark a mirror to enable reflection.

Any marked object remains marked until you mark a new object of that type. For example, you don't need to mark the same center more than once, regardless of how many transformations use it as a marked center.

Sketchpad allows you to construct transformed images of objects using either fixed quantities or dynamic quantities. For instance, you can rotate an object by 45° (a fixed quantity), you can rotate it by angle *ABC* in your sketch (a dynamic quantity), or you can rotate it by the computed quantity (angle *ABC*)/3 (also dynamic). The latter two cases are called dynamic because if the measure of angle *ABC* changes, the rotation changes correspondingly. You will use the other Mark commands—Mark Vector, Distance, Angle, and Ratio— to indicate the objects that establish dynamic quantities to be used in future transformations. Translations can use marked angles, distances, or vectors. Rotations can use marked angles, and dynamic dilations can use marked ratios.

You also use the Transform menu to define and to use complex sequences of transformations called *custom transformations.*

While you can translate, rotate, and dilate with the Selection Arrow tools, you can be more specific about the transformation when you use the commands to perform these transformations. For example, if you use the Rotate tool, you can rotate the selection dynamically by dragging, but you can't specify the precise number of degrees. If you use the Rotate command in the Transform menu, you can rotate the selection by any number of degrees you specify. You can also rotate by a dynamic angle determined by your sketch. As you alter the dynamic angle, the constructed rotation moves to follow it.

Translate...

You can use Translate to create segments of fixed length. For example, to create a one-inch segment, create a point and translate it by one inch. Then connect the two points with a segment.

Constructs an image of the selected objects moved (translated) by some distance.

1. Select the object(s) to be transformed. All geometric objects can be transformed (though loci, text, tables, pictures, and action buttons cannot be).

2. Choose Translate from the Transform menu.

    The Translate dialog box appears. The option By Marked Vector will be available only if you have previously marked a vector in your sketch.

3. Choose the vector of translation.

You can change the units for angles and distances with the Preferences command in the Display menu.

By Polar Vector   Allows you to enter an angle and a distance by which to translate your selection.

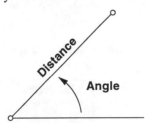

You can enter quantities by typing, or you can used marked quantities. To mark a quantity while the Translate dialog box is open, drag the dialog box by its title bar so that you can see the measurement or the calculated amount you wish to use and click on it. The dialog box will reconfigure accordingly. See Mark Distance and Mark Angle later in this section for more information about marking quantities.

By Rectangular Vector

Allows you to enter a horizontal and a vertical distance by which to translate your selection.

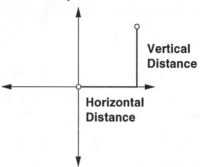

There can be only one marked distance for use in translation at a time. If you wish to use a different measured or computed distance for each direction, select the two quantities and use the Mark Vector command instead of Mark Distance.

You can type in the desired distances as fixed quantities, or you can use a marked distance. (The By Marked Distance checkbox will be disabled if you have not previously marked a distance.)

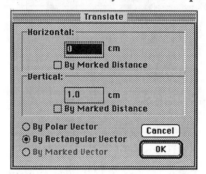

You can mark a distance while the dialog box is open by dragging the box by its title bar so that you can see the measurement or the distance calculation you wish to use, and then clicking on it.

By Marked Vector Allows you specify a dynamic vector by which to translate your selection.

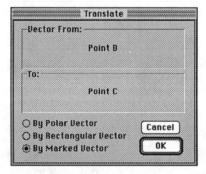

You can specify a marked vector while the dialog box is open by moving the dialog box so that the two points defining the vector are visible and then clicking on the two points in the desired sequence.

If you have marked a rectangular vector using two measurements or computed distances, the dialog box will look similar to that shown below.

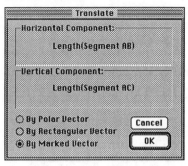

If you have marked a polar vector using a measurement of angle and a measure of distances, the dialog box will look similar to that shown below.

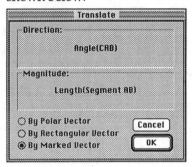

4. Click OK.

Sketchpad constructs the translation of your selected objects by your specified vector.

If you translate by a marked quantity, and subsequently move anything that determines the vector of translation, your translated image will move correspondingly.

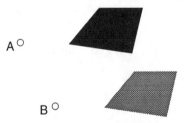

In the example above, the light polygon is the translated image of the dark polygon by a vector from point *A* to point *B*. Each part of the light image is the same distance and direction from the corresponding part of the pre-image as point *B* is from point *A*.

You can use Rotate to create angles of fixed measures. For example, to create a 30° angle, create two points. Mark one point as the center and rotate the second point 30°. Connect the points with rays to form an angle that will remain 30°.

Rotate...

Command constructs an image of the selected objects rotated by some angle about some central point. You must choose Mark Center, described later in this section, before constructing rotations. Additionally, if you wish to rotate by a dynamically-variable angle, you must mark an angle of rotation. See Mark Angle, also in this section.

You can specify the units of rotation—degrees, or radians—in Preferences under the Display menu.

1. Select a point to be the center of rotation.

2. Choose Mark Center from the Transform menu.

3. Select the object(s) to be rotated.

4. Choose Rotate from the Transform menu.

    The Rotate dialog box appears. The option By Marked Angle will be available only if you have previously marked an angle in your sketch.

    You can change the center of rotation while the dialog box is open by clicking on the desired center point in the sketch.

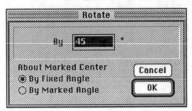

5. Select the angle of rotation.

    By Fixed Angle   Allows you to type an angle by which to rotate your selection. The units of the angle can be set by the Preferences command. (The default unit for angles is degrees.)

    By Marked Angle   Allows you to specify a dynamic angle by which to rotate your selection. A marked angle can be either an angle defined by three points or a measured or computed angle. (See Mark Angle on page 185.) You can specify a measured or computed angle while the Rotate dialog box is open by dragging the dialog box by its title bar so that the measurement is visible, and then clicking on it.

6. Click OK.

    Sketchpad constructs the rotation of your selected objects by your specified angle about the marked center.

If you rotate by a marked angle and subsequently move either the marked center or anything else that defines the marked angle, your rotated image will move to follow the changed center or angle.

In the example shown below the light polygon is the rotated image of the dark polygon by angle XYZ about center point A.

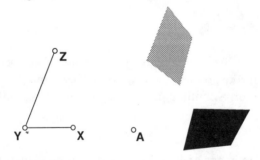

Dilate...

Constructs an image of the selected object(s) dilated by some scale factor about some central point. You must choose Mark Center (described on page 182) before constructing dilations. Additionally, if you wish to dilate by a dynamically-variable scale factor, you must mark a ratio to determine the scale factor. (See Mark Ratio and Mark Scale Factor on page 186.)

1. Select a point to be the center of dilation.

2. Choose Mark Center from the Transform menu.

3. Select the object(s) to be dilated.

4. Select Dilate from the Transform menu.

The Dilate dialog box appears. By Marked Ratio will be available only if you have previously marked a ratio in your sketch.

You can change the center of dilation while the dialog box is open by clicking on the desired center point in the sketch.

3. Choose the scale factor by expressing a ratio.

By Fixed Ratio   Allows you to enter a numeric fraction. The numerator and the denominator must each fall in the range between –10 and +10.

By Marked Ratio   Allows you to specify a dynamic ratio by which to dilate your selection. You can specify a marked ratio of two segment lengths or a measured or computed scale factor while the Dilate dialog box is open by moving the dialog box so that the desired objects are visible, then by clicking on them.

Different scale factors result in different dilations, as shown below, in which x is a scale factor.

$-1 < x < 1$ The dilated image will be *smaller* than its pre-image, and closer to the marked center.

$x < -1$ or $x > 1$ The dilated image will be *larger* than its pre-image and farther away from the marked center.

$x = 0$ The dilated image will not exist (it would be infinitely small).

$x > 0$ The dilated image will have the same orientation as its pre-image.

$x < 0$ The dilated image will appear rotated by 180° about the dilation center.

4. Click OK.

Sketchpad constructs the dilation of your selected objects, toward or away from the marked center, by your specified scale factor.

If you dilate by a marked ratio and subsequently move the marked center or change the marked ratio, your dilated image will move to follow the changed center or ratio.

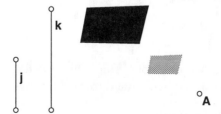

In the example above, the light polygon is the dilated image of the dark polygon by marked vector *j/k* toward center point *A*. Segment *j* is half the length of segment *k*; therefore the scale factor is $1/2$ (or 50 percent). Every part of the light image should be $1/2$ as far from the center as the corresponding part of the dark pre-image.

Reflect

The horizontal or vertical axis can also be marked as a mirror of reflection. See the Graph Menu described on page 197 for more information on axes.

This command creates a mirror image of the selection. First specify a mirror line.

1.   Select a straight object.

2.   Choose Mark Mirror from the Transform menu.

3.   Select the object(s) you want to reflect.

4.   Select Reflect from the Transform menu.

     Sketchpad constructs the image of your selected object(s) reflected through the marked mirror.

Self-Translate… /Self-Rotate… /Self-Dilate… /Self-Reflect

Use Self-Dilate to resize constructions that get too large for your Sketch window. It can be used like the magnifying glass tool that you find in other Macintosh programs, as can the Dilation tool.

You can transform existing selected objects in your sketch instead of constructing new transformed images. These commands are available only if you press Option when choosing the Transform menu from the menu bar.

Applying a self-translation, self-rotation, or self-dilation to a selection is equivalent to dragging it with the corresponding Selection Arrow tool. When you translate, rotate, and dilate objects with the mouse, though, it's sometimes hard to achieve a precise transformation. Use self-transformation when you want to specify a transformation of an existing object *precisely*, such as dilating the object by exactly 50 percent.

To self-transform an object, follow these steps.

1.   Select the object.

2.   Hold down the Option key.

3.   Choose the self-transformation from the Transform menu. Self-Rotate and Self-Dilate will only be available if you have previously marked a center for the transformation. Self-Reflect will only be available if you have previously marked a mirror.

     For all transformations except Self-Reflect, a dialog box will appear allowing you to specify additional quantities important to the transformation.

4.   If necessary, enter the distance, the vector, the ratio, or the angle of transformation as described in the Translate, Rotate, and Dilate sections earlier in this chapter.

5.   If necessary, click OK.

     Sketchpad transforms the selected objects, moving any of their children appropriately.

If the objects cannot be moved because they are rigidly constructed, a warning appears explaining the rigid construction. See Dragging Restrictions in the Toolbox Reference chapter for more information.

Mark Center

Rotations and dilations require a center point from which Sketchpad calculates the transformation, whether you use a tool or a command to perform these transformations.

Specifying the center of rotation or dilation

1.   Select a point.

2.   Choose Mark Center from the Transform menu.

The current selection appears in the command name.

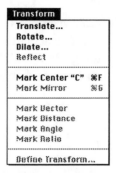

The point displayed in this command is the currently selected point or the most recently selected point, if more than one is selected. The point flashes briefly when you choose this command to show that it is the center.

The marked center remains in effect until you delete it, undo it, or mark a new one. You do not have to mark the same center over and over again.

The keyboard shortcut for this command is ⌘F. You can also mark any point as a center by double-clicking it with the Selection Arrow tool or by clicking on it while the Rotate or Dilate dialog box is open.

Mark Mirror

Reflections require a mirror line to calculate the transformation. This reflection line is the line of symmetry.

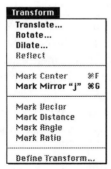

Specifying the mirror line

1. Select the segment, the ray, or the line to be the mirror line.

2. Choose Mark Mirror from the Transform menu.

    The current line label appears as part of the command name.

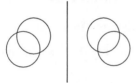

The marked object flashes briefly to confirm its selection as a mirror.

The keyboard shortcut for this command is ⌘G. You can also mark any straight object as a mirror by double-clicking it with the Selection Arrow tool.

Mark Vector

Translations by marked vector require a dynamic vector. A dynamic vector can be specified either by two points or by two measurements or calculations. Two distances determine a rectangular vector—the first distance specifying a horizontal displacement and the second specifying a vertical displacement. A distance and an angle determine a polar vector.

Marking a vector with two points

1. Select any point as the initial point, or *tail*, of the vector.

2. Shift select a second point as the terminal point, or *head*, of the vector.

3. Choose Mark Vector from the Transform menu. Sketchpad confirms the marked objects with a brief animation.

Marking a rectangular vector with two measured or computed distances

1. Select any measurement or computed quantity that has distance units. This will be the amount of translation in the horizontal direction. (Positive distances translate to the right.)

2. Shift-select a second measurement or computed quantity that has distance units. This will be the amount of translation in the vertical direction. (Positive distances translate up.)

3. Choose Mark Rectangular Vector from the Transform menu. Sketchpad confirms by flashing first the horizontal, then the vertical quantity.

Marking a polar vector with a measured distance and angle

1. Select any measurement or computed quantity that has distance units. This will be the amount of translation.

2. Shift-select a second measurement or computed quantity that has angle units. This will determine the direction of the translation. (Angles are measured counter-clockwise from the zero direction, which is to the right.)

3. Choose Mark Polar Vector from the Transform menu. Sketchpad confirms by flashing first the two quantities.

You have now established a vector. Any subsequent translation by the marked vector will construct an image translated by this vector. If the vector is defined by two points, the image will be the same distance and direction from its pre-image as the head of the marked vector is from its foot. If the vector is defined by two measured or calculated distances, the image will be translated in the horizontal direction by the first quantity and in the vertical direction by the second. If the vector is defined by a measured or calculated distance and angle, the image will be translated in the direction given by the angle and an amount determined by the distance. As you move anything in the sketch that changes the vector, the image moves accordingly.

See Translate on page 177 for more information.

Mark Distance

Dynamic translations may use a marked distance as part of their definition. A distance is a measured or computed quantity whose units are distance units; e.g., inches or centimeters.

1. Select the desired measurement or computed quantity.

If the Mark Distance command is disabled, you may have more than one object selected, or you may have selected a measurement or calculated quantity whose units are not distance units.

2. Choose Mark Distance from the Transform menu. Sketchpad confirms the marked quantity by briefly flashing it.

You have now established a marked distance that may be used as part of the definition of a translation. As you drag objects in your sketch that change the result of the measurement or computation, any translated images based on this quantity will move accordingly.

Mark Angle

Rotations by marked angle require a dynamic angle. Dynamic translations may use a marked angle as part of their definition. A marked angle may be specified by three points (the second of which is the vertex) or by a measured or computed quantity whose units are angle units.

Marking an angle with three points

1. Select a point on the initial side of the angle to mark.

2. Select the point at the vertex of the angle.

3. Select a third point on the terminal side of the angle.

4. Choose Mark Angle from the Transform menu. Sketchpad confirms the marked objects with a brief animation. You have now established an angle determined by the three selected points.

Marking an angle using a measured or computed quantity

1. Select the desired measurement or computed quantity expressed in angle units.

2. Choose Mark Angle from the Transform menu. Sketchpad confirms the marked quantity by briefly flashing it. You have now established an angle determined by a measurement or computed quantity.

If the Mark Angle command is disabled, you may have more than one object selected, or you may have selected a measurement or calculated quantity whose units are not angle units.

In transformational geometry, angles are *directed*—they have direction as well as magnitude. The order in which you select the points indicates whether the angle opens clockwise or counterclockwise. In the following illustrations, a polygon has been rotated by two marked angles. Each of the marked angles is 90° in magnitude. In the first, however, the points are selected in an order that marks a counterclockwise angle, and thus the image is rotated 90° counterclockwise from its pre-image. In the second, the angle is marked as a clockwise angle, and thus the image is rotated 90° in the other direction.

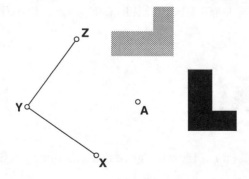

Above, the light polygon is the rotated image of the dark one by counterclockwise angle *XYZ* about center point *A*.

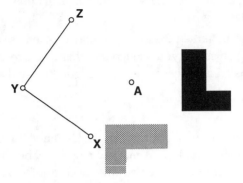

Above, the light polygon is the rotated image of the dark one by clockwise angle *ZYX* about the same center.

See Rotate described on page 179 for more information.

Mark Ratio and Mark Scale Factor

Dilations by marked ratio require a dynamic scale factor. The scale factor is expressed as a ratio of the lengths of two segments or as a dimensionless measurement or a calculated quantity.

Marking a ratio using two segments

1. Select a segment to serve as the numerator of your ratio.

2. Select a second segment to serve as the denominator.

3. Choose Mark Ratio from the Transform menu. Sketchpad confirms the marked objects with a brief animation.

You have now established a ratio which is determined by the lengths of the two selected segments. If the first segment is longer than the second, then the numerator is greater than the denominator, so your ratio will *increase* the size of dilated images. If the first segment is shorter than the second, the ratio's numerator is less than its denominator, and dilations will *decrease* the size of the image.

Another way to think of your dilation ratio is that the first selected segment is the dilated length of the second length. The selection order of lengths is first *image*, then *pre-image*. In the following illustrations, a polygon has been dilated by two marked ratios. Each of the ratios involve the same lengths, but the selection order of these lengths is reversed between them.

Sketchpad can display the numeric value of your segments' ratio. Select the two segments just as you would for Mark Ratio, but instead choose Ratio from the Measure menu. You might want to display the measure of a marked ratio if you're studying transformations from a numeric or analytical perspective.

Above, the light polygon is the dilated image of the dark one by ratio *j/k* toward center point *A*.

Above, a similar dilation by ratio *k/j*.

Marking a scale factor using a measured or computed quantity

If the Mark Scale Factor command is disabled, you may have more than one object selected, or you may have selected a measurement or calculated quantity that is not dimensionless. Only a dimensionless quantity can be a scale factor.

1. Select the desired measurement or computed quantity.

2. Choose Mark Scale Factor from the Transform menu. Sketchpad confirms the marked quantity by briefly flashing it. You have now established a scale factor determined by a measurement or a computed quantity.

In a dilation, if the scale factor is greater than one, the image will be larger than the original and farther away from the marked center than the original. Likewise, if the scale factor is less than one, the image will be smaller than the original and closer to the marked center than the original. If the scale factor is negative, the image will be the inversion of the original; i.e. projected through the marked center to the other side. The illustration below shows this. The light polygon is the image of the dark polygon dilated by –0.60 through the point *A*.

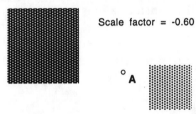

Scale factor = -0.60

See Dilate above for more information.

Advanced Application   In that length is always a positive value, dilations constructed by the ratio of two lengths always have positive scale factors. As discussed above, a computed quantity used as a scale factor can be negative. Another way to get negative scale factors is to mark and to measure ratios determined by the *signed distances* between three points. See the Advanced Applications chapter at the end of this manual for more details.

Define Transform...

Creates a custom transformation based on the transformational relationship between two selected objects. Custom transformations are sequences of individual transformational steps, such as those given below.

*   Translate by vector from point *A* to point *B*.

*   Rotate by 45° around center point *C*.

*   Reflect about mirror segment *k*.

Use custom transformations to encapsulate and to repeat sequences of transformations about known quantities, such as fixed or dynamic angles, ratios, centers, vectors, and mirrors.

Defining a custom transformation

1. Select any two objects, one of which is a transformed image of the other.

    The two objects must be transformed images of each other. That is, one of them must be the constructed image of the other by any number of intermediate transformational steps. No nontransformational steps can exist between them. You can define a custom transformation between a pre-image polygon and its rotated, translated, and dilated image, for instance, but you cannot construct a custom transformation between a segment and the rotated, translated, and dilated image of its midpoint—the midpoint is not a transformed image of the segment.

2. Choose Define Transform from the Transform menu.

    Sketchpad lists the individual transformational steps that relate the two objects. Custom transformations can have between one and thirty individual steps.

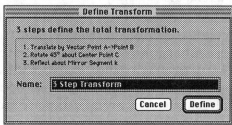

Sketchpad assigns a unique number to the first nine custom transformations in the Transform menu. You can apply the transformations to selected objects by typing this number while holding down the ⌘ key.

3. Type a name that describes the transformational sequence.

4. Click Define.

    Sketchpad creates the custom transformation and adds its name to the bottom of the Transform menu.

Applying a custom transformation

1. Select the object or the objects you wish to transform.

2. Choose the name of your custom transformation from the Transform menu.

When you define a multistep transformation, Sketchpad remembers the formatting you've applied to each step's image—whether you've colored it, or hidden it, and so forth. When you apply the transformation to new objects, Sketchpad creates intermediate images with exactly the same formatting. If you are interested only in the final image of the sequence of transformational steps, and not in the intermediate images, hide each intermediate image between your two selected objects before defining the transformation.

Sketchpad's four transformations—translation, rotation, dilation, and reflection—are considered the four fundamental transformations in a plane. Some geometers consider a fifth transformation, glide-reflection, to be equally important. Define glide-reflection in Sketchpad. First, translate any object by a vector. Then construct the reflection of the translated image about a mirror. Define a transformation based on this reflected translated image of your first pre-image, and name it Glide Reflection.

Saving custom transformations

Custom transformations are saved automatically when you save your sketch and can be reused in the same sketch the next time you open it.

Remove Transform...

Once you have defined a custom transform, a new menu command, Remove Transform, appears on the Transform menu. To remove a custom transform, follow these steps.

1. Choose Remove Transform from the Transform menu.

2. The Remove Transform dialog box appears. From the drop-down list box in the dialog, select the custom transformation you want to remove.

3. Click the OK button.

    The custom transform is removed.

If a transformation depends upon any marked quantities such as a particular point as center of rotation, Sketchpad will remove the transformation if you undo or delete the object upon which it depends.

Measure Menu

The commands on the Measure menu display the quantities that can be measured. The Measure menu works in a way similar to the Construct menu. You select the objects that you want to measure and then choose the appropriate command from the menu. The different measurement commands require different types and numbers of selected objects.

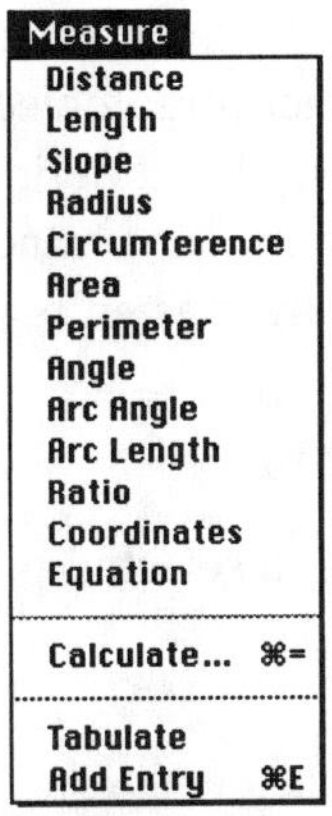

```
Measure
  Distance
  Length
  Slope
  Radius
  Circumference
  Area
  Perimeter
  Angle
  Arc Angle
  Arc Length
  Ratio
  Coordinates
  Equation
  ─────────────
  Calculate...  ⌘=
  ─────────────
  Tabulate
  Add Entry     ⌘E
```

The result of a Measure menu command is a measurement.

The unit displayed with the measured quantity varies appropriately with your selection. Use Preferences in the Display menu to change the current units. Units of length can be displayed either as inches, centimeters, or pixels. Angle units can be displayed either as degrees, radians, or directed degrees.

When you create a measure, it appears in a default location in your sketch. You can use the Selection Arrow tool to move the text anywhere you want. You can change the text characteristics with the Text Style and Text Font submenus in the Display menu. Measurements may appear in either Math Format or Text Format. (The default is Math Format, but you may change the default with a preference. See page 168.) Typical measurements, shown in both formats, are shown below.

Text Format	Math Format
Length(Segment CD) = 2.61 inches	m $\overline{CD}$ = 2.61 inches
Angle(ABC) = 30°	m$\angle$ABC = 30°
Area(Polygon CABD) = 1.53 square inches	Area CABD = 1.53 inches^2
Circumference(Circle DE) = 5.1 inches	Circumference $\odot$DE = 5.1 inches
Perimeter(Polygon FGHI) = 7.84 inches	Perimeter FGHI = 7.84 inches
Arc Angle(a1) = 108.181°	arc angle $\overgroup{HIJ}$ = 108.181°

You can change the format of a given measurement by double-clicking on it with the Text tool and by setting the format in the resulting dialog box. As shown below, you can then change the text that comes before the measurement and the text that comes after.

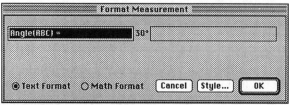

Measurements become the children of the prerequisite object(s) they measure, so be careful cutting or copying measures to the Clipboard. If you copy a measure without copying the object it measures, you break its relationship to the measured object. When you paste it, it will no longer measure any object, and so its value will be undefined. On the other hand, if you copy a measure and its object, the relationship remains intact, and when you paste them, the pasted measure will change if you change the pasted object.

Distance

The distance from a point to a straight object is measured along a perpendicular. Thus, the distance from a point to a ray or a segment is actually the shortest distance between the point and the extended line on which the ray or segment lies.

Displays the distance between two selected points, or a selected point and a selected straight object.

Prerequisite: Two points or a point and a straight object.

Unit: Inches, centimeters, or pixels.

Length

Displays the length of a selected segment.

Prerequisite: One or more segments.

Unit: Inches, centimeters, or pixels.

Slope

Remember that the slope of vertical lines is undefined.

Displays the slope of a selected segment, ray, or line.

Prerequisite: One or more straight objects.

Unit: None

Radius

Displays the radius of the selected circle, circle interior, arc, arc segment, or sector.

Prerequisite: One or more circles, circle interiors, arcs, arc segments, or sectors.

Unit: Inches, centimeters, or pixels.

Circumference

Displays the circumference of a selected circle or circle interior.

Prerequisite: One or more circles or circle interiors.

Unit: Inches, centimeters, or pixels.

Area

Displays the area of a selected polygon interior, circle, circle interior, arc segment, or sector.

Prerequisite: One or more circles, circle interiors, polygon interiors, sectors, or arc segments.

Unit: Square inches, square centimeters, or square pixels.

Perimeter

Displays the distance around a selected polygon interior, arc segment, or sector.

Prerequisite: One or more polygon interiors, sectors, or arc segments.

Unit: Inches, centimeters, or pixels.

Angle

Displays the measure of the angle defined by three selected points. The order of selection determines the angle, with the second point being the vertex of the angle.

Prerequisite: Three points. The second point is the vertex.

Unit: Degrees, radians, or directed degrees.

Arc Angle

Measures the arc angle defined by an arc. The angle is implied by the center and two endpoints of the arc. If the prerequisites of the measurement are a circle and two points, the resulting measurement is always of the number of degrees in the minor arc; but if a circle and three points are given, the measurement will be of the arc from the first point through the second to the third, and may be a major arc.

Prerequisite: One or more arcs, sectors, or arc segments. Or, a circle and 2 points on the circle, or a circle and three points on the circle.

Unit: Degrees, radians, or directed degrees.

Arc Length

Measures the length of an arc.

Prerequisite: One or more arcs, sectors, or arc segments.

Unit: Inches, centimeters, or pixels.

Ratio

Ratio can also compute the signed ratio of three points, if you are investigating negative scale factors. See Advanced Applications at the end of this manual for more details.

Measures the ratio of two selected segment lengths. The first selected length is the numerator of the ratio; the second is the denominator.

Use the Ratio command as a shortcut for measuring two lengths and for explicitly dividing them with the calculator. To display the numeric value of the marked ratio used by dynamic dilations, select the two segments determining the ratio and choose Ratio from the Measure menu. (Make sure you select the segments in the same order you selected them to Mark Ratio!)

Prerequisite: Two segments.

Unit: None.

Coordinates

Displays the coordinates of the selected point or points, using the current graph coordinate form. (For more information on coordinate forms, see the section entitled Graph Menu on page 197.) Graph axes will be created if they have not already been created.

Prerequisite: One or more points.

Unit: None.

Equation

Sketchpad will not display an equation for a line segment or a ray becuase not all points that satisfy the equation would lie on the ray or segment. If you need to, you can construct a line collinear to the segment or ray and display the equation of this line.

Displays the equation of the selected line(s) or the circle(s) using the current graph equation form. (For more information on equation forms, see the section entitled Graph Menu on page 197.) Graph axes will be created if they have not already been created.

Prerequisite: One or more lines or circles.

Calculate...

This command allows you to calculate and to evaluate arithmetic expressions using the values of selected measurements. When the measured objects change, the measurements and calculations change accordingly.

Calculating with measurements

You can enter many interesting expressions. For example, the area of a circle with radius r is equal to πr^2, so having measured the radius of circle CR, you could build the expression "π•(Radius ⊙ CR)²" to measure its area.

1. Select the measurements you want to use in the calculation.

2. Choose Calculate from the Measure menu.

    The calculator dialog box appears.

You can similarly observe the ratio of two quantities by dividing one measured quantity by another. Many interesting geometric ratios remain constant, and when you transform the figure, you can see that the values resulting from these calculations will not change.

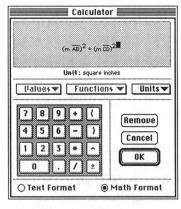

3. Create the expression you wish to evaluate.

Another way to enter values into your expression is to move the Calculator dialog box so that the desired measurement is visible in the sketch and click on the measurement with the mouse.

•   Choose any of your selected measurements from the Values pop-up menu.

Values for individual coordinates and the coefficients of equations for lines and circles appear as submenus in the pop-up as shown below. The submenu gives you access to the *x*- and *y*-coordinates of a point, and the coefficients of an equation such as the slope of a line.

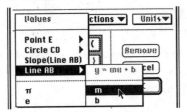

- Choose math operators and numeric digits from the graphic calculator. (You can also type these symbols from the keyboard.) The values for π and *e* (base for the natural logarithms) are available from the pop-up menu of values. Available math operators include those shown here.

      + addition   * multiplication
      – subtraction   / division
      * multiplication   ^ exponentiation
      ± negation (changes sign from positive to negative and vice versa)

As you build the expression, it appears in the display area at the top of the dialog box with a black rectangle showing where the next insertion will appear.

You can switch between Math Format and Text Format using the radio buttons at the bottom of the calculator. In Text Format the expression may appear on more than one line in the dialog box, but it will appear on a single line in the sketch.

- Choose built-in functions from the Functions pop-up menu. Available functions include those shown below.

      sin[*x*]   trigonometric sine of *x*
      cos[*x*]   trigonometric cosine of *x*
      tan[*x*]   trigonometric tangent of *x*
      arcsin[*x*]   trigonometric arcsine of *x*
      arccos[*x*]   trigonometric arccosine of *x*
      arctan[*x*]   trigonometric arctangent of *x*
      abs[*x*]   absolute value of *x*
      sqrt[*x*]   square root of *x*
      ln[*x*]   natural logarithm of *x*
      log[*x*]   logarithm base 10 of *x*
      round[*x*]   *x* rounded to the nearest integer
      trunc[*x*]   *x* with any fractional portion removed (i.e., rounded toward zero)
      signum[*x*]   returns –1 if *x* < 0, 0 if *x* = 0, and +1 if *x* > 0

If *x* does not have angle units, trigonometric functions interpret *x* as an angle in the current angle units. Use the Preferences command (see page 167) in the Display menu to change the current angle units.

After choosing a function, enter a value for *x*—which may be a calculated expression itself—and click on the **)** button (the right parenthesis), indicating the end of the functional argument.

- Choose units from the Units pop-up menu. Units are only available next to a numeric quantity. One use of the units menu, as shown below, is to keep the units within an expression consistent. Sketchpad shows the units that will results from a calculation as you build the expression. (Calculations with mixed units are allowed but may not be meaningful.)

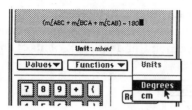

$$\frac{\text{Area } ACDB}{(1.0 \text{ cm})^2} = 8.17$$

Another use of the units menu is to convert an expression from one unit to another. In the example at left, an area expressed in cm^2 is converted to a dimensionless quantity so that it can be used in a dynamic dilation.

Sketchpad presents the expression as you build it in the display area at the top of the calculator. Click Remove to remove the last added term if you make a mistake.

4. Click OK.

The expression and its calculated value are added as a measurement to your sketch.

Order of evaluation in calculations

Sketchpad evaluates expressions in the standard order of mathematical convention.

Exponentiation ($\wedge$) and negation ($\pm$) have highest precedence.
Multiplication (*) and division (/) have intermediate precedence.
Addition (+) and subtraction (–) have lowest precedence.

Operators of the same precedence are evaluated from left to right. You can change the order of evaluation by using parentheses.

Unit preservation in calculations

If you formulate a complex expression with the calculator, Sketchpad preserves the units implied by measured quantities that appear in the expression. For instance, the sum of two distances appears with a distance unit (inches, centimeters, or pixels), the product of two distances appears as a square distance (e.g., square inches), and the ratio of two distances appears as a unitless quantity.

Use Sketchpad's calculated units as indicators of the correctness of a proposed calculation. If you're attempting to find the volume of a cube modeled in Sketchpad, for instance, and you compute a result in square centimeters, then you know your calculation is incorrect, because volume is measured in *cubic* centimeters. Unit analysis can be a valuable tool in many numerical investigations.

Sketchpad can only preserve units when your calculation uses similar terms. If you attempt to add distances to angles—proverbial apples and oranges—Sketchpad displays no unit with the calculated result. (It will display "mixed units" in the Calculator as a warning that your calculation is not using like terms.)

Removing preserved units

To display a calculation *without* its preserved unit, follow these steps.

1. Choose the Text tool from the Toolbox.

2. Double-click the calculation to edit its appearance.

The Measure Editing dialog box appears.

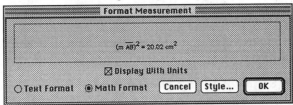

3. Click Display With Units to remove the check box.

The check box and the calculated unit disappears.

4. Click OK.

Later, you can recheck Display With Units to redisplay the preserved unit. Note that you can only remove the displayed units of calculations, not of simple measurements.

Removing a calculation's unit affects only the display of the measurement, not its use. If you use the measurement as a marked quantity or in a calculation, it will still be interpreted with its (undisplayed) units.

Tabulate/Flip Direction

Tabulate collects selected measurements into a single table. Sketchpad tables contain entries describing a set of measurements' values at different points in time.

Creating a table

1. Select the measurements you want to appear in the table, in the order in which you wish them to appear.

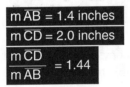

2. Choose Tabulate from the Measure menu.

The measured values appear in a new table. The row labels are in Text Format, not Math Format. (If you are recording your actions in a script, a step will be added to the script describing the tabulation.)

Length(Segment k)	2.889
Length(Segment j)	5.778
Ratio(k/j)	0.500

The table initially has only one entry, representing the value of the measurements at the moment you tabulate them. When these measurements change, you can add new entries to the table with the Add Entry command.

A table acts like any other object in Sketchpad—you can hide or show it, move it about with the Selection Arrow tool, change or hide its labels, and delete it. Tables are bound to the measurements they tabulate: they are the children of the measurement parents. Do not delete any of its parental measurements if you wish to continue adding entries to a table! However, you may choose to hide the measurements and leave the table showing if the measures are only cluttering your sketch.

Flip Direction is only available when you have a single table selected, and it replaces the Tabulate command in the Measure menu. This command changes the orientation of a selected table.

Flipping directions in a table

1. Select the table to flip.

   In the example below, the table tabulates three data and has two entries. The entries extend horizontally.

Length(Segment k)	2.889	4.126
Length(Segment j)	5.778	8.252
Ratio(k/j)	0.500	0.500

2. Choose Flip Direction from the Tabulate menu.

   The orientation of the table flips. The entries now extend vertically.

Length(Segment k)	Length(Segment j)	Ratio(k/j)
2.889	5.778	0.500
4.126	8.252	0.500

   When Sketchpad displays a table in this orientation, it makes the columns as wide as the widest table label to avoid overlapping labels.

   By editing the labels into shorter form, you can make the table take up less room. To edit a table label, double-click it with the Text tool.

k	j	k/j
2.889	5.778	0.500
4.126	8.252	0.500

   You can flip a table back to its previous orientation by selecting it and by choosing Flip Direction again.

Add Entry

This command adds an entry to a table containing the current values of the table's measurements. It is only available when a table has been selected.

Adding an entry to a table

1. Select the table.

2. Choose Add Entry from the Measure menu.

   A new entry appears in the table, containing the current values of the table's measurements.

Shortcut: You can also add an entry to a table simply by double-clicking it with the Selection Arrow tool. Again, Sketchpad will automatically add an entry unless you have just previously added an entry that already describes the current values of the table's measures.

You can add as many entries to a table as you choose, though Sketchpad will not let you add an entry if you have not altered your sketch in any way since the last time you added an entry. This prevents duplicates from appearing in your table. Each entry represents the values of the table's data at the moment is was entered, allowing you to view the evolution of measured relationships over time.

Graph Menu

The Graph menu is the home of commands relating to coordinate and analytic geometry. In Sketchpad a coordinate system is defined by an origin and a unit length, each of which may be changed dynamically. The Graph menu provides commands that allow you to create and to display a coordinate system, to determine the form in which coordinates and equations are displayed, and to place points in the coordinate system.

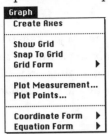

Create/Hide/Show Axes

This command allows you to create or to define a coordinate system and control whether the coordinate system's axes are showing or not. The command allows you to create a coordinate system if a coordinate system has not yet been defined. Once you have done so, it toggles between Show Axes and Hide Axes.

Before you have created axes, the action of the command depends on what you have selected.

When the distance unit has been set to pixels, the graph units are set to 10 pixels per unit (dekapixels).

Create Axes Applies when nothing is selected. Creates a coordinate system with its origin at the center of the window and a unit corresponding to the current distance unit (inches, centimeters, or pixels).

Define Unit Circle Applies when a single circle is selected. Creates a coordinate system with its origin at the center of the circle and a unit equal to the radius of the circle.

Define Unit Length Applies when a distance measurement or a segment is selected. Creates a coordinate system with its origin at the center of the window and a unit corresponding to the distance measurement or the length of the selected segment.

Define Origin Applies when a single point is selected. Creates a coordinate system with its origin at selected point and a unit corresponding to the current distance unit.

Define Axes Applies when a point (the origin) and a segment or a distance measurement (the unit length) is selected.

Once a coordinate system has been created, its origin and unit length respond dynamically to changes in the objects that define them. For example, when axes are created with nothing selected, both the point at the origin and the point at $x = 1$ may be dragged, and the coordinate system will respond accordingly.

The default labels for axes are x and y, but axes may be labeled with the Text tool.

Even when the axes are not showing, measurements of point coordinates and equations for lines and circles are valid.

You can permanently remove a coordinate system from a sketch by deleting either axis, or any of the objects that define the coordinate system (such as the origin).

Show/Hide Grid

This command toggles whether a grid corresponding to the coordinate system is showing. When you show the grid, snapping to the grid will be turned on. When you hide the grid, snapping to grid points will be turned off. In either case, you can override this default behavior with the Snap To Grid command.

Snap To Grid

Snapping can have surprising consequences! A line segment or a circle may appear to vanish as you drag because the two defining points have snapped to the same grid point.

Use this command to toggle whether or not dragged objects snap to the nearest grid point. A check mark appears next to the item when snapping is turned on. With snapping turned on, dragged points snap to a grid point unless constraints prevent it. Dragging other objects will also cause Sketchpad to attempt to snap the points that define that object to the grid.

Grid Form

Use this command to switch between a rectangular (x, y) grid and a polar (r, θ) grid. The form of the grid is independent of the form in which coordinates and equations are displayed, but it determines the way in which the Plot Measurement command (see below) works.

Plot Measurement...

This command requires a selection of one or two measurements. If the grid form is rectangular, the command takes one measurement and allows you to plot it as either an x- or a y-value. The result is a line perpendicular to either the horizontal axis or the vertical axis. The measurement is treated as a pure number without regard to its units.

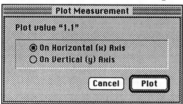

If the grid form is polar, the command takes one measurement and allows you to plot it as either an r- or a θ-value. In the first case the result is a circle whose radius is set by the value of the measurement. In the second case the result is a ray extending from the origin that makes an angle with respect to the positive x-direction set by the value of the measurement.

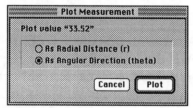

If two measurements are selected, the command is "Plot as (x, y)" or "Plot as (r, θ)," depending on the grid form. The first selected measurement is used as the x- or r-coordinate, and the second selected measurement is used as the y- or θ-value, again depending on the grid form. In either case, the result is a single point plotted at the position of the selected coordinates.

Plot Points...

This command allows you to type in the coordinates of points you wish to plot in the coordinate system. You can also paste in tabulated data from other applications such as spreadsheets. You can constrain the points to stay at the designated coordinates regardless of how the coordinate system's origin and unit change, or you can let them be freely draggable in the sketch.

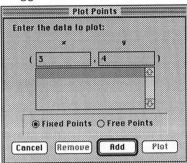

Enter a point by typing its x-coordinate and y-coordinate. Then press the Add button. (Pressing Return has the same effect as pressing the Add button.) Enter as many points as you want; points are not plotted until you press the Plot button.

If you have copied coordinate values (e.g., from a spreadsheet) onto the clipboard, and have not yet typed any data into the entry area, choosing the keyboard equivalent of Paste (⌘-V or F4) will put the clipboard data into the list of points shown in the dialog box.

Select a line containing a coordinate pair to edit its values. Use the Remove button to remove the coordinate pair from the list. Use the Change button to substitute edited values for the originals.

Choose Fixed Points to plot points that will stay at their designated coordinates, or choose Free Points to plot points that you can move with the Selection Arrow tool.

Press Plot to create points in your sketch at the desired coordinates.

Plot Table Data...

This command takes data you have gathered in a Sketchpad table and uses the values in the table to plot points. To enable the command, select a table that is tabulating exactly two measurement values. The first value will be used as the x-coordinate and the second will be used as the y-coordinate. In the resulting dialog box, specify whether the plotted points should be fixed to the coordinate system or freely draggable.

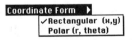

Coordinate Form

This command determines the form of currently selected and subsequent measurements made with the Coordinates command in the Measure menu. (See Coordinates on page 192.) Because unselected measurements are not affected by this command, you can have both the rectangular and polar coordinates of a point visible at the same time.

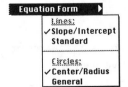

Equation Form

This command determines the form of currently selected and subsequent measurements made with the Equations command in the Measure menu. (See Equation on page 192.) Equations for lines have two forms, shown here.

Slope/Intercept: $y = mx + b$

Standard: $Ax + By + C = 0$

Equations for circles also have two forms, shown here.

Center/Radius: $(x - x_1)^2 + (y - y_1)^2 = R^2$

General: $x^2 + y^2 + Dx + Ey + F = 0$

To display the equation of a line or circle, select it and choose Equation from the Measure menu. The calculator allows you to use the coefficients of each equation form in calculations.

Work Menu

The commands on the Work menu allow you to create a script based on a sketch's selected objects, to activate an open sketch or script, and to automatically play a script.

Make Script

Make Script is handy if you forget to record a script for a wonderful but complicated construction.

This command creates a script that describes the construction of objects that are selected.

1. Select all of the objects in a construction for which you want a script.

    The objects must be related to each other to create a script. If your selection contains no related objects, there would be no steps in a script. The Make Script command is enabled only if you have selected related objects. The easiest way to select all of the objects in a sketch is with Select All in the Edit menu.

2. Choose Make Script from the Work menu.

    A new script appears with the construction described in words.

    When played back, the script constructs the same objects as were selected, but your construction method may not be used. However, the geometric relationships between selected objects remain intact in the script.

Making a Recording Script

Normally, Make Script creates a complete script. Sometimes when you make a script, however, you'll want to add more steps to it later, either to extend its geometric constructions or to set up recursive loops. In this case, hold down Option while choosing Make Script from the Work menu. (The menu command will now appear as Make Recording Script.) This will create the same script as described above, but will leave the script recording. You can then add steps to it just as if you'd pressed Record yourself. Be sure to press Stop on the script before trying to play it back!

Active Scripts and Sketches

The bottom section of the Work menu lists the names of the open scripts and sketches. You can make a script or a sketch active by choosing its name from the menu.

If you select a script's prerequisites and then hold down Option while choosing that script from the Work menu, Sketchpad will automatically play it into the active sketch.

Use the Work menu to extend Sketchpad's construction capabilities. Choosing a script from the Work menu (with the Option key down) is just like choosing a command from the

Construct menu, except—by writing the scripts—you get to choose exactly what sort of constructions are available.

Help Menu

When used with System 7, Sketchpad supports Balloon Help. When turned on, Balloon Help gives brief explanations of menu commands, of window components, and of dialog controls. Point to any of them with the mouse, and an explanation will appear. Use Show Balloons to turn Balloon Help on, then Hide Balloons to turn it off.

Toolbox Reference

The Toolbox contains tools for creating, for selecting, and for transforming points, circles, and straight objects (segments, lines, and rays), Text and Information tools, and tools defined by scripts:

	Selection Arrow tools (Translate, Rotate, Dilate)
•	Point tool
⊙	Compass tool
/ ↗ ↗	Straightedge tools (Segment, Ray, Line)
✍	Text tool
?	Object Information tool

 **Script Tools tool**

If you have chosen a Script Tool Folder in the Advanced Preferences dialog box, you will also see the Script Tools tool. This tool allows you to use scripts that you've created as interactive drawing tools in your sketch.

 **Viewer tool**

If you are demonstrating your sketch across a System 7 network, you will also see the Viewer tool, which allows you to track the viewers of your demonstration.

Click with the mouse on any tool to make it the active tool. You can also change the active tool by pressing the arrow keys. The Up and Down Arrow keys move from tool to tool without affecting the variants of the Selection and Straightedge tools.

Selection Arrow Tools

The Selection Arrow tool palette contains arrows that select and transform objects. You can use each tool to select objects in the same way, but the transformation function of each is different. The various methods for selection are discussed in depth in the Sketches chapter.

Translate	Selects objects and moves selections without changing their size or orientation.
Rotate	Selects objects and rotates selections around a point previously marked as the center of rotation. (Use Mark Center in the Transform menu to mark the center.)
Dilate	Selects and shrinks or enlarges the selection toward or away from a point previously marked as the center of dilation. (Use Mark Center in the Transform menu to mark the center.)

☞ Get into the habit of using the Option key to invoke the Selection Arrow tool. This action will save time during class demonstrations.

Using optional selection

If a drawing tool is active, you can temporarily invoke the current Selection Arrow tool by holding down the Option key; when the pointer is in the sketch plane it becomes a Selection Arrow.

Automatic change from Selection Arrow to Text Tool

If the Selection Arrow tool is on top of an object's label, it automatically changes to the Text Tool. With the text tool you can move and edit the label. (See the full description of the Text Tool on page 210.)

Choosing a tool from the Selection palette

1. Move the pointer to the current Selection Arrow tool in the Toolbox.

2. Press and hold down the mouse button. The palette displays the Selection tool choices.

3. Drag to highlight the tool you want to use.

4. Release the mouse button.

    The Toolbox displays the Selection Arrow tool you specfied.

You can create a point at an intersection by clicking an existing intersection with a Selection Arrow tool. If you are using another tool, you can hold down Option and click the intersection.

Using the keyboard to switch Selection Arrow tools

You can switch to a different Selection Arrow tool without using the mouse by holding down Shift and pressing the spacebar. Each time you press the spacebar, the tool cycles to the next one on the palette. The tool must still be chosen to be the active tool. You can change the active tool with the mouse or by pressing the Up or Down Arrow keys.

Translate Tool

The Translate tool is a freehand transformation tool. The direction and distance you move the mouse control the translation.

This tool selects one or more objects. With this tool you also drag, or translate, objects. (If you want to specify the amount of translation numerically, see the Self-Translate command in the Command Reference chapter.)

Translating selections with the Translate tool

1. Choose the Translate tool.

2. Select the object(s) you want to move.

3. Move the pointer to the selection until the pointer becomes a drag arrow.

The drag arrow appears when you move the pointer near an object that can be dragged.

4. Press and hold down the mouse button.

5. Drag the selection to the new location.

    The selection is translated, and all objects that depend on the selection adjust automatically.

6. Release the mouse button.

The Rotate tool is a free-hand transformation tool. The way you move the mouse controls the angle of rotation.

Rotate Tool

This tool selects one or more objects as described in the Sketches chapter. This tool also rotates the selected objects. (If you want to specify the angle by which to rotate numerically, see the Self-Rotate command in the Command Reference chapter.)

Rotating selections with the Rotate tool

1. Choose the Rotate tool.

2. If you have not already marked a center of rotation, select a point to be the center, and choose Mark Center from the Transform menu.

3. Select the object(s) you want to move.

4. Move the pointer to the selection until the pointer becomes a drag arrow.

The drag arrow appears when you move the pointer near an object that can be dragged.

5. Press and hold down the mouse button.

6. Drag the selection around the center of rotation until it is in the position you want.

   The selection is rotated, and all objects that depend on the selection adjust automatically.

7. Release the mouse button.

Dilate Tool

This tool selects one or more objects as described in the Sketches chapter. This tool also dilates the selected objects. (If you want to specify the scale factor for the dilation numerically, see the Self-Dilate command in the Command Reference chapter.)

The Dilate tool is a free-hand transformation tool. The way you move the mouse controls the scale factor.

Dilating selections with the Dilate tool

1. Choose the Dilate tool.

2. If you have not already marked a center of dilation, select a point to be the center and choose Mark Center from the Transform menu.

3. Select the object(s) you want to move.

4. Move the pointer to the selection until the pointer becomes a drag arrow.

The drag arrow appears when you move the pointer near an object that can be dragged.

5. Press and hold down the mouse button.

6. Drag the selection toward or away from the center of dilation to the place you want.

   The selection is dilated, and all objects that depend on the selection adjust automatically.

7. Release the mouse button.

Dilation by Negative Scale Factors

The Dilate tool also permits dilation by a *negative* scale factor. Negative dilation involves a 180° rotation around the center of dilation. This half-turn can be visualized as an inversion of the figure through the center point. The size of a dilated image is determined entirely by the magnitude of the scale factor, not by its sign.

In the following illustration, the two dark triangles are images of the light triangle dilated about center point X. The image on the left has been dilated with a scale factor of negative one-half; the image on the right with a scale factor of positive one-half. Note that the images are the same size and shape (they are *congruent*), but their orientations differ by 180°.

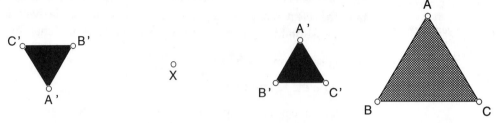

With the Dilate tool, you can drag selections "through" the center of dilation. As you pass through the center, your selections invert and emerge from the other side, rotated 180°.

Dilating by negative scale factors with the Dilate tool

1. Choose the Dilate tool from the Toolbox.

2. If you have not already marked a center of dilation, select a point to be the center and choose Mark Center from the Transform menu.

3. Select the object(s) you want to move.

4. Move the pointer to the selection.

The drag arrow appears when you move the pointer near an object that can be dragged.

5. Press and hold down the mouse button.

6. Drag the selection toward the center of dilation. The scale factor approaches 0, and your selected objects grow smaller and closer to the center.

   At the moment the Dilate tool passes over the center, the scale factor is 0. Your selected objects are infinitely small—they have been dilated to a point.

   Keep dragging as you emerge on the opposite side of the center. Your selected objects—now inverted through the single point—begin to grow larger and farther away from the center.

   Move back and forth, toward and away from the center until your selected objects are where you want them.

7. Release the mouse button.

Point Tool

Use this tool to create points. You can create points anywhere in the sketch plane or on existing objects.

If the point is on an object, it will remain on that object throughout any transformations you do to the point or the object. If a point is at the intersection of two objects, the point will remain at the intersection when you make changes to the objects.

You can also create a point at an intersection of two objects by clicking the intersection with a Selection Arrow tool.

Creating points

1. Choose the Point tool in the Toolbox.

2. Move the pointer to the sketch plane.

   The pointer changes to a crosshair when it is in the sketch plane.

3. Click to place a point.

Compass Tool

With a physical compass you are accustomed to drawing arcs rather than entire circles. Though you can construct arcs with Sketchpad, circles are preferable because your constructions will hold together when you drag things around.

This tool constructs circles based on a point at the circle's center and a point on the circle's circumference. Create circles by dragging: The spot where you press the mouse button defines the center of the circle, and the spot where you release it determines the radius. If points don't already exist at these locations, Sketchpad will create them.

Drawing a circle

1. Choose the Compass tool in the Toolbox.

2. Move the pointer to the sketch plane.

   The pointer becomes a circle.

3. Press and hold the mouse button where you want the center of the circle to be.

4. With the mouse button down, drag until the circle is as large as you want it.

   Note that the point on the circumference determines the radius of the circle. Moving this point changes the radius. If you want to construct a circle so that it always passes through an existing point, make sure that you release the mouse button when the pointer is over that point. It isn't sufficient for the circumference of the circle to pass through the point.

5. Release the mouse button.

Straightedge Tools

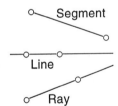

These tools create straight objects: segments, rays, and lines.

Segment   A straight object defined by two endpoints: The point where you press the mouse button and the point where you release it.

Ray   A straight object defined by an endpoint where you press the mouse button and a second point where you release the mouse button. The ray extends infinitely in the direction in which you dragged.

Line   A straight object defined by two points: the point where you press the mouse button and the point where you release it. The line extends in both directions.

If points don't already exist where you press and release the mouse button, Sketchpad will create them. These points may be placed in blank parts of your sketch, on existing objects, or at the intersection of existing objects.

Choosing a tool from the Straightedge palette

1. Move the pointer to the current Straightedge tool in the Toolbox.

2. Press and hold down the mouse button.

   The palette displays the Straightedge tools.

3. Drag to highlight the tool you want to use.

4. Release the mouse button.

The Toolbox displays the Straightedge tool you specified.

Using the keyboard to switch Straightedge tools

You can switch to a different Straightedge tool without using the mouse by pressing the spacebar. Each time you press the spacebar, the tool cycles to the next one on the palette. The tool must be highlighted to be the active tool. You can change to different active tools by pressing the Up and Down Arrows.

Constraining straight objects to 15° increments

You can use the Shift key to draw segments, rays, and lines at angles of exactly 0°, 15°, 30°, 45°, 60°, 75°, and 90°.

1. Choose the Straightedge tool.

2. Begin dragging to construct the straight object.

3. Press and hold down Shift.

4. Continue dragging (holding Shift down) to specify the construction.

    Sketchpad constrains the straight object to angles of 15° increments.

5. Release the mouse button.

6. Release Shift.

Segment Tool

This tool creates a segment. You can place the endpoints in unoccupied space on the sketch plane or attach one or both to objects in the sketch.

Constructing a segment

1. Choose the Segment tool.

2. Move the pointer to the sketch plane.

    The pointer becomes a crosshair.

    -+-

3. Press and hold the mouse button.

    An endpoint of the segment appears. If there is an existing point at the same location, Sketchpad locks onto that point; if there is no point at the location, Sketchpad constructs one.

When you draw a segment with the Segment tool, Sketchpad automatically creates endpoints that are the parents of the segment if they don't already exist in the sketch.

4. Drag the mouse until the segment appears as you want it.

5. Release the mouse button.

    A segment appears with one endpoint where you pressed the mouse button and the other endpoint where you released the mouse button. If there is an existing point at the same location, Sketchpad locks onto that point; if there is no point at the location, Sketchpad constructs one.

Ray Tool

This tool creates a ray. You can place the defining points in unoccupied space on the sketch plane or attach one or both to objects in the sketch.

Constructing a ray

1. Choose the Ray tool.

2. Move the pointer to the sketch plane.

    The pointer becomes a crosshair.

    -|-

3. Press and hold the mouse button.

    The endpoint of the ray appears. If there is an existing point at the same location, Sketchpad locks onto that point. If there is no point at the location, Sketchpad constructs one.

4. Drag the mouse until the ray extends in the direction you want.

5. Release the mouse button.

    A ray appears with its endpoint where you pressed the mouse button and passes through the point where you released the mouse button. If there is an existing point at the same location, Sketchpad locks onto that point; if there is no point at the location, Sketchpad constructs one.

Rays are drawn in Sketchpad so that they appear to continue indefinitely in one direction beyond the border of the sketch window. A ray that is printed or copied to the Clipboard will display an arrowhead.

Line Tool

This tool creates a line. You can place the defining points in unoccupied space on the sketch plane or attach one or both defining points to an object in the sketch.

Constructing a line

1. Choose the Line tool.

2. Move the pointer to the sketch plane.

    The pointer becomes a crosshair.

    -|-

3. Press and hold the mouse button.

    A point appears, and the line extends through it in the direction in which you drag until you release the mouse button. If there is an existing point at the same location, Sketchpad locks onto that point. If there is no point at the location, Sketchpad constructs one.

4. Drag the mouse until the line extends in the direction you want.

5. Release the mouse button.

Lines are drawn in Sketchpad so that they appear to continue indefinitely in both directions. A line which is printed or copied to the Clipboard will display arrowheads at each end.

An infinite line appears passing through the points where you pressed and released the mouse button. If there is an existing point at the location where you released the button, Sketchpad locks onto that point; if there is no point at the location, Sketchpad constructs one.

The Tool Status Box

The tool status box at the bottom of a Sketch window displays helpful information about the active tool in the current sketch. You can use it to determine what object you are about to select, or to know if you've put the cursor in the right position to construct a point on an object or a point at an intersection. (You can also use it to select and draw using the keyboard rather than the mouse—see Keyboard Selection and Construction Interface on page 217. You can even use it to type in menu commands—see Command-Line Interface on page 221.)

The tool status box can be resized and repositioned.

- To resize the tool status box, place the cursor over the right edge of the box. The cursor becomes a right-and-left arrow. Click and drag to the right or the left to make the tool status box longer or shorter.

Text Tool

This tool displays, hides, and moves labels for objects, creates captions, allows you to edit existing text, and allows you to specify whether a label will be used in a script. Sketchpad labels all objects in the order in which they are created. You can also use the Text tool to display or hide these labels.

Note that you can't display their labels for captions, measurements, and imported pictures. The default labeling scheme is shown in the table below. You can change the way new objects are labeled as described in Label Options and Relabeling on page 163.

Object type	Labels used
Points	Capital letters starting with A
Straight Objects	Lower-case letters starting with j
Circles	Numbers prefixed by c (c1, c2, . . .)
Arcs	Numbers prefixed by a (a1, a2, . . .)
Interiors	Numbers prefixed by p (p1, p2, . . .)

Displaying an object's label

Another way to display labels is to use the Show and Hide Label commands as described on page 152. This command can be very convenient for hiding and showing labels of a group of objects.

1. Choose the Text tool in the Toolbox.

2. Move the pointer to the sketch area.

   The pointer turns to a hand.

3. Move the pointer to an object.

   The hand pointer turns black.

The axes of the coordinate system may be separately labeled with the Text tool in the same way that other objects are labeled.

4. Click the object.

    The object's label appears.

     A

Hiding an object's label

1. Choose the Text tool if it is not already chosen.

2. Move the pointer to an object displaying a label. The black hand indicates that you are pointing at an object whose label can be shown or hidden.

3. Click the object.

    The label disappears.

Changing an object's label

Labels can contain as many as 32 of any characters you can type on the keyboard.

Sometimes you may want to use a more descriptive label than a simple letter or number. You can use words for labels.

1. Choose the Text tool if it is not already chosen.

2. Move the pointer to a displayed label until a letter *A* appears inside the hand pointer.

3. Double-click the label you want to change.

    The label dialog box appears.

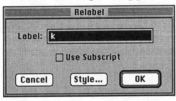

If you have measured an object and then change its label, the text in the measurement also changes to reflect the object's new name.

4. Type the label you want to use, using up to 32 characters.

5. Click OK.

    The new label replaces the old label.

You can use the Relabel Objects command in the Edit menu to change the labels of a whole group of objects at one time. (See Label Options and Relabeling on page 163.)

Moving a label

Once a label is visible, you can move it around the perimeter of the object it labels.

If the label is not on top of a geometric object, the Selection Arrow tool will automatically change to the Text tool when the pointer is over a label.

1. Choose the Text tool if it isn't already chosen.

2. Move the pointer to a displayed label until a letter *A* appears inside the hand pointer.

3. Click and drag the label to a new location. You will notice you cannot drag the label very far away from the object, but you can position it aesthetically in relation to other objects.

Creating a caption

Use captions to annotate or to title constructions in your sketch.

1. Choose the Text tool if it isn't already chosen.

2. Move the pointer to a blank area in the sketch plane where you want the caption to begin.

3. Press the mouse button and drag.

As you drag, you establish the corners of a rectangle in which to display the caption. The caption may be as wide as you want, although its height will be determined by how much text the caption contains.

4. When the dimensions of the caption rectangle are as you want them, release the mouse button.

    An I-beam appears at the top of the blank caption.

5. Type your caption. Sketchpad automatically wraps lines at the right margin of the caption's rectangle.

6. When you are done typing your caption, click anywhere outside the caption's rectangle.

    You have now successfully created the caption.

Resizing a caption

You can resize a caption to change its width and its height after you've created it.

1. Select the caption with a Selection Arrow tool.

    When selected, the caption displays four resize handles in the corners of its rectangle.

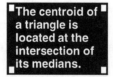

2. Click and drag any resize handle to change the caption's rectangle.

    As you drag, Sketchpad realigns the caption's text to the new rectangle.

3. Release the mouse when the caption is positioned properly.

Working with captions

Captions act like other objects in Sketchpad. You can move them with Selection Arrow tools, you can show and hide them, and you can delete them. Unlike geometric objects, captions do not have labels, cannot be traced, and do not appear in color.

To change the text of a caption, click the caption with the Text tool. You can enter new text, and select, cut, copy, and paste existing text as usual. When you are done changing text, click outside of the caption's rectangle.

To change the text format of a caption, select the caption with a Selection Arrow tool and choose new text formats from the Text Style and Text Font submenus in the Display menu.

To delete a caption, select the caption with a Selection Arrow tool. Then choose Clear from the Edit menu, or press the Delete or Backspace key on your keyboard.

Changing the text of a measurement

You can use the Text tool to alter the text displayed with a measurement.

1. Choose the Text tool if it isn't already chosen.

2. Move the pointer near the measurement you want to change.

   The pointer displays a letter *A* when it is near text that can be edited.

3. Double-click the measurement you want to edit or to change.

   A dialog box appears in which you can change the measurement to Text Format. (It may already be in Text Format.)

   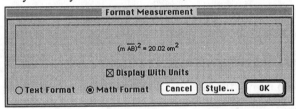

4. After choosing Text Format, the dialog box should look like this.

   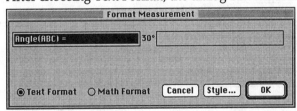

5. Make the changes you want. You can drag to select characters and double-click to select words. The Delete key deletes selections, and typing replaces selections. The ⌘ key commands for cutting, copying, and pasting sequences also work.

   The dialog box allows you to edit or to add text both before and after the measurement. You can add text after the measurement to provide units for calculations where no units appear or to embed the measured quantity in a complete sentence.

If you don't change the text of a measurement, the text will be updated automatically any time you change the label of the measured object.

The text before the measurement is normally updated if the measured object's label changes. For example, if you change the label of a segment from `k` to `Horizontal`, the measurement of that segment would automatically change from `Length(Segment k)= 2.5 inches` to `Length(Segment Horizontal)= 2.5 inches`. But if you change the text of the measurement itself so that the measurement reads `Width = 2.5` inches, any change in the segment's label will no longer be reflected in the text of the measurement.

6. Click OK.

☞ Get in the habit of using the ⌘ key to invoke the Text tool. This will save you time when you are demonstrating in class.

Temporarily using the Text tool

You can hold down the ⌘ key to invoke the Text tool temporarily while another tool is active. This is particularly handy when you want to label only one object in the middle of a construction session. You don't have to switch from the tool you are using.

Object Information Tool

This tool provides three levels of information about objects: a selection list showing the currently selected objects in the order of their selection, summary balloons with brief information on any visible object in the sketch, and information dialogs with more detailed information about objects, their parents, and their children.

Selection List

Click and hold on the Object Information tool in the Toolbox to see a selection pop-up menu listing the names of all objects currently selected in the order in which they were chosen. You can choose one of the objects in the list to see an Object Information dialog box which describes the object and its parents and children. Consult the selection list to verify that you have selected the appropriate prerequisite objects for constructions, measurements, animations, and scripts.

The order of selection in the information list is very useful for setting up selections for matching Givens in scripts.

Displaying the selection list

1. Move the pointer to the Object Information tool in the Toolbox.

2. Press and hold the mouse button.

    A pop-up menu displays the list of currently selected objects.

    ```
    Current selections:
    1. Segment j...
    2. Segment k...
    ```

    Drag down to the name of any object on the list in order to display full information about that object.

Summary Information

Click on any object with the Object Information tool to see a summary balloon showing the object's name and how it was constructed.

Don't confuse Sketchpad's summary balloons with System 7's Balloon Help. Balloon Help is available only under System 7, and gives hints about how to use the Sketchpad program. Summary balloons, on the other hand, are available under both System 6 and System 7, and explain how objects in sketches were initially constructed.

Displaying summary information about an object

1. Choose the Object Information tool from the Toolbox.

    The pointer changes to a question mark in a balloon, indicating that you are using the Object Information tool.

2. Move the point of the balloon directly over the object you want information about.

3. Click the mouse button.

    A summary balloon appears, briefly describing how the object was constructed.

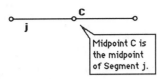

4. Click anywhere there is no object to make the summary balloon go away.

Object Information Dialog

Double-click on any object with the Object Information tool to see an Object Information dialog box for that object. The Object Information dialog shows the object's name and how it was constructed, and allows you to specify whether the object's label is showing and whether the object is hidden. The Object Information dialog provides a list of all of the object's parents and children, and allows you to view the same Object Information about these parents and children.

Displaying full information about an object

1. Choose the Object Information tool.

2. You can access the Object Information dialog box in several ways.
   - Hold down Shift while you click an object.
   - Double-click an object.
   - Press and hold on the Object Information tool in the Toolbox, and then choose an object's name from the selection list pop-up menu that appears.

   The Object Information dialog box appears, and the selected object blinks on the sketch plane.

If you can't see the blinking object, you can move the dialog box by dragging it by the title bar.

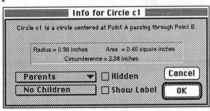

3. Click the appropriate option if you want to change whether or not the object's label shows or to specify if the object is hidden or not.

4. Press the Parents pop-up menu to see a list of the parents of the current object. You can choose from this menu to see a parent's Object Information dialog.

5. Press the Children pop-up menu to see a list of the children of the current object. You can choose from this menu to see a child's Object Information dialog.

   Continue to examine related objects by choosing from the pop-up menus.

6. Click OK to dismiss the box and execute the changes in object and label visibility you have specified. If you click Cancel, any changes you made are revoked.

Information about action buttons

When you examine an action button's Object Information dialog, you'll be able to set that button's In-sequence Delay—the time period for which Sketchpad will pause when it performs that action button as part of a sequence under the control of a sequence button.

For more information, see the description of Action Buttons in the Command Reference chapter.

Information about Traces

When you examine a traced point's Object Information dialog, you'll be able to choose the type of traces Sketchpad displays for that point. Discrete traces show the point's locus as a collection of individual points at different locations. Continuous traces show the point's locus as a single continuous line, indicating the path that the point traced. By default, Sketchpad assumes that traced points have continuous loci.

For more information on tracing, see Trace on page 165.

Information about Loci

The Object Information dialog lets you change the number of samples used to construct that locus. The more samples, the smoother will be the locus constructed from a point and the more numerous will be the repeated images of other objects. As with the Object Information dialog for a traced point, the Object Information dialog for a locus constructed from a point lets you set the locus to either discrete points or a continuous curve.

For more information on tracing, see Locus on page 175.

Script Tools Tool

The Script Tools tool appears when you have set a Script Tool Folder in the Advanced Preferences dialog box. Use script tools as a way of adding your own customized drawing tools to Sketchpad's toolbox.

1. Press the Script Tools tool with the mouse.

    Sketchpad presents the Script Tools list, which contains every script in the Script Tool Folder. Scripts stored in sub-folders of the Script Tool Folder appear as hierarchical submenus (up to five levels deep).

By default, script tools have the same names as their documents. To give a script a customized tool name, enter the customized name as the first line of the script's comment before saving the script.

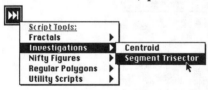

    You can add scripts to the list by saving them directly into your Script Tools Folder, or by moving or copying them there from someplace else.

2. Choose a script from the list.

    The chosen script becomes the active drawing tool. In the Tool Status Box, you are prompted for the next given object to match. You may either click on an existing object to match, or you may click in a blank area of your sketch to create a new object to match the given.

If you want to read the script associated with a script tool, press the Option key before choosing the script from the menu. This will cause it to be opened in its own window, rather than used as a drawing tool in your sketch.

3. Continue clicking until all given objects are matched and your script is done.

    When you're done, the Script Tools tool remembers your last chosen script. If you want to use it again at some later point, just click on the Script Tools tool. If you want to choose a different script, press on the Script Tools tool and choose a new script from the menu.

    If you want to change your Script Tool Folder or stop using script tools, use the Advanced Preferences dialog box.

Viewer Tool

The Viewer tool appears in sketches that you are demonstrating across the network. Networked demonstrations, and consequently the tool, are available only under System 7. Use the Viewer tool to keep track of the various viewers of your demonstration.

1. Press the Viewer tool with the mouse.

   Sketchpad presents the Viewer list, a pop-up menu containing the names of all users viewing your demonstration.

   Beneath the names of viewers are registered the names of users—if any—who were previously viewing the demonstration but are no longer. These names appear dimmed, and, in parentheses following each name, Sketchpad lists the reason for which that user is no longer viewing.

Stop   Indicates that you've explicitly stopped the viewer from viewing (as explained later in this section).

Cancel   Indicates that the viewer has explicitly stopped you from demonstrating (by closing or by typing ⌘ and the period key in your demonstration's window).

Network   Indicates that an error occurred between you and the viewer on the network.

2. Choose any name from the Viewer list for more information about that viewer.

   The Viewer Info dialog box appears.

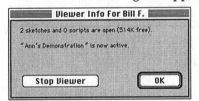

   The Viewer Info dialog box displays the number of sketches and scripts this user is currently working with, the name of the active sketch or script, and the estimated amount of free memory the user's Sketchpad has available.

3. To continue without interrupting the viewer, click OK.

   If you want to stop the viewer from following your demonstration (leaving a copy of your demonstrated sketch on their desktop), click Stop Viewer. If you want to *cancel* the viewer (which removes your sketch from their desktop), press down the Option key and click Cancel Viewer.

Keyboard Selection and Construction Interface

The tool status box in the lower left corner of a Sketchpad window provides a keyboard interface for selecting and constructing objects. Assuming you do not have an active text object, typing the label of an existing object and pressing Return causes that object to be selected. Similarly, typing the label of a point that does not yet exist causes that point to be created.

Creating a new point

To cancel what you have started in the tool status box, press ⌘-period or the Esc key. But you do not need to explicitly cancel the keyboard interface action. It will be canceled automatically when you proceed with your next action.

1. In a new sketch, type an uppercase *A*. Notice that the tool status box says "Draw Point A" and contains a blinking text cursor.

2. Press Return. A point labeled *A* is created at a random position in the window.

Creating a new line segment

1. Type an uppercase A. If your sketch contains a point *A*, the tool status box reads, "Select Point A"; otherwise it reads "Draw Point A."

2. Type a space. Nothing appears to happen in the tool status box, but the space is necessary to separate one label from another.

3. Type an uppercase B. The tool status box reads, "Draw Segment from A to B." (You can change to Ray or Line by successively typing "/".)

4. Press Return. A new segment is constructed with point *B* chosen at random within the window.

Selecting objects

1. Type the name of the object you wish to select. The tool status box will show what object you are going to select.

2. Press return to select the object.

Creating and selecting other kinds of objects

Five keys control what kind of object you create or select.

Comma	Circle
Period	Point
Slash (/)	Segment, ray, or line (repeatedly pressing this key cycles through the options)
Semicolon	Arc
Apostrophe	Polygon

1. Type the key corresponding to the type of object you wish to create.

2. Type the labels of your object's parental points, separated by spaces. (Sketchpad will create new points for any parents you don't type or for labels you type that don't match existing points in your sketch.)

3. Press Return to complete the construction.

Advanced Applications

If you use The Geometer's Sketchpad frequently, you'll realize the software "scales" well from modeling simple problems to constructing complex geometric systems. In this section, you'll find an assortment of techniques and features provided for users who are already familiar with Sketchpad's basic operation and want to extend their proficiency. Some of these features are hidden from the novice user, in an attempt to keep the complexity of the program from overwhelming first-timers. These tips, techniques, and features are arranged in no particular order and cover a diverse range of topics. Some may be applicable to your situation or interests, and others not.

If this is your first time through the manual, you may wish to skip this section now and come back to it once you've gained experience with the more standard ways of operating the program.

Keyboard Shortcuts

While Sketchpad provides a keyboard shortcut for most of its commands, two are fundamental. Pressing the Option key at any point substitutes the Selection Arrow tool for the current tool (for as long as Option is held down). Pressing the Command key (⌘) similarly substitutes the Text tool. By using these shortcuts, you can virtually eliminate the need to choose new tools from the Toolbox, as these two tools are used far more frequently than the others in conventional Sketchpad activities.

Advanced Sketchpad users keep one hand on the mouse and the other hovering above the keyboard. Depending on your keyboard dexterity, you'll find accessing *all* of the Toolbox's tools much faster with keys than with the mouse.

Keyboard Shortcuts for Choosing Tools

Option	Temporarily invokes current Selection Arrow
Command (⌘)	Temporarily invokes Text tool
Up Arrow (↑)	Invokes next higher tool in Toolbox
Down Arrow (↓)	Invokes next lower tool in Toolbox
Space Bar	Rotates current Straightedge tool
Shift+Space Bar	Rotates current Selection Arrow

Calculator Values

When using the calculator, you can use the keyboard to enter the digits (0-9) and various mathematical operators (+, −, etc.) visible in the calculator. You can *also* use the keyboard to access the selected measures in the calculator's Values pop-up menu. Though for legibility these shortcuts are not listed in the menu, the first nine selected measures are assigned numeric command keys beginning with ⌘1. Thus if you have selected the five interior angles of a pentagon and wish to sum them with the calculator, you can do so using only the keyboard by typing ⌘1 + ⌘2 + ⌘3 + ⌘4 + ⌘5.

Ratio of Three Points

Dilation by a negative scale factor produces a half-turn about the center of dilation. This effect is described in the Toolbox Reference chapter, and is significant in many advanced transformational applications, such as planar inversion through a circle.

Using the Mark Ratio command, you can indicate dynamic scale factors to be used in transformational dilations. The default method of indicating a ratio is by selecting two segments; the scale factor is the ratio of the length of the first to the length of the second. In that segments always have positive length, however, it is impossible to indicate negative dynamic scale factors using segments.

Sketchpad allows you also to mark a ratio of the *signed distances* between three points. Given three points A, B, and C, the signed ratio between them is equal to AC/AB. If the angle BAC is greater than ninety degrees—that is, if B and C fall on opposite sides of A—then the ratio is negative. If B and C fall on the same side of A (and therefore, $BAC \le 90°$), then the ratio is positive.

When the three points are collinear, an easy way to visualize their signed ratio is as the scale factor that would dilate B onto C if A were the center.

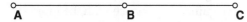

When you use the Dilate tool, you are actually dilating by the signed ratio of three points. The first point is the marked center of dilation. The second point is the one at which you pressed the Dilate tool when you began dragging your selections. These two points are fixed during the dilation. The third point, which changes continually as you drag, is determined by the present location of the Dilate tool.

In the illustration above, B is the midpoint of segment AC. The following signed ratios are present in the construction:

A-B-C = AC/AB = 2.00   *B and C are on the same side of A (positive)*

A-C-B = AB/AC = 0.50   *C and B are on the same side of A (positive)*

B-C-A = BA/BC = -1.00   *C and A are on opposite sides of B (negative)*

B-A-C = BC/BA = -1.00   *A and C are on opposite sides of B (negative)*

C-A-B = CB/CA = 0.50   *A and B are on the same side of C (positive)*

C-B-A = CA/CB = 2.00   *B and A are on the same side of C (positive)*

To mark the ratio of three points, select them and choose Mark Ratio while holding down Option. You may then construct dilations by marked ratio normally. (Don't forget to mark a center as well!)

You may also measure the signed ratio of three points numerically. Select them in the same order as you would to mark them, and choose Ratio from the Measure menu while holding down Option.

Arc By Center and 2 Points

Under normal circumstances, an arc is constructed either to go through three points or to have one point as its center and two other points as its endpoints. But it is occasionally desirable to relax these requirements slightly and allow one point that determines an arc to be neither the arc's center nor one of its endpoints. To allow this construction, hold down the Option key before activating the Construct menu. Arc On Circle changes to Arc By Center And 2 Points. Like Arc On Circle, this command constructs an arc based on three points or on a circle and two points.

If three points are selected, the first point determines the center of the arc. The second point determines the radius and starting point of the arc, and the third determines the direction for the end of the arc. The arc extends counter-clockwise from the second point to an imaginary ray drawn from the center point to the third selected point.

If a circle and two points are selected, the circle determines the center of the arc, but not its radius. The first point determines both the radius and starting point of the arc, and the second determines the direction for the end of the arc. The arc extends counter-clockwise, about the circle center, from the first point to an imaginary ray drawn from the circle center to the second point.

Scrolling Off the Plane

In most Macintosh programs, your documents are views into a space of fixed area: a page of paper of some size, or several pages. In Sketchpad, however, documents are views into the infinite geometric plane. As you construct and manipulate objects, you continue to expand in this plane without hitting artificial barriers of the printed page. The scroll bars' range expands appropriately, allowing you to scroll anyplace you've constructed objects, but preventing you from scrolling off to infinity.

Computer programs are notoriously bad at calculating infinity. Sketchpad's notion of the infinite plane is actually only an area about 5750 square feet large.

While in most cases this behavior is exactly as you'd want it, occasionally it would be handy to scroll "just a little way" closer to infinity than the program will allow—to place a caption beneath your construction, for instance. (To solve this, you may have dragged an object off the edge of the window in the desired direction so that you could then scroll toward it.)

To extend the dimensions of the scrollable area by a small amount, press Option while clicking the left, right, up, or down scroll arrow. (Click the scroll arrow repeatedly while pressing Option to move farther into the plane.)

Hiding All Labels and Turning Off All Tracing

You can rapidly hide all visible labels by choosing Select All (⌘A), and then choosing Show Labels (⌘K) twice. The first time you choose it, Sketchpad will show all objects labels; the second time, because all objects already have their labels showing, Sketchpad will hide all the labels.

Similarly, you can turn off all tracing by typing ⌘A, ⌘T, ⌘T (Select All, Trace Objects, Untrace Objects).

Command-Line Interface

Sketchpad is a rich and flexible environment, and is used by teachers, students, researchers, and artists. Sometimes, the needs of one group of users is very different from the needs of another. For instance, a teacher who has customized her Sketchpad environment (by setting up a certain group of Script Tools, and by changing the available geometry menus) may not want her students to be able to change this customized environment. Because of these diverse needs, Sketchpad provides a number of commands which are only available by typing their name on a special command-line. This keeps regular users from ever encountering such commands, but makes them available to advanced users who absolutely need them.

To access one of these hidden commands:

1. Make any sketch window active.

2. Hold down the Option key and type \.

In the Tool Status box, Sketchpad displays the command-line, asking you for your command.

3.	Type the name of the command. (You only need to type the first few letters: Sketchpad will guess and display the rest of the command name.)

4.	Press the Return key to enter the command.

The following commands may be typed into the command line interface.

Protect	Disables access to Advanced Preferences by removing the More button from the Preferences dialog. A teacher or system administrator can prevent students from changing the advanced preferences—such as available geometry menus, current Script Tool folder, or number of networked demonstrations—by protecting the student's version of Sketchpad.

Deprotect	Undoes the effect of a previous Protect command, by reenabling access to Advanced Preferences.

Close All No Save	Closes all open documents without saving their contents, and without asking whether their contents should be saved. Presenters conducting workshops may often find themselves with a dozen or more open windows which they wish to close instantly (without saving). Warning: This command will cause you to lose any work you've made in unsaved, open documents.

Quit No Save	Quits the program instantly. It's useful if you want to eliminate many windows without explicitly telling Sketchpad that you don't need to save each one. Warning: This command will cause you to lose any work you've made in unsaved, open documents.

Any menu command	Any enabled menu command can be entered in the command-line interface. This includes commands from geometry menus which are not currently available (because they have been supressed in the Preferences dialog). It does not include disabled commands, however. Thus, with one or more segments selected, you may execute the Point at Midpoint command whether the Construct menu is available or not. You could not execute this command if you did not have one or more segments selected.

Math Format Text

Normally, the text you enter for Sketchpad's labels and measurements is standard Macintosh text—characters from the keyboard, displayed in your desired font, size, and style. Sketchpad can also display a text in a rich variety of standard mathematical notations that are not conveniently entered from a keyboard. You see some of this ability when viewing measurements in Math Format as opposed to Text Format. Authors using Sketchpad to prepare illustrations for publication may wish to read this section to learn how to control Sketchpad's ability to display more sophisticated notation than simple text.

In Sketchpad, every visible object label or measurement text is governed by a Math Format String, which describes in symbolic language the Math Format appearance of the text. This symbolic language consists of commands interpersed with regular text. An example of a Math Format String (MFS) command is:

{u: *text*}

This particular command is used to superscript the appearance of *text*. (u is a mnemonic for up.) Thus the Math Format String x{u:2} appears as

$$x^2$$

and the Math Format String x{u:2{u:4}} appears as

$$x^{2^4}$$

As this example shows, MFS commands can be nested to produce more complicated displays.

The total library of MFS commands includes those shown below.

Math Format Command	Meaning	Example Math Format String	Example Result
{u:*text*}	*text* as a superscript	inches{u:2}	inches^2
{l:*text*}	*text* as a subscript	P{l:1}	P$_1$
{A:*text*}	*text* with an arc overbar	{A:ABC}	$\overparen{ABC}$
{L:*text*}	*text* with a line overbar	{L:AB}	$\overleftrightarrow{AB}$
{R:*text*}	*text* with a ray overbar	{R:AB}	$\overrightarrow{AB}$
{S:*text*}	*text* with a segment overbar	{S:AB}	$\overline{AB}$
{D:*text1*}{*text2*}	*text1* (numerator) divided by *text2* denominator	{D:3}{4}	$\dfrac{3}{4}$
{(:*text*}	*text* surrounded by parentheses large enough to fit	{(:{D:3}{4}}	$\left(\dfrac{3}{4}\right)$
{@:*text*}	*text* surrounded by absolute value bars large enough to fit	{@:{D:3}{4}}	$\left\|\dfrac{3}{4}\right\|$
{V:*text*}	the square root of *text*	{V:3}	$\sqrt{3}$
{!:C}	the circle symbol	{!:C}AB	⊙AB
{!:A}	the angle symbol	{!:A}ABC	∠ABC
{!:*}	the multiplication symbol	3{!:*}4	3·4
{!:[}	the { symbol	{!:[}3, 4{:!]}	{3, 4}
{!:]}	the } symbol	{!:[}3, 4{:!]}	{3, 4}
{!:T}	the Greek letter theta	{!:T}	θ

Math Format Command	Meaning	Example Math Format String	Example Result
{!:P}	the Greek letter pi*	{!:P}	π
{!:D}	the Greek letter delta*	{!:D}	Δ

*If you are creating sketches that use π and Δ, and you wish them to display properly under the Windows version of Sketchpad, you should use these format strings.

When these commands are nested, they can display text of considerable complexity. For instance, the MFS command

$$\{V:\{!:D\}x\{u:2\}+\{!:D\}y\{u:2\}\}$$

displays as

$$\sqrt{\Delta x^2 + \Delta y^2}$$

To alter the MFS command which controls the display of a label or measurement

1. Cause the label or measurement to appear in the sketch by normal means.

2. Choose the Text tool in the Toolbox.

3. While holding down the Ctrl key, double-click the measurement or label.

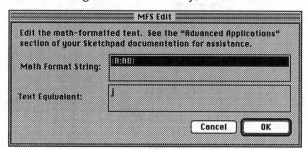

A dialog appears, listing both the Math Format and Text Format representation of the label or measurement.

4. In the Math Format portion of the dialog, enter your desired Math Format String command. The maximum length of the Math Format String is determined by the maximum allowable length of either a measurement prefix or label.

5. Click OK.

Sketchpad redisplays the label or measurement according to your command.

Changing the Order of Script Givens

When you record a script interactively, Sketchpad enumerates the script's given objects in the order you create objects in your sketch. When you manufacture a script retroactively (using the Make Script command), however, Sketchpad chooses the order of given objects by rules of geometric precedence. While the order of given objects in a single script rarely matters, if you are authoring a collection of scripts for wider use, it may be desirable to change the order in which they appear (and therefore, the order in which they must be matched) for purposes of consistency or clarity.

To change the order of givens in a script:

1. Make the script the active window, and scroll so you can see the list of givens at the beginning of the script.

2. While holding down the Option key, press the mouse button on the given in the script you wish to reposition.

   A gray line appears in the script window, indicating the current position of the given object.

3. Drag up or down to the desired position.

   The gray line moves up or down within the list of given objects, indicating possible new positions for the given object.

4. Release the mouse button.

   The given object moves to the position that you have indicated.

File Formats (Macintosh/Microsoft Windows)

There are versions of Sketchpad available for both the Macintosh and PCs running Microsoft Windows. The Command Reference chapter describes how to import files created in one version into the other using PC Exchange. However, many other software tools are available for routine translation of files between DOS and Macintosh disk formats.

If you use a different utility for converting files, you may need information about Sketchpad's file extensions (for DOS), types, and creator (for Macintosh). These attributes of a file are used by an operating system to determine which application created the file. If your conversion utility requires this sort of information, the following table may help you set-up automatic translation of Sketchpad files:

	Extension (MS-DOS)	Type (Mac)	Creator (Mac)
Sketches	.gsp	GSPk	GSP!
Scripts	.gss	GSPc	GSP!

Preferences files are not compatible, and should not be exchanged between Macintosh and Microsoft Windows computers.

What's New in Version 3

The Geometer's Sketchpad has evolved to meet the increasing needs of the tens of thousands of teachers and students who have been using it. Research at Key Curriculum Press, supported by the National Science Foundation, has enabled the designers to visit classrooms, talk with teachers and students, consult with researchers, and try out new designs. Version 3.0, the third incarnation of the software, incorporates important new features and a myriad of small improvements. The aim has been to make the program both easier to use and more versatile. Here are listed some of the most important changes, referring you to the appropriate section of this manual for the details.

Arcs, Arc Segments, and Sectors

You can now construct arcs by three points, by a circle and two points on the circle, or by a center and two points. Given an arc, you can measure its arc angle and arc length. From an arc you can construct an arc segment or a sector. Arc segments and sectors are filled and may be colored and shaded in all the ways that polygons can. You can measure areas and perimeters of arc segments and sectors, and you can place points on their perimeters.

See   Tour 5: Measuring Circles, Angles, and Arcs on page 47
       Arc on Circle on page 174
       Arc Through 3 Points on page 174
       Arc Sector Interior on page 174
       Arc Segment Interior on page 175
       Arc Angle on page 191
       Arc Length on page 191

Analytic Geometry

Sketchpad 3.0 allows you to create a coordinate system and measure the coordinates of points, the equations of lines, and the equations of circles. You can drag the origin of the coordinate system and dynamically change the unit length. The axes of the coordinate system are Sketchpad objects on which you can construct points and which can be used to construct parallels and perpendiculars. Coordinates of points are available for use in calculations, as are parameters that define the equations of lines and circles. The coordinate system has a grid that you can show or hide, and dragging can be constrained to snap to the grid if desired. You can set the coordinate grid to be either rectangular or polar, and you can display both forms of coordinates for a point simultaneously.

See   Tour 10: Coordinates and Equations on page 68
       Coordinates on page 192
       Equation on page 192
       Create/Hide/Show Axes on page 197
       Show/Hide Grid on page 198
       Snap To Grid on page 198
       Grid Form on page 198

Graphing

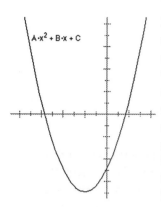

Measurements, calculated values, and data can be plotted in the coordinate system. For example, you can measure the side length and area of a square and use these two values as an (x, y) pair to plot a point. The point will move as you drag the side of the square and, with tracing turned on, will trace a parabola. You can use the calculator to build any mathematical expression you like as a function of the x-coordinate of a point on the x-axis and use the result to find the y-coordinate of the function. In combination with dynamic, constructed loci, you now have a powerful tool for exploring algebra within a dynamic geometry environment. You can type in coordinates for individual points and constrain these points to remain at these fixed coordinates. You can import data from other applications and plot this data as points in the coordinate system. Tables generated within Sketchpad can also be used to plot points.

See   Tour 16: Graphing and Locus Construction on page 89
        Plot Measurement... on page 198
        Plot Points... on page 199
        Plot Table Data... on page 199

Marked Measurements for Transformations

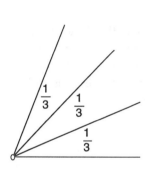

In previous versions of Sketchpad you could create transformations of objects that depended dynamically on marked vectors, angles, and ratios. In Version 3, transformations can depend dynamically on measured or computed values. You can, for example, measure an angle, use the calculator to compute one-third of that angle, and use the result of the computation to construct a trisector of that angle. Marked measurements open up whole new worlds of geometry that were difficult or impossible to reach previously.

See   Mark Distance on page 184
        Mark Angle on page 185
        Mark Ratio and Mark Scale Factor on page 186

Locus Construction

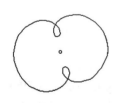

In previous versions of Sketchpad, you could trace an object and this allowed study of curves and envelopes. But the trace would disappear as soon as you went on to do anything else in the sketch. In Version 3 you can construct a locus of one object driven by a point on some path. A locus constructed this way responds dynamically to dragging in the sketch. So, for example, a locus of a point constrained to lie on a parabola shows the entire parabola and changes as you drag the focus or directrix. Constructed loci in combination with plotting measurements and calculations can be used to create dynamic graphs.

With the proper geometric construction or calculation, you can create almost any mathematically defined shape and investigate its behavior as the construction parameters change. You can even place points on a locus and use them to drive an animation or to construct another locus.

See   Tour 16: Graphing and Locus Construction on page 89
        Locus on page 175

Script Tools

You can now specify a special folder where Sketchpad will look for scripts to add to the toolbar as script tools. Whereas scripts played from a script window require you to select the script's givens before you play the script, script tools act like other tools in the toolbar in that they allow you to specify the givens interactively. A script tool for drawing the circumcircle for a triangle will begin showing you the circumcircle as soon as you have selected or placed two of the points and snap into place when you have placed or selected the third.

See   Script Tools on page 134
       Tour 11: Script Tools on page 72

Mathematical Notation

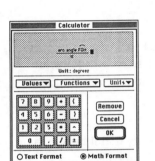

Sketchpad now uses mathematical notation for measurements and calculations. You can set the default to Math Format or Text Format and you can control the format of individual measurements or calculations.

See   Calculate… on page 192
       Changing the text of a measurement on page 213
       Math Format Text on page 222

Enhanced Calculator

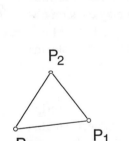

The calculator can display expressions as you create them either in Math Format or in Text Format. There are now three pop-up menus in the calculator: one for values, one for functions, and one for units. Many new mathematical functions have been added, and you can now use decimal fractions as part of your expressions. The Units pop-up menu allows you to specify the units of a part of your expressions. Sketchpad will show you the unit of an expression as you build it. Finally, you may select a measurement directly from the sketch with the mouse while the calculator is open.

See   Tour 5: Measuring Circles, Angles, and Arcs on page 47
       Calculate… on page 192

Enhanced Labeling Options

Labels for objects may be longer than in previous versions and you may subscript them. A group of selected objects may be relabeled simultaneously in a specified sequence. You now have control over the labeling sequence Sketchpad uses as it creates new objects. Whereas in previous versions the only way to force Sketchpad to begin the labeling sequence over again was to open a new sketch, now the label sequence will start from scratch if you Undo All.

See   Label Options and Relabeling on page 163
       Changing an object's label on page 211

Customizable Menus

Using Preferences, you can specify which menus are available in Sketchpad. This gives you the ability to simplify the program by getting rid of some of the menus, or to restrict the available commands to a subset in order to explore what can and cannot be accomplished with that subset.

See   The Advanced Preferences Dialog Box on page 168

Keyboard Interface

You may now accomplish a great deal of construction and selection through the keyboard alone. Keyboard command cues and toolbox assistance appear in the tool status box at the bottom of the sketch window.

See   Keyboard Selection and Construction Interface on page 217
           Keyboard Shortcuts on page 219
           Command-Line Interface on page 221

Other User Interface Improvements

Numerous small changes make this version of Sketchpad even easier to use than previous versions. Some of the changes are listed here.

Automatic change to text tool

When using the Selection Arrow tool, if the arrow is positioned over an object's label, the tool changes automatically to the text tool. This makes it much easier and more intuitive to reposition a label or change a label.

Tool status box

Sketchpad now gives you cues as to what tool you have chosen and what object you are about to select or construct using a tool status box.

Large text for calculator, scripts, and axes

The Preferences dialog box now allows you to specify larger type to be used for display text in the calculator, in script windows, and on axes. This is particularly useful for classroom demonstrations. (See page 168.)

Specifying objects for use in transformations

You may now double-click on a point to specify that it be used as a marked center for rotation or dilation or double-click on a straight object to specify that it be used as a mirror for reflection. While a transformation dialog box is open, you may click on objects and measurements visible in the sketch to specify that they be used as part of the transformation. (See the various transformation command descriptions beginning on page 177.)

Simplification of labels in scripts

It is no longer necessary to specify that a label be used in a script. Givens always get the label of the original object. Objects created in the course of a script will show with their actual labels if you change the label.

General Issues

Floating-Point Units

Some Macintoshes come with built-in floating-point units (FPUs) which will speed up many of Sketchpad's operations. The FPU is an additional processor chip which assists the computer in performing mathematical computations. Some other Macintoshes allow you to install an FPU as an add-on peripheral. Without an FPU, mathematical calculations such as those Sketchpad makes are significantly slower than with an FPU. Power Macintoshes, though they do not have FPU's, do their floating point computation within their central processors are as fast as other Macintoshes that have FPU's.

Multiple Monitors

You can use Sketchpad with more than one monitor. You can expect the following behavior from Sketchpad if you are using multiple monitors:

- Dialog boxes and messages appear on the monitor where the pointer is located.

- When you click the zoom box to zoom a window, it will expand to fill the monitor it is on, or the monitor which displays the largest area of the window if the window appears on two monitors. You can zoom a window from one monitor to another by holding down the Option key while clicking the zoom box.

If color is hard to see on an LCD color projection device, use the Control Panel to turn color off.

If one or more of the monitors have multiple colors or grayscale, don't stretch a window onto two monitors. Doing so slows the program significantly.

If one of the monitors is a color monitor, be sure to use the Control Panel in the Apple menu to put the menu bar on the color monitor. Although Sketchpad works in any color depth, for optimum performance set your monitor to 4-bit color (16 colors) or grayscale.

Memory Management

Sketchpad uses memory to figure out how to draw and redraw the geometric objects you create. It also uses memory to store a list of your actions so that you can undo them. The amount of memory your Macintosh has installed determines just how much number crunching and Undo history storage you can have in any one session using Sketchpad. It is possible to run out of memory, especially if your computer has only the minimum memory required. This section gives you tips for using Sketchpad efficiently.

Flickering When your reserve memory is running low, you can see some deterioration of Sketchpad's function. When you drag or animate objects, Sketchpad draws them crisply and smoothly as long as there is sufficient memory. If your images flicker and look ragged when you drag or animate them, take steps to free memory (such as saving the sketch or closing open sketches and scripts that you aren't using). Flickering doesn't mean that your system is about to crash, it only means that you can improve performance by making more memory available.

If you have a color monitor, try reducing the number of colors used, as described later in this section. The amount of memory required to draw objects smoothly is related exponentially to the color depth of your monitor.

Warnings

Sketchpad gives you warnings when your reserve memory begins running low. When you get the first warning, or as soon after as is feasible, you should save your document (freeing the Undo history) and close any open documents that you are not using.

If you take no steps to free memory, you may exhaust the supply. Sketchpad monitors this process so it can warn you in time to save your document. However, when all memory is exhausted, you may be forced to quit from Sketchpad after saving. You should review the rest of this section to see if you have done everything you can to use your system and Sketchpad efficiently.

Undo Rather Than Delete

To Undo All, hold down Option while selecting Undo from the Edit menu, or press Option-Z.

When you create an object, Sketchpad keeps the construction in a list (the Undo history), specifying how and where you did it. If you select that object and then delete it (with the Delete key or the Cut or Clear commands), Sketchpad not only has to remember that you created the object but also that you deleted it.

You should instead use Undo to remove the last object you created if possible. You can also use the Undo command to step back through the list to undo earlier constructions. Undo shortens the list and, therefore, uses less memory.

Finally, use Undo All to remove every object from the Sketch plane.

Save Often

Saving stores the current document on the disk so that power failures and other mishaps won't cause you to lose your work.

In addition to protecting your sketches and scripts, saving frees the Undo history, thereby increasing your memory reserve. If you are constructing figures for a demonstration and want to keep your Undo history so others can view it, you can still save whenever you want. When the construction is complete, close the document and then open it again. Click the Include Work check box in the Open File dialog box. This makes a limited version of your Undo history available.

Close Documents

It is good practice to close any sketches and scripts you are not using. Of course, if you are using several documents it is a great advantage to be able to flip through them to find what you want. But if you are warned that your memory reserve is low, you can increase the reserve by closing documents.

System Settings

If your technique for using Sketchpad does not free enough memory for efficient operations, you can change your system settings to add to the reserve memory.

Monitors

If you have a color monitor, Sketchpad looks best when set for 16 colors.

All monitors use memory, especially color monitors. You can set your system to make the most efficient use of memory for either color or monochrome monitors.

Color   If you have a color monitor, you can increase the amount of reserve memory by using fewer colors and by reducing the size of the sketch window. If you are getting warnings about the reserve memory, or if images flicker when you drag them, you should check to see that your monitor is set for 16 colors rather than 256 or more. Choose the Control Panel from the Apple menu and then change the setting for Monitors.

Monochrome   While you cannot set your monitor to display fewer colors than black and white, you can still decrease the size of the sketch window to increase the reserve memory.

Multifinder/System 7

If you are using Multifinder you can increase the amount of memory allocated to Sketchpad.

Increasing application memory size

1. At the Finder desktop, with Sketchpad closed, click the Sketchpad icon once.

2. Choose Get Info from the File menu.

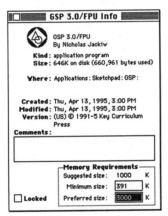

3. Change the number shown in the Application Memory or Preferred Size box, adding 50 percent.

4. Click the close box in the Info window.

5. Open Sketchpad.

RAM Cache

To maximize your available memory usage for Sketchpad, RAM disks and the RAM cache should not be used.

Turning off the RAM Cache

1. Choose Control Panel from the Apple menu.

2. If necessary, set the Off button for the RAM Cache.

3. Click the close box in the Control Panel window.

Virtual Memory

If you have System 7 or higher, you can increase the overall available RAM with the Virtual Memory Control Panel, then increase the Application Memory size as described above.

Adding Memory

If your ability to use Sketchpad is severely limited by the available memory you have, and if you have tried the above techniques and settings, you can have a computer dealer or service center add more memory to your computer.

Index

metafile
    saving a sketch as 141
microphones 108, 151
Microsoft Windows (files)
    exporting files to 139
    importing files from 139
midpoints 32
mirror 60
monitors 233
Move buttons 108, 150
Movie 167
Movie buttons 109
movies 152, 154
Multifinder 233
multi-media capabilities 150
multiple monitors 231
multiple selections 26
multiplication 193

N

natural logarithm function 115, 193
negation 193
negative dilation 205
negative scale factor 205, 220
networks 116, 144
    guests 118
New Script 137
New Sketch 137
non-Euclidean constructions 115

O

Object Information
    for locus 175
Object Information tool 22, 30, 100, 120,
    214–215
objects 93, 94
    animating 114, 165
    changing color of 161
    changing line style of 160
    children of 96
    coincident 99
    constructing 94, 95
    deselecting 98, 99
    dilating 100
    hiding 162
    labeling 110
    on the Clipboard 106
    parents of 96
    rotating 100
    selecting 97
    shade 161
    translating 100
Open 138

opening scripts 124
opening sketches 93
optional selection 203
origin
    of a graph 197

P

Page Setup 141
Parallel Line 8, 173
parents 64, 96, 99
Paste 106, 148
    from other applications 149
    to different applications 106, 107, 148
    using color 107
Paste Picture 149
Paste Sound 152
Path Match
    skip 166
paths
    animating along 165
    Bidirectional 166
    Once 166
    One Way 166
PC Exchange 139
Perimeter 191
Perpendicular Line 173
PICS 154, 167
pictures
    imported 149
Place Points 199
Place TableData 199
PLAY 22, 128
Play Sound buttons 109
playback speeds 168
playing scripts 127–129
Plot as (x, y) 91
Plot Measurement 198
plotting 228
Point At Intersection 67, 172
Point At Midpoint 172
Point On Object 171
Point tool 21, 95, 206
pointer 17, 19
pointing 17
points 26
    coordinates of 192
    creating with keyboard 217
    plotting 199
polar coordinates 199
polygon interiors 42, 174
precision 115, 167, 168
    hundredths 115
    tenths 115